Enjoy your journey
within these pages!

You Are
Powerful Beyond Measure

You are a Light
in the World!

Much Love
Cindy

Praise for

Powerful Beyond Measure

"Cynthia had me at 'hello,' and each page drew me deeper and deeper into a world of profound self-discovery. I loved reading the story of her dark-night-of-the-soul experience and how it led to her inner awakening and the resulting teaching about how we can take our own most challenging experiences and use them to awaken our inner spirit, passions, and gifts—and become *powerful beyond measure*."

—**Debra Poneman**, best-selling author, founder of Yes to Success, Inc.
and cofounder of Your Year of Miracles, LLC

"*Powerful Beyond Measure* is a beautifully written book, filled with wholehearted wisdom, trustworthy guidance and potent tools to awaken you to your power to live the life you came here to live. For those seeking to live an empowered and authentically happy life, Cindy Mazzaferro has created a reliable blueprint for true transformation."

—**Katherine Woodward Thomas**,
New York Times best-selling author of *Calling in "The One."*

"In a world where so many seek power in an unbalanced way, Cindy takes us back to the roots—addressing internal issues to support the reader in embracing a balance of power and heart. A true gift to humanity."

—**John Newton**, founder of HealthBeyondBelief.com

"In *Powerful Beyond Measure*, Cynthia Mazzaferro takes you on an inspirational journey of inner healing gained from her own personal experience. *Powerful Beyond Measure* offers valuable exercises designed to help you claim your own power and gives clear guideposts for your path of self-discovery and self-love.»

—**Hans Christian King**, internationally renowned medium, spiritual teacher,
and author of *Guided: Reclaiming the Intuitive Voice of Your Soul*

"You create your life through the beliefs and thoughts you hold. In Cynthia Mazzaferro's insightful book, *Powerful Beyond Measure,* you'll discover why you've created the life you are living now, and if you aren't completely happy with that life, how to transform it into a life that lights you up. If you find yourself struggling with your own sense of self-worth, or just struggling, then this is the book you've been looking for."

—**Chris Attwood**, NY Times best-selling author of
The Passion Test and *Your Hidden Riches*

"You can't depend on external circumstances for lasting happiness, and *Powerful Beyond Measure* helps you to look deep within and resolve the inner conflicts that are holding you back from achieving your brilliance."

—**Geoff Affleck**, #1 best-selling coauthor of
Enlightened Bestseller, Breakthrough! and *Ready, Set, Live!*

"What if you could let go of the past and harness the power of the most difficult experiences of your life? In *Powerful Beyond Measure*, Cindy Mazzaferro has given us a path for healing ourselves and walking into our future with open hearts. With depth and honesty, she's written an exceptional book that will help you ease emotional pain and transform it into the peace and power that's always been inside of you."

—**Kim Forcina**, owner of Kaleidoscope Spirit -
Coaching for Dreamers and Creatives

"*Powerful Beyond Measure* is a beautiful book of self-exploration. It leads you inside yourself so you can find your true purpose. If you want to have a deeper understanding of yourself, and who doesn't, you must read this book!"

—**Cary Carbonaro**, MBA, CFP®, author of *The Money Queen's Guide:
For Women Who Want to Build Wealth and Banish Fear*

"Cindy Mazzaferro makes a compelling case about releasing the existent gifts we all possess into the various patterns of our life purpose or dharma. By identifying our aptitudes and fortifying them with purposeful skill building, Cindy challenges us to wake up to and sustain the highest callings of our destiny, which are truly 'powerful beyond measure'."

—**William R. Levacy**, PhD

"When I first met Cindy my world looked dark and bleak. The years of mental, emotional, and physical abuse was embedded into every cell in my body, which resulted in numerous serious medical conditions, including multiple cancers and autoimmune diseases. I had fibromyalgia pain for over forty years that was constant and debilitating. Cindy offered to work with me, and after the first Reiki treatment, I slowly stood up and opened my eyes. I remember clearly everything around me: the natural light in the room was brighter, almost shimmering; her flowers and plants all had a fascinating glow to them, and one could feel them to be alive. I couldn't stop watching the beauty all around me; it was as if everything had changed, from a place of profound darkness to God's true light in the world. I was so amazed at the light and love in the room, I hadn't even realized that I was totally pain free, too!

It was such a change in reality, as if I was seeing life and love for the first time. *Powerful Beyond Measure* is Cindy's gift to the world, infused with God's love, powerful words, and healing. For all those waiting for love, peace, and beauty to enter into your life, there's no need to wait any longer; you're only a few pages away from finding your power within and being *Powerful Beyond Measure*. This is a book that you'll want to read over and over again!"

—**Margot Saraceno**

"*Powerful Beyond Measure* is truly a gift. It's a must-read for everyone interested in living life to the fullest possibility."

—**Kasey Mathews**, author of *Preemie: Lessons in Love, Life and Motherhood*

"In my 20s, I made a conscious choice to start having a happy life. I didn't know how that would manifest or what changes it would open up–but more than thirty years later, I still refer to it as the best decision I ever made. Finding and harnessing our own mighty power to change ourselves and the world is a path to happiness. And Cynthia Mazzaferro will lead you there. Combining her own and others' personal stories with the latest neuroscience, she's created a well-written and smoothly flowing guide to what's possible–which is just about everything. As Muhammad Ali said, 'Impossible is not a fact. It's a dare.'"

—**Shel Horowitz**, Transformpreneur.com; lead author of *Guerrilla Marketing to Heal the World: Combining Principles and Profit to Create the World We Want*

"*Powerful Beyond Measure.* That says it all! Cynthia helps us see that we are all 'powerful beyond measure' by helping us tap into the power that we all have within us. She goes through all the limiting factors that keep us from tapping into or even being aware of that power. When we discover that power within us, we become different beings, living life to its fullest. This book will open gateways that you never imagined existed. It's all about the power that you have within you and how you can be *Powerful Beyond Measure.*"

—**Luella May**, cohost of radio show *The Best Years in Life*

"In her new book, Cynthia Mazzaferro helps us cut through the layers of resistance and denial we've crafted to protect ourselves. She challenges us to reexamine our past and face how we perceive our present so we might embrace the full potential of our future. Powerful concepts are supported with real-world data and brought to life with meaningful exercises and thought-provoking questions. If you long to live a fuller, happier life, start today by reading *Powerful Beyond Measure.*"

—**Lisa Dadd**, author of *Finding Fabulous: Paving the Path between Paycheck and Passion*

"*Powerful Beyond Measure* dynamically illuminates the connections between our emotions, physicality, and memories with our current patterns and pains. In a gentle sequence, Cynthia Mazzaferro offers the path of understanding, with tools and support so you can relieve your underlying struggles. Inner healing is now available for everyone with this remarkable book."

—**Susan Steiner**, OTR/L, CST-D; instructor of craniosacral therapy and somato-emotional release, Upledger Institute

"Cindy has taken the time not just share her story but also to motivate and empower the reader to go deep and reflect about their own story. Written with compassion, kindness, and wisdom, *Powerful Beyond Measure* helps the reader to realize the need for self-knowledge, self-growth, and self-love. A truly wonderful book that is a blessing to read and a blessing to share."

—**Lynnis Woods-Mullins**, CHC, CLC, CPI; holistic living and wellness expert; publisher and editor of *Wellness Woman 40 and Beyond* e-magazine

"In her self-help book, *Powerful Beyond Measure*, Cindy Mazzaferro has the courage to open up her personal journey towards self-knowledge and a common ground with her husband and the world. Her professional skills and training as a physical therapist and ergonomist have aided in this assembly of programs that will help guide readers towards personal empowerment."

—**Frank Federico**, master pastelist, PSA

"Cynthia Mazzaferro has provided a profound experience for you to integrate into your quest for your Soul's purpose as you seek for answers to living a life of joy, fulfillment, and peace within. I highly recommend *Powerful Beyond Measure*, as it's a book that you will be interactive with as you discover your true and authentic self."

—**Nancy Ferrari**, multimedia producer/host; intuitive life coach

"There is no longer a reason to suffer, feel alone, and live a life of despair. *Powerful Beyond Measure* gently, but with a concise and effective process, guides you to resolution, healing, growth, and prosperity. Cindy has masterfully shared her own experiences, in addition to providing you with the tools that she has used to heal her life physically, mentally, emotionally, and spiritually. When we find ourselves reactionary to life, it's most often necessary to seek outside influences to help us clear our minds and bodies. This book is a culmination of years' worth of integrated healing mastery. It should be considered an integral puzzle piece to our lives, affording each of us an opportunity to clear our unwanted or unneeded baggage, paving the way to peace, a deeper kind of self-love, and inner as well as outer healing. This book is a must read."

—**Nicole Myers Henderson**, ThM, MRV; president, Earth Essence Inc.; author *of On Sacred Time, Tapping the Power Within*

"Spot on! People are searching for the answers as to what is holding them back in the attainment of their goals. Cindy gives them the road map to get beyond the obstacles. *Powerful Beyond Measure* helps the reader achieve excellence in any and all areas of their life."

—**Lori Boyle**, Airline Pilot (retired), TV & radio show host and producer, internationally syndicated columnist

"Have you ever walked through a door to a place where you could feel the energy and vibration and know that something special and powerful was about to happen?

As you step into the pages of *Powerful Beyond Measure*, you will immediately feel the love, power, and energy that will be there for you throughout the book and experience the profound impact that it will have on you and your life. This is a book you will want to read again and again."

—**Kathleen O'Keefe-Kanavos**, international
award-winning author; TV/radio host/producer

"*Powerful Beyond Measure* offers a clear road map to our true purpose in this lifetime. Understanding that our lives have been scripted before we were even born allows us to realize that life is a playing field for us to grow, learn, and fulfill our destiny.

Reading Cynthia's book allows us to explore ourselves at a deeper level and effortlessly step into our true calling and passion in this life. Thank you, Cynthia, for sharing your passion with the world."

—**Traysiah Spring**, Vedic astrologer and author,
Surviving the Death Sentence: How My Mother Survived Pancreatic Cancer

"*Powerful Beyond Measure* is very well thought out and sensitively written. A fantastic template that will generate lasting and profound changes in one's life. *Powerful Beyond Measure* will be remembered as an empowering guidebook for years to come, the go-to book that empowers oneself to take action to make positive changes, create internal and external healing, and ignite one's passions and purpose for life that sets you on the road to success, happiness, and fulfillment."

—**Debbie McIntosh**, Debonaire Earth Angel

"Discover the world of possibilities and open your heart to fuel your desires as you use this book to find your power within. Create your own 'First Aid Toolbox' of strategies that work for you in both personal and professional areas. Following the P-O-W-E-R Steps in *Powerful Beyond Measure* will bring you results that you once thought were impossible."

—**Magnes Welsh**, principal, Magnes Communications

"You don't have a testimony until after you have a test. Cindy Mazzaferro's testimony *is Powerful Beyond Measure*. Apply the wisdom in her book, and yours will be too."

—**John Brubaker**, award-winning author, speaker, and coach

"*Powerful Beyond Measure* is a book that you cannot put down. Captivating from the start, Cynthia Mazzaferro honestly tells her story of self-doubt, emotional devastation, and the process of transformation she underwent to discover her power within. Beautifully written, you are given tools and a path to take charge of your own thoughts, emotions, and the power to achieve happiness, health, and the success that you want. You'll start the book with a desired outcome but end it with so much more. Empowering!"

—**Debra Kelsey-Davis**, CEO Soul2Soul, author of *The Ruby Slippers Principle*

"*Powerful Beyond Measure* is a living, breathing gift of love, light, and learning. Cindy gives voice to what the reader is feeling, offering crucial validation for the fears, doubts, and struggles we encounter every day. Most importantly, she offers hope that we can overcome all those obstacles and create lives of joy and inner peace.

Cindy shows us how to break down the walls we build to hide our true selves. It's all about finding the answers that come with self-exploration: why we view ourselves through a murky lens of self-limitation and doubt and how our external environment and experience are huge factors in what we see as 'self.'

Powerful Beyond Measure teaches us how to welcome love, acceptance, compassion, and kindness into our lives, making us free to invite others to see the beautiful human beings we are. It will definitely change people's lives—and who knows, maybe the whole world!"

—**Beth Riley**, MA; president and chief editor, BARdamiss Communications

"To think that we hold the keys to our happiness can be daunting, but it's also very inspiring and empowering. *Powerful Beyond Measure* shows you how to do just that in a simple, practical, and life-changing way. Happiness is no longer unattainable."

—**Leila Reyes**, MSW; Master Integrative Coach

Powerful Beyond Measure

3 Steps to Claim your
POWER WITHIN
for a Happy & Healthy Life

Cynthia E. Mazzaferro

NEW YORK

NASHVILLE   MELBOURNE

Powerful Beyond Measure
3 Steps to Claim your **POWER WITHIN** *for a Happy & Healthy Life*

Published in New York, New York, by Morgan James Publishing. Morgan James and The Entrepreneurial Publisher are trademarks of Morgan James, LLC.
www.MorganJamesPublishing.com

To book a speaking event directly with Cynthia Mazzaferro visit www.CynthiaMazzaferro.com or email at info@CynthiaMazzaferro.com.

Shelfie

A **free** eBook edition is available with the purchase of this print book.

CLEARLY PRINT YOUR NAME ABOVE IN UPPER CASE

Instructions to claim your free eBook edition:
1. Download the Shelfie app for Android or iOS
2. Write your name in **UPPER CASE** above
3. Use the Shelfie app to submit a photo
4. Download your eBook to any device

ISBN 978-1-68350-150-3 paperback
ISBN 978-1-68350-151-0 eBook
ISBN 978-1-68350-152-7 hardcover
Library of Congress Control Number:
2016911108

Cover Design by:
Rachel Lopez
www.r2cdesign.com

In an effort to support local communities, raise awareness and funds, Morgan James Publishing donates a percentage of all book sales for the life of each book to Habitat for Humanity Peninsula and Greater Williamsburg.

Get involved today! Visit
www.MorganJamesBuilds.com

This book is dedicated to the One,
The Creator of All,
My God
and all his Creations.
Including You.

May the words in this book
glorify his name, express his unconditional Love,
and serve as an instrument of inspiration and healing
with greater clarity of your divine purpose.

May you awaken the Power Within and
realize that you're Powerful Beyond Measure!
Allow your brilliance, gifts, and passions
be the light that shines upon the world.

CONTENTS

FOREWORD

We are all searching for something. Money, relationships, purpose, health, peace, success … the list is endless. At the core of these goals is the desire to attain an optimal "feeling state"—that deep sense of unconditional love, happiness, and meaning.

Most of us see this optimal feeling state as different or "better" than where we already are. We wonder if what we long for is actually attainable or how we'll ever be able to create the life we truly desire.

We wait for our lives to change; feeling powerless, we pray for someone to save us from our suffering. But the power to create this change is *already part of our soul's nature*. We already have the power to create the miraculous, visionary life of which we dream. We need only delve deep enough, and open ourselves wide enough, to access the limitless reservoir of power that resides within. When we do this, we can manifest our own remarkable and fulfilling lives.

In this book, my colleague and friend Cynthia Mazzaferro delivers this profound message in a relatable, touching way. More, she provides practical tools and interactive exercises to move you through the layers of mental and experiential conditioning which have, up until now, kept your power hidden and out of reach.

Only when we are willing to awaken to, and fearlessly examine, our deepest truths can we access the power within. This power transforms us, creates inner peace, and anchors us in our authenticity. It also connects us directly with the highest aspects of ourselves and the benevolent Universe—the aspects that dwell beyond fear and limitation. To reach our divine core is the journey of a lifetime; to wield its power is the ultimate privilege of living.

If you feel called to undertake this internal quest, you may suffer from doubt, fear, and frustration on a regular basis. You know that your past experiences are holding you back, but you aren't sure how to shed the weight of your old stories. You may cycle through anger, guilt, and emotional pain even though you want more than anything to be happy and contented. You can't seem to make the shift from relating to your traumas as wounds to seeing them as lessons.

You are not alone. Nor are you powerless. Your soul is calling you to a new awakening, and the knowledge in this book is a gateway to a place beyond your current suffering. In it, Cindy shares remarkable stories that show how our thoughts, fears, and beliefs dictate our lives. Her potent strategies give you the strength, support, and knowledge to move beyond *wanting* a joyful, healthy, fulfilling life to actually *claiming* that life in an empowered and sustainable way.

One of the core concepts of this book is the inescapable truth that in order to stand fully in the light, we must come to peace with our own darkness. Our darkness does not come from outside ourselves; it is only, and ever, self-created. When we explore this reality without fear or shame and unravel the mysterious paths where we originally lost our way—from before our birth to the present day—we can finally reveal the power and light that was buried within us all along.

I know that Cindy models and teaches these principles based on her own life experience. I met Cindy in one of my programs and personally mentored her for a few years (you'll read the synchronistic story of how we met in Part 3 of this book). I fell in love with her heart, her message, and her passion. In her work and in this book, she shares her great gifts in helping people live healed and empowered lives.

In my own books, *Happy for No Reason* and *Love for No Reason*, I focus on the importance of finding what we seek on the inside and then bringing it forth into our outer experience. Cindy has followed the same proven pathway here; her stories and strategies are delivered with the intention of transforming old wounds into life lessons and old beliefs into new strengths. Every reader will have a different experience with this book, because our life histories are different, as are our obstacles. However, I can share from personal experience that if you follow this healing formula, you *can* create transformation beyond what you can possibly imagine at this moment.

For many ages, this world has encouraged us to live from the outside in. We, the human race, have struggled to find peace both individually and globally. "Power" has been defined as assertion, control, and dominance over both individuals and the collective. But these tendencies stem from the very misconception that keeps us stuck in daily life: that true power (and love, and happiness, and success) can only be gained externally, and at someone else's expense.

Real power—the power of our divine nature—can only come from within us. This is the power to love ourselves and others; the power to find compassion in the face of anger and despair; the power to live completely in the present, each and every day. It is my hope that this book's vital message will guide you beyond your perceived limitations and allow you to live the truth that *you* are powerful beyond all measure.

Wishing you love and true power beyond measure,

Marci Shimoff, #1 *NY Times* bestselling author of *Happy for No Reason* and *Chicken Soup for the Woman's Soul*

ACKNOWLEDGEMENTS

Writing a book has been a vision of mine since I was a young girl. I always thought the title would have been *The Power Within* until recently, when I realized that when you acknowledge your Power Within, which is the connection to your divinity and Source of Creation, you become *Powerful Beyond Measure*!

I am forever grateful for Thomas Mazzaferro, my dear husband, soulmate, partner, best friend, and my biggest supporter and cheerleader throughout these past two years. Your strength, stability, encouragement, humor, and love light my life and allowed me to fulfill the passion that lay within and was waiting to take form. For all the many household responsibilities you took on and the many date nights that were canceled without complaint, I so appreciate all that you did and went without. You've been my rock, and you were always there to support me in every way during this writing process and so much more. I thank you, Tom, for letting me share our story, with its difficulties and successes, to help others who will read this book and understand how our past influences our present. Your caring heart is always present. I love you and am so happy you're in my life.

My heart and soul gives endless thanks to my mother, Janet Moore, a remarkable, faithful, loving, caring woman who overcame great odds by raising five daughters alone. Your path has not always been easy, but your heart and love are always present. I've enjoyed our spiritual journey together and the personal growth that we both have shared. Thank you for your unconditional love throughout my life and your unending support and encouragement. It is beyond measure!

Thomas and Daniel—my a-*mazz*-ing sons who I adore and have always thought of as my greatest gifts to the world—thank you for your love, encouragement, and praise as I wrote this book, which I also hope becomes a gift for many to love and treasure. Nicole, my lovely daughter-in-law who recently joined our family, I thank you for your love and support, and I embrace your ever-present smile.

A very special thanks is sent for the miraculous relationship that initially began through synchronicity and ultimately grew to give me a dear friend for life—Marci Shimoff, my mentor and the woman who has been a major influence in the culmination of seeing my vision turn into a reality. You've been with me throughout these two years, and I thank you for all your love, guidance, and wisdom in helping me achieve my dreams, passion, and purpose. I so love and appreciate that you wrote my foreword to *Powerful Beyond Measure*, this miracle that has been a creation in constant divine flow, and I am forever grateful.

To Kim Forcina, my life and "birthing" coach, for helping me personally grow and become *powerful beyond measure*, and for helping me bring my baby to full term and deliver her to the world. I now openheartedly wait for this divinely created baby, *Powerful Beyond Measure,* to become the treasure that it was born to be in this world. To a lifelong friendship and never-ending easy conversations.

To my remarkable editor, Beth Riley who brought her wisdom, grace, and insight, "rearranging the furniture" and polishing my divinely inspired words and message, letting them shine brilliantly. I knew you were the right editor because the messages and personal growth that lies within these pages resonated for you so deeply. Thank you for all the time, dedication, and love that you put into its beautiful creation. Acknowledgement goes to the other editors who aided in the process of development of *Powerful Beyond Measure*, Brookes Nohlgren and Jon VanZile.

Many thanks go to the four creators of the Enlightened Bestseller program (Marci Shimoff, Janet Bray Attwood, Chris Attwood, and Geoff Affleck) for their expertise, brilliance, and the wealth of knowledge they provide for enlightened authors and their creation. Thank you to each and every one of you for your specialized focus, attention, and support. If any aspiring author wants to learn, understand, and have the resources to bring your vision to print, this program is top-notch and one I highly recommend. Please tell them I sent you!

To the many authors and authors-to-be who were part of my support team: Carol-Ann Marshall, Debra Kelsey-Davis, Mary Johnson, and Lisa Dadd, I thank you all for your support and love.

To my wonderful webmaster, Don March, your beautiful heart, creative ability, and support of my vision and passion has always been present and is visually evident on my website. Many thanks for all the long hours and commitment to bringing the various components into creation. You are an artistic master of design.

Many thanks go to my publishing team at Morgan James Publishing. David Hancock, the founder of Morgan James Publishing, is a fabulous and heartfelt individual whose primary focus is bringing great literary work into the public eye. I felt so at home from the first time we spoke. Thanks for all your love and attention to details in making *Powerful Beyond Measure* the jewel I hoped and knew it would become. Many thanks go out to Margo Toulouse, my managing editor; Jim Howard, publishing director; Nickcole Watkins, the senior marketing relations manager, and all the other integral people who made up the fabulous Morgan James design team that helped to make *Powerful Beyond Measure* a classic beauty that will be treasured for years to come.

During these years, I've been blessed to participate twice in the "Year of Miracles." Debra Poneman and Marci Shimoff are co-creators and facilitators of this program, which is specifically tailored to women who are creating miracles in their lives, and it is nothing short of a miracle in itself. Debra, your love and support is never-ending, and I personally want to thank you for *all* that you've offered me along this wonderful road. Marci, once again, your overflowing, happy heart is always open and willing to give unconditionally. Much love and endless gratitude to you both, my dear friends. To the various miracle sisters in my YOM inner-circle group, thank you for your love, encouragement, and intentional flow and support, where miracles are abundantly present.

Bill Levacy and Traysiah Spring are both Vedic astrologers who are highly skilled at reading the stars, planets, and houses to reveal the strengths, gifts, and destiny we possess the moment we are born into the world. The amazing insights you both offered and the peace I experienced confirmed that my path and purpose is aligned with the heavens. Bill, thank you for providing valuable insight about important dates to optimize the cycles that bring the greatest results and are beyond our understanding: 6-16-16 was the day I signed with Morgan James. "616" in *Angels 101* by Doreen Virtue means "Look only at possibilities and not at material illusions. You are powerful and can overcome any situation using a positive mindset."

Additional thanks go out to Joel Roberts in the production of my video and messaging in your course, The Language of Impact. Your insightful, passionate gift of language and turning the spoken word into an inspiring, profound message is simply miraculous.

To my partner in our Intuition Mastery Summit, Lynnis Woods-Mullins, thank you for our wonderful collaboration with the intuitively created Intuition Mastery Summit that brought us together and offered us expansion, credibility, and a beautiful platform to reach out and bring the importance of intuition into people's lives. Thank you for allowing me to be an integral part in your beautiful and far-reaching e-magazine, *Wellness Woman 40 and Beyond*.

Many thanks for all the podcasts, workshops, presentations, sponsored events, OLLI and MILE classes that allowed me to speak and spread the many messages that are found within *Powerful Beyond Measure*.

For all the stories of students and clients who have allowed me to be part of their lives, I have been forever changed by your light. Thank you for allowing me to share a bit of you within these pages, for others to see how pain can be healed and the growth that is always waiting patiently for us to embark upon.

To Master Reiki Practitioner, Lourdes Gray at John Gray Reiki Institute thank you for being a wonderful, energetic leader that trained me to Master

Reiki Level and all the fabulous light workers that I had the privilege to work alongside.

Many thanks to Mary Summa for her photographic brilliance in capturing my light and love. Mary took the beautiful photograph of me for *Powerful Beyond Measure*.

To my dear friends Lina Alpert, Madeleine Diker and Carol Kovaly for all the wonderful Thursday evenings and toasting my successes over the years. For all my extended family: sisters, cousins, in-laws, etc. and all my friends in art, tennis, and social groups, I love you all and thank you for your support and love. For all those who have touched my life in some way—and there are thousands— know that I love and appreciate your beautiful souls.

INTRODUCTION

I'll never forget the devastating day when my husband told me, in a broken, calm voice, that he still loved me but couldn't live with me any longer. I could feel his agony and regret as he spoke, unfamiliar tears spilling down his cheeks. My throat tightened and my heart lurched as my own tears started to flow. I stood there for a moment in disbelief. My mind raced as I tried to grasp the magnitude of what he was telling me. How could this be happening? What did he mean, he *loved* me but couldn't live with me any longer? How could he destroy all that we had created? What about our commitment, our vows in front of God—for better or worse, 'til death do us part?

I struggled to understand. Why was he doing this? Was our life so bad? We had two healthy, smart, ambitious sons who had both recently struck out on their own and were well on their way to independence. Tom had achieved professional success and was able to retire early. Wasn't this *our* time for freedom, to explore and do what we wanted without family obligations pulling at us?

Tom was always a gentle man, avoiding confrontation at all costs. Although he may not have been as emotionally expressive as I needed or wanted, I always felt he would walk the world for me. He told me there wasn't another woman.

Intuitively, I knew that was true, but the realization that he would rather be alone than with me cut me to the core.

My world was crumbling. I begged him to stay. I was angry, hurt, and defensive. I criticized myself for being a failure. I fought to regain my bearings as a storm of shame, profound sadness, loss, and grief swirled within me. I felt completely broken.

As Tom went upstairs to pack a few things, I sat alone in our family room, unable to move, tears flooding uncontrollably. I felt hopeless, deserted, and unable to speak. I knew that no words I spoke today would change his mind. My mind raced. How would I survive? How would this affect our sons? What were the financial implications? How could I protect myself?

During the terrible hours and days that passed, I had frequent flashbacks to my first experience with abandonment. I was only seven years old when my father deserted my mother, my four sisters, and me. I know now that my father's rejection some fifty years ago triggered the profound feelings of abandonment, commitment, and loss of love that affected me in ways I'd carry throughout most of my life, but at the time, all I knew was that it was happening all over again. I was living my worst nightmare. Was I such a bad person? Had I done something to create this? Why was I being rejected by another man who told me he loved me? Had I always worried deep in my heart that Tom would leave me, like my father had? I couldn't understand why the men in my life who were supposed to love and nourish me would just turn and walk away.

I was nauseated most of the time, unable to eat, and filled with a profound emptiness. I spent hours reflecting on our life together. I had given everything to my family and marriage. Tom had worked long hours, occasionally traveling overseas, while our boys had maintained busy schedules with school and sports. I had put my career as a physical therapist and ergonomist on hold so I could support them in their passions, and I took great pride in my roles as wife and mother.

Tom moved into a hotel. We talked on the phone occasionally about household matters. I asked him to come back so we could work things out, but he said he needed space. I felt that if I pushed more that would only drive him farther away. Maybe we both needed time.

After ten agonizing days, we agreed to meet at a local coffee shop. It felt wonderful to see him, to feel his presence. I was thrilled that he hugged me when he came in. Our time together was engaging, each wanting to know how the other was doing. It was evident that we both were hurting, and we listened to each other closely, really trying to hear what was being said. I could feel that he still had very mixed emotions. He hugged me again as we left.

A few days later, he called to tell me that he was going to move into our second home on the lake; spring was approaching, and it had to be opened up anyway. I felt a stab of resentment that he was going to be enjoying himself alone in our beautiful play house, the one we'd created together. How would that help resolve the situation?

I had a strong gut reaction—intuition was speaking: I needed to go up to the lake house. I found these inner thoughts really bizarre. I couldn't believe I was feeling like I should go there. I was so afraid of being rejected once again. What would he think? How would he feel about me coming there uninvited? Would it make the situation worse? But with each question my mind offered up, my heart continued to tell me I just *had* to go. This was one of those choices in life when you have to decide whether to follow your intuition, even when it's in direct contrast to what your mind is telling you. I actually had to trust my inner feeling: I was supposed to go there, to help clean up and open our beloved waterside house. I know it sounds crazy, and my mind was telling me all the reasons not to, but I followed my heart. I decided not to call him or ask permission to meet; I just followed that inner voice that told me to *just go*.

Well, I certainly surprised him when I showed up! When he asked why I'd come, I said I just *had* to, that this was *our* home. Amazingly, he was receptive, and I started to help clean and open the house. As I cleaned, tears flowed at all the memories that filled the walls. We had so much to be happy for, and his leaving was just throwing all that we had been blessed with back at God, without a shred of gratitude. It hurt so much!

Later in the day, Tom and I started talking. Really talking. We talked and cried together for hours, expressing our deepest thoughts and desires. I encouraged him to return home so we could work it out. Thankfully, in what I knew was a very difficult decision for him, Tom agreed to move back to our primary home and continue to work on resolving our problems.

Over the next few months, I found myself trying desperately to change the things about myself and my behavior that I thought bothered Tom. Since he didn't show his emotions easily or openly, I avoided getting into deep, emotional conversations or saying anything that could be construed as instructions or telling him what to do. I even stopped asking what he had planned for the day, in case it might seem like I was being controlling. I was experiencing a constant inner tug-of-war. I was unsure of what to say, and I worried about everything: what our boys would think, what the future would look like, if our marriage would survive.

As I dealt with all the questions and internal unrest, I began to realize that there was something deeper going on inside me. I needed to find the answers within myself—to understand the underlying root cause of my feelings and the behaviors I'd developed to cope with them. I needed to understand the defense mechanisms I'd created to protect myself and, more importantly, how to heal my emotional wounds so I could move forward and embrace the fulfilled, loving, grace-filled life I wanted and was meant to live.

Thus began my journey toward self-knowledge. I dove deeply into the internal investigative work necessary to bring personal healing and the resolution of events from my past. It wasn't until I actually starting to deal with the original wound—my father leaving—that I gained some relief from its emotional pain and gained the power to change my present. I had wondered as a child if somehow I had been responsible for Dad leaving, but when I started to look at my parents' divorce from an adult viewpoint, I realized it had nothing to do with me. I had to consciously reverse my old patterns of belief and insecurities and put the ownership of my father's behavior back on him instead of myself. I began to see myself as a person with substantial worth and value, and I learned to recognize that my dad's inability to be committed and show love to his children was his issue; it was his choice, and the absent role he played may have been exactly what I needed for my soul's growth.

This process of personal resolution, development, and healing wasn't always easy. When I would deal with one aspect, another door would open, revealing another layer I needed to resolve. I had been holding on to so much emotional pain from my childhood—as we all do—and it negatively affected me in almost every aspect of my life.

I had to catch myself when self-doubt started to creep in and my mind tried to remind me of all the reasons I wasn't able, capable, worthy, or entitled to. It took some time, but once I was able to identify the falsehood—the triggers—and understood that my father's abandonment had nothing to do with me, I was well on my way to changing the physical, mental, and emotional responses that I would normally internalize, making me feel like a victim or someone lacking. Once I started to see myself as worthy, loveable, and important, then I could apply this inner feeling of harmony and self-love to my relationship with Tom and others. I was able to be more open. I stopped worrying about rejection or abandonment and shed the fear that I was somehow not good enough. My life was proof of the philosophical Law of Attraction: what we put our attention on and how we think about it reflects energetically onto ourselves. I was discovering that we create much of what we think and feel, and we manifest and control exactly what we live and experience! Powerful, but scary at the same time.

Our marriage did indeed survive, but it wasn't always easy. It took a lot of time, hard work, patience, and compassion, but we got through it together, and our marriage is stronger than ever. As difficult as that experience was, it had a profoundly positive impact on my life. It forced me to face myself in ways I hadn't before. If I'd been completely honest with myself, many aspects of my own personal life were far from tranquil and harmonious. Tom's leaving was a wake-up call: something within me needed to be addressed, a lesson needed to be learned. Tom and I both needed to grow.

As an adult woman, I look back and realize now that each step of my life was a rung on a ladder that brought opportunities for personal growth and development. Using the dynamic, empowering process I've laid out for you in this book, I was able to identify emotionally triggered memories that played a very significant role in who I became. As I continued to grow and recognize the wounds from which I needed to heal, I became alive. I could see what I struggled with and the life lessons I needed to learn. I can pick any point along my lifetime continuum, see the potential lessons that availed themselves to me, and acknowledge how each experience has significantly contributed to where I am in my life. This process has been incredibly rewarding for me personally and is the foundation of my work in the world today.

Did I ever envision writing this book, reaching thousands with this profound healing work, and enabling people to be **Powerful Beyond Measure**? The answer, quite simply, is *no*, but miracles were ever present and pathways unfolded beyond what I could ever have imagined, facilitating my purpose work. I actually had to learn not to be small and accept that this was my divine calling and gift to the world. I believe we each walk our paths so we can learn and share those lessons with others. I feel so blessed, recognizing that my life is only a mere extension of my life's purpose. I embrace the people and opportunities that come into my life as part of my understanding and growth. This knowledge and realization has been life-changing for me on so many levels. Soon, you'll experience the same transformation in your own life as you read and delve into this book; miracles will unfold, and your heart will be overflowing with love and happiness.

I have found time and time again that our struggles are opportunities the Universe creates so we can learn and grow. I learned how to open myself up to the lessons the Universe had so patiently been trying to teach me. Most importantly, I discovered my own inner power, the ***power within*** that was allowing me to be **Powerful Beyond Measure**! I now had the power to take charge of my thoughts, emotions, life, and my destiny.

This power is in you, too. It's in all of us. We sense it when we have that "gut feeling" or hear that inner voice we call intuition—the one that whispers, "You *know* what's right for you. Life *can* be better. You *can* be happy. You *deserve* love, respect, and compassion."

Are you ready to unveil your inner strength—to become **Powerful Beyond Measure**? The most important step on any journey is taking that first one. Congratulate yourself—you took that first step when you decided to read this book. You are following your intuition: you've acknowledged that you have the desire, commitment, and willingness to change and that you want more, you deserve more, and, most importantly, you want to be happier on the inside and outside. You're seeking answers to all the same questions I asked myself.

The good news is that I can help you find those answers. This transformational book will show you exactly how to reveal and harness your inner power. You'll learn how to understand and take control of your emotions and embrace a life filled with vibrancy and passion, where each new day brings adventure, awe, and true happiness. During this process, you will understand and accept that *you* are the one who must be in harmony with your *self* and that transformation will ultimately bring you a profound sense of *oneness* and inner peace. You will discover that you are **Powerful Beyond Measure** and fall in love with yourself once again.

Powerful Beyond Measure will be a valued resource that you'll return to frequently to unravel new aspects of truth that need to be revealed and incorporated into your life. The concepts in this book will exceed your greatest expectations as they facilitate enlightenment, healing, forgiveness, awareness, personal transformation, directional shifts, and even miracles that will support your passion and purpose. To obtain the greatest benefits from this book, I strongly encourage you to actively participate in all the exercises, start a journal, be courageous as you move outside your comfort zone, and commit to following the intuition that has led you to this book at this time. All exercises, templates, and meditations are available to download or print and can be found at <u>www. PowerfulBeyondMeasureBook.com/forms</u>.

Becoming Your True Self

The search for your true self is central to the **Powerful Beyond Measure** process. Are there times when you struggle with who you really are and ask, "Is this all there is?" Do you find it hard to believe that you are unique, important, and here to play a beneficial role in the world?

We have been molded and shaped by what we have been taught, told, and accepted as truth. These imprints from family, institutions, cultures, and religions have infiltrated our perception of ourselves. Many of us blend in with the masses, feeling like we've lost touch with our true essence.

Using the powerful key steps found within this book, you will learn to connect with and be true to your authentic self—who you really are, not what you believe others want you to be, what you've been told you should be, or the persona you've come to believe is you. That self-image is based on filtered, distorted, and misperceived notions. Who allows us to be judged and evaluated, accepting others' perceptions of us as our own? *We do!*

Within these pages, you'll find the tools you need to empower *yourself* to heal the root cause(s) of your pain, change your behavior, beliefs, thoughts, and defense mechanisms, and achieve true emotional freedom and expression. You'll look at your past situations, current scenarios, and repetitive cycles to discover your *Soul lessons*. You'll learn how to accept the events in your past, both "good" and "bad," as integral components that will help you learn those lessons. All these parts are intimately woven together, and when they're incorporated, you'll be able to embrace new experiences, joyfully embark on the life you were meant to live, and use your gifts and passions in support of the larger world. How wonderful would that feel? If this sounds too good to be true, it's not. It may sound impossible right now, but I am here to tell you that you hold the key that will unlock everything you seek.

It all starts with understanding the impact of your past and how it continues to influence your life today. Our life experiences are often laced with difficulties and struggles. As a result of these experiences, we become wounded—emotionally, mentally, physically, and sometimes even spiritually. We misinterpret and personalize these untruths, holding onto them (possibly throughout our whole lives) and devaluing ourselves in the process.

I am sure you can recall very difficult times in your life when you felt like you could barely breathe. You felt devastated, depleted, and hopeless. During those trying moments, it's hard to have a clear perspective, but later you often see that the hardest times were actually launching points toward resolution, opportunity, and growth. Our oldest, most painful memories ultimately have the greatest influence on who we become. I believe these same memories hold the keys to the lessons we need to learn in the present.

Everyday life can be marred by a profound sense of confusion, loss, dissatisfaction, depression, or feelings of unworthiness. You might not understand where these emotions come from, and you may even blame yourself. *You are not alone.* Each of us carries painful emotional weight from situations, relationships, and our own inaccurate perceptions of our past, present, and even our future.

This emotional weight is the anchor that keeps you stuck in your limiting self-beliefs. It can actually take up residence within your body, affecting your life force energy and impacting your health. The good news is that you have the power to let go of this emotional weight, and I will show you how to let go, permanently release these toxic emotional energies, and begin the healing process.

In Part I, **Explore Your Past and Ease Your Pain**, you will gain clarity and greater inner wisdom by identifying the triggers and misperceptions you've internalized up to this point: your emotional wounds, self-limiting beliefs, and the defensive behaviors and protective walls that you created. You'll investigate your past, your memories, and the imprints that continue to bombard your mind. You will see how your self-image has been contaminated by your past impressions, negative feedback, and, ironically, even your own misguided perception of what you thought to be true. You will start to see a common thread—a repetitive theme of concepts, values, and beliefs that need to be focused on and addressed. As you go through this process, you'll start to make the life-changing shift from victimhood to empowerment. You'll see that you have the power within to forever break those old habits and patterns. You'll discover that you are the source of your own worthiness, abundance, love, and you'll no longer need the excuses or benefits your self-limiting beliefs were providing you.

After working with thousands of individuals, I've found that emotional health affects every aspect of life, including physical, mental, and spiritual well-being. When your emotions create internal stress, they negatively affect your actions and beliefs, and they even have detrimental physical effects on your physiology, chemistry, and energy. When you identify and reduce your emotional stressors, they'll no longer trigger harmful negative emotions, thoughts, and outcomes that can sabotage you. The only way to reduce this stress is to deal with the repressed emotional energy from your past.

In Part II, **Empower Your Present and Embrace Your *Self***, you will learn how to heal and release those emotional pains that have kept you weak, afraid, and small. The key to release is reframing these difficult times. "Reframing" means assigning new meaning to an event. Often, we are weighed down by the memories of traumatic experiences long after they have occurred, but if we *reframe* those memories, we can find the opportunity to learn and grow from them. This is a critical component in the healing process. Our lives can be profoundly altered by pain, sorrow, loss, guilt, anger, and the belief that there is something wrong with ourselves and/or the world. But what if we look at it another way: what if we *never* had difficulties, struggles, or hard times? How would we learn to overcome, succeed, and persevere? If life were always perfect, would we be truly happy and content? The truth is that our own struggles are invaluable opportunities for personal development. They help us develop forgiveness, generosity, kindness, strength, confidence, and, of course, love.

During my career, I owned an ergonomics company which focused on preventing injury and reducing stress by creating efficiencies and optimizing the relationship between individuals and their environment. We can apply many of these same concepts to relieve stress in our mental and emotional lives, too; I call it emotional ergonomics. This part of the book specifically deals with living in the moment and empowering you to be in control of your thoughts, how you choose to feel, and what steps you decide to take.

In Part II, you'll learn how to reduce your emotional stress with the *Emotional Health and Fitness Program*. The exercises will rekindle the *you* that is longing to be awakened by learning to love, forgive, and accept yourself. You will fortify your emotional fitness with a full *Range of E-motions* that support, facilitate, and empower you to be healthy and authentic to yourself. You'll examine the walls you erected to protect yourself and the defensive behaviors you have relied on and allow them to be removed so you can begin your journey of freedom, expansiveness, and continued healing. With this freedom, an inner peace, acceptance, and love will be gifted to you.

"What you seek is seeking you!"
—**Rumi**

All the personal growth work that you will accomplish in Parts I and II will prepare the soil for you to plant your seeds of passion and desire—your unique, special spiritual gifts that are meant to be nurtured and developed. Your life is beckoning, asking you to find your inner power, honor your gifts, and realize your special life purpose. With such a universe of gifts and empowerment awaiting, you might ask yourself why your life has been so difficult and why you haven't found happiness. The best news is that *you* hold every answer to these questions—as well as the ones that haven't even been formulated yet—but the real question is: What are *you* going to do now? Part III, **Envision Your Future and Expand Your Possibilities**, focuses on empowering you to create your own future and use those gifts to bring great joy to yourself and others.

For some, feeling alive, living with a realized purpose, and seeking great joy, fulfillment, and love that comes from making a difference in service to others can be scary and may seem unrealistic. To think that you have a specific purpose can be daunting and even overwhelming, but rest assured that you are unique and wonderful, and reawakening that miraculous being will change your life in ways you can't even imagine. In a way, it will be the rebirth of your beautiful spirit.

Can you imagine what our world would be like if each one of us lived the purposeful life we were created for? How could each of our unique, caring, and thoughtful acts transform this chaotic, violent world? Can you even imagine a world of harmony, love, and cohesiveness? What if that desired outcome couldn't be realized without you playing your integral part? I believe that love of self and others is the ultimate lesson we are all here to learn and the truth we need to uncover. When you embrace this realization, your life becomes the playing field upon which to learn, excel, and evolve, and when you're aligned within and truly love and see your value, miracles will be abundantly present in your life.

In this final powerful section, templates are provided to help you create action steps to manifest the future that you want to live in the present—your treasure chest of dreams, visions, passions, and goals. You'll explore how to follow your intuition to reveal your passions, desires and life's purpose(s). In addition, I will show you a variety of techniques that will aid in your physical, emotional, and energetic healing and open you up to living a life of abundance, success, and happiness. This will totally transform how you feel and what the Universe brings to you. Many of my clients say things like: "I have never felt this happy before! I had no idea that I had this power to change, and I can't believe how everything has been impacted for the better. I didn't know freedom and happiness was so empowering!"

Your Creator has a plan for you.

I believe that we are each a part of the Creator and that we all have our own unique, important roles to play in this world. Each of us is a single thread, intertwining with all the billions of other brightly colored threads to construct this glorious tapestry of life designed by our Creator, but we each need to fulfill our part to create this beautiful masterpiece.

What if your Creator has a special plan for you? What if you are the missing piece to the puzzle? What if you've been uniquely gifted for a specific, loving, life purpose that brings value to the world? You don't have to be intimidated by these questions. When you recognize that you belong to something greater—that you, with the specific talents and gifts that only you possess, are a divine being—then you can reclaim your spirituality and live your destiny. Your life is part of a greater vision, but you need to explore, be brave, and live your truth.

Your existence matters. You have important work to do. If we all fulfill our roles, both singularly and collectively, can you imagine how amazing our world could be? We cannot see the master plan, but know that you are one irreplaceable piece that contributes to the whole. Your life matters!

Many people say to me, "but I am 50, 60, 70 years old. What can I do now?" Trust me, it is never too late to acknowledge who you are, awaken your Soul, follow your passion, and live the life you were meant to live. Sometimes just learning to love yourself and be happy is the greatest gift you can give to yourself and the world.

How to Use this Book

I encourage you to approach this book with self-love, self-compassion, and self-acceptance so that you can literally transform every part of your life. You'll receive the greatest benefit if you take the time to connect closely and personally with the exercises. These tools are extremely powerful in obtaining the answers that you seek because they continue to build upon each other, bringing you to a deeper and higher understanding. The more honest, vulnerable, and engaged you are, the more profound your clarity will be. Only then will you be able to clearly identify the steps you need to take in order to resolve your inner struggle and find the passion, inner peace, and wisdom that's been calling you all along —your *essence*.

Some sections may be more challenging than others. Be patient with yourself. The speed of your journey is not the critical component; it's all about learning your Soul lessons so you can open your heart and mind and let the healing begin.

As we go through the various steps, I will be sharing some of my personal stories, along with several others from my students and clients, to demonstrate how the process works and the revelations that brought self-awareness, inner-peace, and personal transformation. Many of these reflections will speak to you on a personal and visceral level. Even though their stories may be different from yours, you'll be able to relate and gain greater understanding and enlightenment for your own personal healing.

If you've been somewhat reluctant or even resistant in the past to let your guard down and allow yourself to be vulnerable and authentic, ask yourself, "What am I afraid of?" No matter what the reason has been in the past, today is the perfect day to start your new life. It's never too late! Open yourself up to the capacity for a greater personal understanding and healing so that you can realize your true authentic potential and share your gifts and purpose with the world. Honor yourself and explore what you're seeking, for therein lies freedom, love, and peace.

It is my hope that through the many stories I share with you in these pages, you'll see that you are *not alone* and that you can change how you feel about yourself and acknowledge how the world can open up to you. You're here for a reason. Be excited and trust that you are exactly where you need to be. You have a Universe of support: guides, angels, God/Creator/Source, and even this **Powerful Beyond Measure** community. Your journey and your destiny have been divinely inspired and created for you; now it is time for you to choose to claim that inner calling.

I encourage you to take a deep breath, quiet your mind, let any misgivings pass out of your thoughts, and give yourself the greatest gift—become **Powerful Beyond Measure** *within yourself and in your life*. It's time for you to start your own personal journey of self-exploration. Be excited, because today you're taking the next, most powerful step forward, the one that will ultimately bring you everything you ever wanted.

I feel honored and blessed to be with you throughout this powerful process of personal transformation, and I know that you'll achieve the results that you desire and maybe even ones that you might not be aware of.

> *"What lies behind us and what lies before us are tiny matters compared to what lies within us."*
> —**Ralph Waldo Emerson**

"The unexamined life is not worth living."
—Socrates

Part I

Explore Your Past And Ease Your Pain

In the introduction to this book, I shared very briefly the story of how my parent's divorce impacted me, but let me share a few more details.

I was one of five girls; each of us was born approximately two years apart. My father, John, was a U.S. Air Force B-52 pilot who wasn't home very often. My mother, Janet, was a wonderful, loving, faithful woman who was very dedicated to raising and keeping her children together, regardless of the stress and difficulties.

I have very few memories of my father, and the ones I do have are mostly of his absence. I recall my mom bringing us to the tarmac in our Sunday best to meet his plane. As the band played, excitement, anticipation, and energy permeated the air. I remember him emerging as the airplane door opened, descending the stairs in his pilot's uniform as his six beauties waited for his loving embrace and sweet, endearing comments. I remember feeling proud of my father and his service and dedication to our country—but I always wished there was more time for us, for me!

I longed for my father's love, his physical embrace, protection, and support. Even before my parents' divorce, his constant absence created an inner need that made me search for external love and confirmation to fill an inner void.

Not having a dad in my life was a constant reminder of rejection and abandonment. Even though I had a beautiful, loving mom, she couldn't fill the paternal void. There was always an empty seat at the kitchen table, at my graduation, recitals, and sporting events. He wasn't there to walk me down the aisle and give me away at my wedding. I didn't get to feel his embrace as he proudly waltzed me through the traditional father-daughter dance. He wasn't there to watch my sons grow up. Each one of these experiences, and so many more, were a constant reminder that he had walked away, discarding us—me—as if we were trash. The pain, the emptiness, and loneliness were often hard to come to grips with. Was it really too much to ask that he simply love me?

I grew up feeling stressed, biting my nails, slightly overweight and constantly concerned about what I did and how I did it. I became a tomboy, loving to play outside with the neighborhood boys. I guess I was searching even then for the masculine support and love that I so desperately wanted and needed. I was a happy, extroverted little girl, but I was unsure of myself and I was always seeking approval. I desperately wanted to be liked, and I often held my emotions in until, eventually, they would explode. In some ways, I was like a volcano, the pressure building until I couldn't hold it in anymore.

I couldn't understand how a father could leave five beautiful daughters who ranged from nine months to nine years of age, as well as a wife who was committed and faithful to him. Even as I write these words, after much inner work, I can still feel the sadness of a relationship that never was, but the negative energy has finally been released. Thank Goodness! This one event changed the trajectory of my life, but in hindsight, I can see clearly now that it offered me exactly what I needed for personal growth and empowerment to enable me to follow my destiny and do the work I was born to do.

How can I stop the past from hurting me in the present and future?

My story is living proof that, even as we continue to age, our subconscious mind constantly replays events from our past: surviving a terrible accident; the suffering of a friend; the devastation of a business; financial loss; the death of someone close; abusive relationships; dependency on drugs or alcohol—the list could go on forever. If they aren't dealt with in a healthy way, memories can create a never-ending cycle of fear, judgment, anger, worry, misgivings, doubt, anxiety, and a loss of self.

Tell me *one* thing that you were unable to survive. If you're here, then you're alive and there is nothing that you haven't been able to endure. No matter what experiences you've had—happy or sad, short or long, devastating or joyful—you managed to navigate through them all, and life carried on. You may have regrets or wish things had turned out differently, but you somehow found a way to get through them. However, the indelible memories of those experiences, deeply coded within your mind, continue to play a huge role in your physical, emotional, and mental health. These memories cannot be changed or altered in any way, but what you'll learn to do in these pages is to acknowledge and accept these *past* events and memories and choose to release the trapped emotional imprint and live in the now, from a state of acceptance and love.

My life is only a mere extension of my life's purpose.

Of course, you can't just press the delete key and make those memories disappear, and you really don't want to erase them. Everything that has happened to you has occurred for a reason, even though you might not be able to see it clearly yet. Your task is to choose whether you'll let these wounds continue to hold you hostage or look for the gift that lies in your experience. As odd as it sounds, the truth is that your gifts lie next to your wounds. Transforming your personal challenges into your greatest gifts will help to reveal your destiny.

The first step in the Powerful Beyond Measure process is to look at your past in terms of the opportunities life has already presented to you and the lessons you've learned and haven't learned—both positive and negative. This is an integral step in resolving the problems that allow memories to harm your emotional health. It can also be the most challenging, because acknowledging and experiencing these thoughts, feelings, and images again can often be filled with sadness, regret, blame, and anger. Trust me, you won't have to relive the past, but through exploration, you'll be able to uncover the triggers that wounded you. If you don't learn these lessons, you'll probably find that the Universe will continue to provide opportunities to try again and again, often escalating in intensity until you do.

Understanding Your Past

Why do our past images, thoughts and emotions come to mind so frequently?

Why do we relive the negative aspects of our past?

What are we supposed to learn from those experiences?

These are the crucial questions you will explore in Part I of the Powerful Beyond Measure process. You will see how your past and the emotional weight associated with your experiences have been imprinted on your subconscious, how they are often replayed throughout your life, and how you can learn and grow beyond these experiences and memories even today.

If the events of your past hadn't occurred, then your perception, beliefs, and defense mechanisms would also have *not* been created. Those old perceptions of self and the defense mechanisms you've developed must be changed and lowered to allow you to address your Soul lessons and grow.

As you go through the Powerful Beyond Measure process, you will see that your memories carry a persistent theme that reveals your Soul lessons. You will examine your patterns of behavior and see that your thoughts and emotions feed into your subconscious programming—what you learned from people and experiences in your past—and holds you back today. Unfortunately, we give more emotional weight to the negative events in our lives, so they have more power over us. The good news is that this negative information is actually where your growth and Soul potential lies. Once you can articulate the areas or lessons that you need to address and release the emotional weight that is associated with them, true healing and growth can occur.

*You are **not** your past, unless you **choose** to live in that space.*

The first vital step is to realize that your memories cannot hurt you unless you allow them to. The past is in the past and you never have to relive those painful moments again unless you *choose* to. If you keep watching that old mental rerun or listening to that same, tired record play again and again, *you* are choosing to give power to the emotional environment associated with that past experience. You need to ask yourself, "Why do I need to see or listen to this again? What am I not understanding? What can or should I do? What lessons were there to learn? When can I finally put this memory in long-term, permanent storage?"

"He who does not remember the past is condemned to repeat it."
—George Santayana

When you become engaged and work toward your Soul growth, something magical happens. You become awakened, your breath expands, your heart rejoices; there is an excitement and change in intention that propels you forward. You start to see the world as if your sight has suddenly been restored after a long, dark night—everything looks brighter, colors are more vibrant, and an exhilarating energy fills everything within you and all around you. You'll see amazing bits of synchronicity in your everyday life, and you'll find yourself awestruck, wondering, "Is this *really* how wonderful life can be?"

This is a time for self-exploration, which is a vital component of your understanding so that you can look at your past in a more loving way. I like to think of it as being your own spiritual private investigator. Private investigators seek information, capture pertinent data, and draw objective conclusions. They look at just the facts. When you can use this method—taking a step back to look at your life without passion or judgment, you can figure out which of your emotions are true and which ones are *reactions* to your perception of past events.

As you approach your past and memories with this private investigator mindset, you'll learn to look at this new knowledge with enthusiasm and realize that current situations are presenting themselves so you can work on these similar concepts for Soul growth. We all have blind spots, just like when we're driving, that make us unable to see all that is going on around us. The same is true when it comes to looking at our lives; we see the most obvious details and emotions, but we have an unsettling feeling that we're missing something, and we can't quite put our finger on it.

It is important that you don't judge yourself as to why you have to learn these lessons or why it has to be so difficult. Recognizing these Soul lessons will bring you into harmony, where you are aligned with your destiny. Everything will continue to support your growth and purpose. Embracing your past and letting go of your judgment will allow you to see more clearly so you can get in touch with your passion, inner power, and desire. You *can* become content, accepting, and loving of yourself and understand why you are here and the value that you are meant to share with the world.

Are you ready to begin, asking questions and looking inward for answers will help identify what you need to acknowledge and work on? This exercise encourages you to do just that: find out what you're looking for and where you hope to end up.

Before you begin this exercise, take a few minutes to contemplate, breathe consciously, and release any stress or worry. You may even want to meditate. You want to be open and willing to reflect on your past and identify those aspects that have played a role in your unhappiness.

Remind yourself that you are safe and nothing can hurt you. When you feel relaxed and ready to begin, you will be stepping through the first door of your transformation. Realize all that you observe, gain as knowledge, and identify as emotional weight (pain) are jewels of wisdom that will guide you in the search for your Power Within, which in turn will allow you to be *Powerful Beyond Measure*.

Please don't just read the questions to this Self-assessment form, but actually answer them. They will provide great insight and serve as a baseline. To obtain a printed copy of self-assessment form, go to www.PowerfulBeyondMeasureBook. com/forms.

Powerful Beyond Measure: Self-assessment Form

Date: _____

1. What would you like to accomplish by reading this book?

    _____

    _____

2. What is it that you seek—spiritually, physically, mentally, and emotionally?

    _____

    _____

3. What are your greatest attributes/strengths?

    _____

    _____

4. What are your greatest weaknesses?

    _____

    _____

5. What is your greatest fear?

    _____

    _____

6. Can you list any inner "knowing" of what you consider your spiritual gifts?

    _____

    _____

7. Are you living a life that is in harmony with your divine purpose? If so, what is it?

    _____

    _____

8. On a scale from 1 (sad) to 5 (very happy), how happy are you right now?

    _____

9. On a scale from 1 (low) to 5 (high), rank how you feel about yourself.

    _____

10. If you could wish one thing for yourself, what would it be?

    _____

    _____

11. What part(s) of your body do you feel you hold your emotional weight and pain?

    _____

    _____

12. On a scale of 1 (slight) to 10 (severe), what is the pain level of the conditions/symptoms you associate with your emotional weight? (e.g., stomach symptom level 8, wrist symptom level 4).

    _____

    _____

"What we find changes who we become."
—Peter Morville

Power of your past
In the beginning …

Let's begin your journey of awakening through exploration, empowerment, and enlightenment.

What if you I told you that you chose to come to Earth, into your family, to learn certain lessons and grow spiritually? Would you look at your life or family any differently?

I believe we each have Soul lessons to learn and grow from during our lifetime. The Universe presents us with different windows of opportunities—scenarios and environments that support our spiritual growth. There is no right or wrong, just what is. How we respond, interact, feel, and understand is a choice we make.

In this chapter, I invite you to explore your youngest years. These are the most critical because the understandings and beliefs you took on then formed the template that has influenced you throughout your life. As we begin to explore our past and how it continues to impact us even today, we need to understand how we took on our beliefs and develop a personal understanding of Self.

Power of Memory Recall

The Power of Memory Recall happens all the time. It's the movie that replays in your mind even when you don't want it to. You've watched it a million times; you can recall the characters, the environment, the dialogue, the climax, and, ultimately, the outcome. Of course, time has a way of changing and twisting the details to fit your understanding and make it more comfortable (even casting blame on others), and most likely that memory isn't even accurate any longer.

Some of you may feel your memories haven't played a significant role in your life, while others feel their past is to blame for all the misery and unhappiness they experience today. There is a wide continuum of how people allow their past to influence their lives. Even so, it's critical to identify the elements of your memory recall because they are the root of what lives, breathes, and grows in your mind, body, and spirit.

Earliest Years

Let's start at the very beginning. Understanding the mindset, feelings, and environment of your parents when you were in utero may be very interesting, and it can give you insight as to how you felt loved and wanted. Children are fragile individuals who are constantly being impacted by their environment, as well as their own perception of their experiences. The brain begins to mature in utero, and this growth process continues through most of our lives. A baby enters the world with a still-primitive cerebral cortex, and those first few years of life contribute to their emotional and cognitive maturation. Children's conscious minds are immature, waiting to be stimulated for learning and developing.

What we learn as children lays down neural circuitry that still influences us as adults. Between conception and six years of age, our immature, conscious mind is greatly affected by what we see, hear, and feel. As a result, we create long-lasting beliefs, expectations, and behaviors that continue to be the neural template we take with us into adulthood. As a child, you were unaware of the profound messages that were shaping your personality and behaviors, but that doesn't mean they weren't laying the foundation for who you were to become.

Your mind is like a sponge, taking in information and forming perceptions around the dynamics that occur in your life. Your senses are constantly bombarded with stimuli; in response, you form understandings and beliefs. This concept is very important to understand, because as thinking, mature adults, we can consciously change our old neural ingrained pathways and create new positive, healthy circuitry that can promote health and happiness.

Our perception, whether it is accurate or not, is one critical element that can totally transform how we look at ourselves, others, and the situation at hand. For example, a daughter who always sees her father roughhouse with his sons can perceive that Dad doesn't love her as much, since the physical activity is not the same. Of course, this is one child's perception. Is it accurate or inaccurate? Who's to say? In this child's perception, she takes on the belief that unless someone is physical with her, then she is not loved. You can see how our perceptions can trigger the false, self-limiting beliefs we take on and how they influence the choices we make.

Reflecting back on your childhood can bring clarity about when, where, and how your perceptions, beliefs, and behaviors were born. Expectations, the role you played (or thought you should play), the way you were treated, your environment, the cultural and religious beliefs you were taught—these are just a few elements that contributed to your belief system. The key is learning to recognize how your impressionable years impacted you and what potential lessons you have to learn. Unfortunately, we don't live in a society that values this type of inner exploration. When are we taught how to create and promote a loving environment, both *internally* and externally? Where and when are children, and even adults, taught to deal with emotions in a healthy way so they aren't made to carry painful wounds throughout their lives?

It's easy to blame our parents or a specific person or event for our pain, but I don't encourage it. When we do this, we make ourselves out to be victims, and we feel helpless. I believe it is very important for us to acknowledge that we are also an integral component of our understanding and cannot hold our parents and environment completely responsible for our self-limiting beliefs and who we've become as adults.

Memories are formed even before we're born!

With life, as with everything, there is always a beginning. We do not know when our spirit, our Soul, was created, but many believe that our physical birth begins at the moment of fertilization. The joining of two single cells creates a miraculous being—you! Each of us is a unique and special Soul whose emotions and personality start to form even before our birth.

At around ten weeks, a fetus is already wiggling and stretching his tiny limbs. At twenty-three weeks, he hears and responds to his mother's voice and other sounds, and may even develop a taste for the food she eats. He is preparing for life after birth.

The brain of the unborn baby is still very much developing. The cerebral cortex, which is the last to develop in utero, is responsible for our mental processes: conscious experience, voluntary actions, remembering, and feeling. Studies show that in the final trimester, fetuses are actually capable of simple forms of learning. (For further information, see "Will my baby learn anything in the womb?" at www.babycentre.co.uk/a1049781/will-my-baby-learn-anything-in-the-womb#ixzz45uxFvX88.)

New research by Patricia K. Kuhl, PhD, suggests that babies begin to absorb language when they are inside the womb during the last ten weeks of pregnancy—which is earlier than previously believed. "Newborns can actually tell the difference between their mother's native tongue and foreign languages just hours after they are born. Their brains do not wait for birth to start absorbing information," she writes (see "Babies Listen and Learn While in the Womb" at www.webmd.com/baby/news/20130102/babies-learn-womb).

It only makes sense that the way the mother feels also influences her developing baby. David Mendez, MD, a neonatologist at Miami Children's Hospital, says that the best thing that expectant moms can do for themselves and their baby is to maintain a stress- and chemical-free environment. "Talk to your baby as much as possible in a calm and relaxing way," he says. "Avoid screaming, yelling, and other violent language."

As you can see, a great deal of research supports the idea that a fetus is already experiencing the world around them in utero, and they can even feel how they are loved and valued!

"My hands will do great things."

Elizabeth Noble, a pioneer in the field of prenatal psychology, has written a number of books on childbirth, including her 1993 book, *Primal Connections: How Our Experiences from Conception to Birth Influence Our Emotions, Behavior, and Health*. She writes that what you experience in the womb and during birth can shape your emotional, mental, and physical well-being later in life. Noble believes that cells have both emotional and physical memory, that our earliest experiences may explain profound emotions and chronic conditions that are resistant to traditional treatments, and that with regression hypnosis and visualization, patients can access their deepest memories.

I attended one of Noble's workshops with a large group of medical professionals. She had us lie on mats and led us into a meditative state, taking us back until we were only an egg or sperm, talking us through conception, the time we grew in utero, and then, eventually, through the birthing process.

During this exercise, I experienced my own profound prenatal recall. I had an amazing clarity about my movements, emotions, feelings, and visual awareness of that time and space. I actually experienced myself as an egg drifting down the fallopian tube, and I began to physically jerk as the sperm tried to penetrate the membrane of the egg to complete fertilization. This was not only a sensing or an internal knowing; I actually felt my body gyrating on the floor in the class. Of course, I was aware of my movements—I even felt self-conscious about them— but since everyone was lying on the floor with their eyes closed, I opened myself up to experience without judgment.

I had an overwhelming sense of total peace and awe. My arms and legs felt like they were physically moving in an outward direction, transforming from stubs into extremities. The most profound image (which I can still recall) was seeing my hand extended in utero. I watched in awe with absolute knowing that my hands were special and would do remarkable things. I can still recall the posturing of my hand in space even today and sense the miracle potential we all hold.

My cells recalled their earliest, most primal physical and emotional memories. At the conclusion of the workshop, I shared my experience with my mother. She told me that after I was born, she had experienced complications and wasn't allowed to see me for several days (delivery protocols were much different in the 1950s). She also recalled that, as a young toddler, I would tell her that my hands were special and that they would do great things. Of course, at the time, neither one of us understood what to make of that.

Your Environment Affects Your Biology

Of course, your cellular memory doesn't turn off after birth. In fact, your very biology is profoundly influenced by the home and family you were born into. In 1982, Dr. Bruce H. Lipton, one of the medical community's leading voices about mind/body medicine and spiritual principles, published a breakthrough study on the cell membrane, revealing that the outer layer of the cell was in essence an organic computer chip—the cell's brain. Furthermore, his pioneering work in stem-cell research confirms the idea that the environment affects our cells on a very deep, physiological level—and can determine what type of cells they become (how healthy they are) simply by altering their *environment*.

Since science has proven that a cell is a living organism that can be profoundly changed by its external surroundings, it shouldn't come as a surprise that our emotions, thoughts, and feelings influence our cells (and, subsequently, our health) based on the internal environment that we create. If we can impact our internal chemical and hormonal environment in a positive or negative direction, clearly we can affect the health of our bodies, too.

Your birth order matters, too!

When my father *abandoned* our family, each of us girls reacted differently, in part because of our ages, personalities, individual perceptions of the events, personal needs, and the Soul lessons we each were meant to learn. Significantly, our reactions were also affected by our positions within the family.

With a firstborn child, the family is typically proud of every sign of progress and frightened by every potential injury. Many of my students who are the oldest child in their family have told me that growing up, it was their "job" to take care of their sister and brothers. A middle child occupies the "in-between" space: he is often dominated by the firstborn (who takes on the leadership role) and usually plays a silent role in comparison to the youngest. By the time the youngest child arrives, parents are usually worn down and worn out.

Scientific research supports the idea that birth order plays an important role in our lives. Even with the same parents and events, each child will have different perceptions, emotional wounds, impacts, and outcomes that play influential roles in their lives and health. Dr. Gail Gross, a human behaviorist and parenting expert, confirms that birth order implies certain characteristics. "Some researchers believe birth order is as important as gender, and almost as important as genetics. It gets back to the old nurture versus nature business," she says. "I know that no two children have the same set of parents, even though they live in the same family. Because parents are different with each of their children, no two children ever take the same role." Dr. Gross continues with these words of advice: "Children need to be allowed to find their destiny, whatever their role in the family may be, and as a parent, your most important job is to support their individual journey." How powerful is that statement?

I don't believe that parents really understand the significance of the impact we have on our children. We play an undeniable role that influences who our children become and how they perceive themselves. This is *not* to cast blame on parents, because children, in fact, take on their own perceptions from their experience.

Lisa's Story: Belonging

I'd love to share a story about a client of mine. Lisa had a beautiful home, a company car, and all the money she would ever need, but one day she decided that something was definitely wrong. She started to realize that she needed a sense of purpose, meaningful relationships, closeness, commitment, and to *feel wanted*, but these needs weren't being met at work or at home. She experienced self-doubt and questioned her self-worth. She knew that she had to make a personal transformation.

Lisa had already begun to connect the dots. In some ways, she had been aware of these feelings, but she had intellectualized them until that fateful day when she finally realized that her heart was telling her that her life was missing something. At that point, after achieving professional success, position, and wealth, she left her job and a six-figure salary in search of happiness. She had no plans, but she desperately wanted to know how to change her mindset and her behavior. She yearned to be more receptive and expressive, but had no idea how to go about it.

I told her my story about my absent father and how it impacted me, and before I knew it, Lisa began to share her own experience without a father. He would come and go, but he eventually left her mother when she told him she was pregnant. Her mother struggled with the decision to continue the pregnancy to full term, and even her parents' marriage counselor had suggested that she have an abortion. One can understand the dilemma her mother faced, but what emotional impact might those feelings have had on her unborn child? Could her parents' feelings have been transferred to Lisa in utero?

Growing up and watching her mother struggle as a single mom, Lisa didn't share any of her struggles, worries, and hurts with her mother because she didn't want to be an additional *burden*. This was Lisa's *perception*. Since she already felt unwanted in many ways, she took on a persona that didn't add additional strain. "It wasn't that my mother wasn't loving. She was," Lisa says, "but not having a father in any form was devastating." She was crushed to think that even before he had seen her, this man had discarded, rejected, and abandoned her.

Like me, Lisa was a tomboy, and she felt most comfortable with boys. Perhaps you can see how this may have filled her emotional need to be wanted by the opposite sex. She avoided being with the girls who openly displayed their emotions, which Lisa had learned so effectively not to share.

Lisa told me that she had always felt that she didn't *"belong."* This feeling had haunted her throughout her life. Most people who meet Lisa don't understand this because she is one of the most loving, kind, gracious, and supportive individuals in the world. She was very good at hiding her true emotions. She became a strong, independent woman, proud of her accomplishments and her self-sufficiency. Everyone thought Lisa was so put together that she *never needed anything from anyone.* When I asked her how that made her feel, she said, "It's okay, being alone. I don't need to rely on anyone for help. Actually, I'm almost too good at it, and that's one of my challenges."

The defensive walls Lisa had built didn't allow anyone to enter her protected space, where she belonged to no one but herself. To avoid feeling hurt or abandoned, she had built a persona of strength in her aloneness—an independence that kept her from reliving the feeling of rejection.

I suggested that she had separated herself from emotional support, companionship, intimacy, and unconditional love. Her protective space had become her downfall: the defense mechanisms she had created for safety and security but represented the Soul Lesson she would have to learn. She had learned to accept *alone*-ness, and that was the subtle energy she gave off unconsciously: "I'm okay by myself. I do not need you," and that was the complete opposite of what her Soul lesson was about and what she in fact desired.

Lisa is now far along on her Soul's intended path. She's spent the last couple of years on a personal quest, seeking out and talking with other people whose journeys were like hers—people who left behind the emotional and spiritual emptiness of the corporate world in search of greater meaning and fulfillment.

Powerful Beyond Measure: Earliest Years of Understanding

Now it's your turn to tell your story.

Just like Lisa, you've created walls that you believed would keep you safe. In some ways they have, but now you have to tear them down and open yourself up to being able to receive on all levels. The beautiful, authentic person that you are will to be revealed when you let people in and experience love. Understanding the dynamics, the relationships, the environment, and the struggles you've endured will give insight into your story.

If you're interested in exploring your earliest moments of growth and understanding, here are some questions to ask your parents or people who knew you as a very young child. If your parents or other relatives are not available, this exercise may be a difficult to complete, but go through the questions regardless, and try to recall your earliest memories from conception to infancy. See what your intuition reveals to you. Your Soul was there and knows all. You may be surprised at the answers that come to you.

1. How long were you in utero? Were you full-term or premature?
2. Was it a normal, healthy pregnancy?
3. What were your mother's feelings about being pregnant? Your father's feelings?
4. Was your mother ill during the pregnancy?
5. Were there complications with the pregnancy?
6. How was your birth?
7. Were there complications for your mother during the birth?
8. Were there complications for you (the baby)?
9. Were you with your mother/father post-delivery?
10. How were you received into the family?

Your takeaway:

_____

_____

_____

_____

_____

I believe the Soul lessons that become an integral part of our personal growth can best be learned from our emotional wounds and limiting beliefs. Our past lies parallel to the lessons we need to learn.

Knowledge is power, and your "discovery" can help you to piece the puzzle together and gain a better understanding of who you are today: the emotions you experience, the pain that you still hold within you, your self-imposed limitations and beliefs, and even the scope of your success and/or failures. Some of you will eagerly embrace this opportunity as a vehicle to heal, while others may be apprehensive about exploring this aspect. Don't be afraid; you have the strength to take this step toward the greater understanding that is waiting for you.

Here are two ways to begin your personal exploration and retrospection of your past. For a printed copy of this exercise, go to <u>www.PowerfulBeyondMeasureBook.com/forms</u>.

1. **<u>Journal Along Exercise</u>**
A pen and a blank piece of paper can serve as one of your most powerful life tools. Research shows that journaling has a positive impact on physical well-being. Writing about stressful events can help you reduce their impact on your physical health. Regular journaling can strengthen immune cells and even decrease the symptoms of asthma and rheumatoid arthritis. Writing reduces stress, removes mental blocks, and allows you to use your brain and feel your emotions; this helps you understand yourself and others better. Journaling allows for increased focus and clarity, opening the way to a deeper level of learning. It helps to release the emotional charge, process events, and bridge the truth about the limitations and beliefs you've taken on. Journaling will help you heal your past, move toward forgiveness, and let go of events that should no longer impact

you. You'll be able to integrate and reveal patterns, increase your self-image and confidence, and become more open to creating positive change in your life. (For more information on the health benefits of journaling, see http://psychcentral. com/lib/the-health-benefits-of-journaling/.)

When you put pen to paper, your inner voice can be expressed in a way that awakens your deepest desires, passions, gifts and purpose. Many "A-ha!" moments, miracles, and synchronicities will appear as you take this private time to connect with your inner-self. You'll probably even find yourself saying, "Where did *that* come from?"

I suggest that you gift yourself with a beautiful journal to record your most private thoughts and emotions. Honor your Soul's need by carving out time each day to allow yourself to explore that which is buried within, as well as the experiences that occur throughout your day.

I also encourage you to *express gratitude* in your journal on a daily basis. This simple act signifies to the Universe your appreciation for the blessings in your life and your willingness to receive more abundance and regift it back to the world.

At this time, choose a story or a specific memory that is significant to you—maybe the one that replays so often in your mind. You know the one! See the story without reliving it. Focus on *why* and *how* you *felt* a certain way, instead of just the specific details of the event. This way you can begin to understand the belief, emotion, and behavior that you took on in response to the event(s). Try not to place judgement, blame, or guilt on anyone, including (and especially) yourself. That event happened long ago, and the personal understanding you gain from this exercise will start the healing process and set you free to move forward.

As you write in greater detail about your event, try and connect to your emotions and make sure you address these questions—how you *felt hurt*, what you would have *liked to say*, *why it happened*, and what you could *learn from the experience*.

2. **Journey Along Exercise**
Use the form below to answer the questions that will help you explore different aspects of your life: how you were wounded as a child (or even presently in

response to another event), along with your perceptions, behavior, and beliefs. Most importantly, listen to your intuition. Your inner wisdom will guide you along your journey of growth, awareness, and transformation. Although these memories can be positive, they often have a negative component and are filled with strong feelings of guilt, loss, illness, loneliness, trepidation, regret, or severe pain—just to name a few. Remember, there are no right or wrong answers. You're safe to experience the truth that you feel deep within.

I encourage you to use this form for many situations and events, including those that are going on in your life today. Information and understanding is **power**. If you prefer to type on a form on your computer instead of writing on paper, use this link to download additional forms: www.PowerfulBeyondMeasureBook.com/forms .

Take a deep breath, quiet your mind, and allow your self-exploration to begin. Take a few minutes to just be still *and sense within your presence the images or memories that come to you.* For a printed copy of this exercise, go to www.PowerfulBeyondMeasureBook.com/forms.

Journey Along: Significant Events in Your Life

Choose memories of two events (ones that either happened in the past or are happening in the present) that have touched you deeply, shaken you to your very core, and left you questioning yourself and your life. Have one of the memories be from your early years, (preferably before you were eight years old), and the other can be from any time. Describe the event, the people involved, your thoughts and feelings about it, the outcomes for you, and whether it still has a long-lasting impact. Even though you are looking at the different roles people played and how they made you feel, this is not about them; it's all about *you* and your healing, growth, happiness, and empowerment.

Memory #1

When: _____

Who: _____

Incident:

_____

_____

_____

_____

Outcome:

_____

_____

_____

_____

Thoughts/Feelings during the event:

_____

_____

_____

_____

Thoughts/Feelings after the event:

_____

_____

_____

_____

What understandings and perceptions did you take away from this event? Are they true or false? How has it harmed you? What would you have to do to stand up to these *untruths*? This may be one of your Soul lessons.

Understanding:

_____

_____

_____

_____

True or False? _____

How has it harmed you?

_____

_____

_____

_____

What do you have to overcome to stand up to these untruths?

_____

_____

_____

_____

Memory #2

When: _____

Who: _____

Incident:

_____

_____

_____

_____

Outcome:

_____

_____

_____

_____

Thoughts/Feelings during the event:

_____

_____

_____

_____

Thoughts/Feelings after the event:

_____

_____

_____

_____

What understandings and perceptions did you take away from this event? Are they true or false? How has it harmed you? What would you have to do to stand up to these *untruths*? This may be one of your Soul lessons.

Understanding:

_____

_____

_____

_____

True or False? _____

How has it harmed you?

_____

_____

_____

_____

What do you have to overcome to stand up to these untruths?

_____

_____

_____

_____

Please do *not* judge, critique, or stress about what you wrote in the exercise above. This is your first attempt to identify the powerful memories that are ever-present in your mind and uncover why they continue to impact your life.

Congratulations! You have just taken the first step toward identifying an important aspect that may be preventing you from feeling happy and learning your Soul lesson(s).

Own your story
Your perception is your reality

Isn't it time to fall in love with who you really are?

Our personalities are unique to us, but they can be altered by our perceptions of who we are—what we see as our strengths and weaknesses. As we develop, we take on understandings of where we fail, succeed, and what we lack. We constantly view ourselves based on those understandings; this can result in behaviors that are completely different from who we truly are. Are your behaviors a result of taking on what someone else had you believe and what you perceived, causing you to be untrue to yourself?

Here's a good example: if you *perceive* yourself as an introvert, you probably wouldn't want a high-profile sales job. This environment would make you very uncomfortable and cause you to contract, which would probably result in poor sales. Choosing occupations and relationships that resonate with your false *perception* of self may allow you to feel comfortable, but inauthentic choices cause an internal struggle of inadequacy, feeling less, and dissatisfaction.

A healthy sense of *self-awareness* is crucial to achieving success and happiness. It creates the template for what you attract and expect to experience. Your internal awareness of self is actually the determining influence on how you experience life.

The more you learn about yourself,
the broader your self-awareness becomes.

Self-awareness is the psychological state of being aware of ourselves as separate entities—our viewpoints and perceptions of ourselves and our traits, feelings, and behavior—and it's one of the first components of the self-concept to develop. Research suggests that self-awareness begins to emerge around the age of 18 months. Who would have guessed that it begins so early? This awareness of self starts as children but continues throughout our lives.

As you become aware of self, you start to understand your personality, strengths, weaknesses, thoughts, beliefs, emotions, reactions, and your perception of others' opinion about you. This self-assessment is necessary for you to function, but it can also create a lot of internal unrest as you strive to fit in, to be liked, and to be accepted according society's norms.

The best news I can share with you right now is that it's never too late to explore and develop your self-awareness, and you can start right now as you go through the questions and exercises in this chapter. Listening to your internal truth and finding answers about why you took on your beliefs and perceptions will be eye-opening and life-changing.

Your self-awareness is an imaginary neon sign, flashing messages about who you are: you're a victim or a victor, a winner or a loser. When you judge yourself, your failures and successes become integrated into your self-awareness about your capabilities and expectations. If the behavior and outcomes becomes repetitious, this only strengthens that aspect of your self-awareness and your belief system about what you can achieve.

Your self-awareness holds the greatest potential that affects
your long-term happiness and success.

Healthy self-awareness doesn't mean you have to be perfect, because perfection doesn't exist. The most important aspect of self-awareness is forming a *positive view of yourself* that is based on truth. We are constantly viewing ourselves, and based on those understandings, our personalities and behaviors may become disingenuous to who we truly are.

How would you answer these three questions right now?

- How do you *feel* about yourself? _____
- How do you *see* yourself? _____
- How much *self-love* do you have? (1 low, 10 high) _____

It's so easy to read questions that are posed and move on, but I encourage you to contemplate each one deeply and allow yourself to experience and learn about yourself. What you find will become what you need to work on in your healing and transformation for growth.

How is "Self" created?

You aren't born with self-awareness, but it doesn't take long before the outside world starts to affect how you see yourself. The way you're treated by your parents, siblings, and other significant people in your life significantly affects your perception and understanding about who you are. As sociologist Dr. Neal Houston suggests, "The quality of your life is based 10% on what happens to you and 90% on how your respond to what happens to you."

There are two types of self-awareness: public self-awareness and private self-awareness. Public self-awareness is how others view us, which often causes us to adhere to social norms and blend in to be accepted. Private self-awareness is your external view of self—what you see when looking in the mirror or interpreting internal signals like sensations and emotions.

When people become overly concerned about their awareness (often through self-judgment), they can experience self-consciousness. Some can tend to be overly sensitive about their feelings and beliefs, and that can have negative health consequences, with symptoms like increased stress, depression, and anxiety. As your self-awareness develops, you make changes in your thoughts and interpretations which impact your emotional response.

Childhood Zest for Life

When we're young, we rarely experience limitations on our capabilities, and we explore life eagerly. It's how we learn, grow, and prepare for our life's purpose— one that uses our unique gifts and passions.

Take a few minutes to think about the things that you were really excited about as a child.

- What did you *love* to do as a youngster, and why?
- What was your favorite activity? Who did it involve? Where did it occur?
- Were you encouraged or discouraged to participate in those activities?

Our **behaviors**, habits and routines are often *reactive*, rather than *responding*. This often creates less than desirable results. One may question why those negative behaviors exist in the first place and when they were created. Are those behaviors learned responses to earlier experiences?

Understanding your **feelings,** which create your **emotional responses,** is integral to knowing how they impact your behavior and thoughts. Emotional self-awareness plays a vital role in our happiness. If you suppress or ignore your emotions, this will undoubtedly have a negative impact on your self-awareness and how you function in the world.

Your self-awareness allows you to utilize your **strengths** and helps you to cope with your perceived **weaknesses**. If you're articulate and enjoy talking, then you might gravitate to a speaking career, whereas if you're quiet but have strong language and writing skills, you might seek a job creating documents, pamphlets, and books. Finding the job that utilizes your strengths and passions and places you in an environment where your gifts can be utilized and your inner presence positively expressed.

I would like to add though, that what we see as our **weakness are not necessarily true**; rather, they come from the learned perception that you took on at an earlier age. For example, one of my children had difficulty with pronunciation and stuttered under stress, but as he grew, he turned this perceived weakness into a strength, and he is now a vice-president for one of the largest banks in the world. You have a choice to walk away and believe that you aren't qualified or good enough, but is that in fact really the "truth" that you want to continue to believe?

So What's Self-Esteem?

Your self-awareness provides much of the information that guides the development of your self-esteem. While self-awareness is about learning, perceiving, and viewing yourself, self-esteem is about placing *value* on yourself and what you do. The word esteem means that someone or something is important, special, or valuable. Your self-esteem is fluid and evolving; just like self-awareness, it begins to form in childhood and continues on into our adult lives.

Babies have no judgement of self; they don't see themselves as either good or bad. They don't think, "I'm great!" until they hear praise from the people around them. They don't see themselves as demanding, incontinent, and incapable, just as what they are—a Soul in a body that relies on nurturing from parents and other people. As children grow older, their self-esteem develops based on feedback from others and how they view themselves.

Parents, teachers, coaches, parents, and peers can boost or hurt your self-esteem, which can have a long-lasting impact on your self-awareness. Studies show that if parents tend to yell in the home, that affects their children's self-esteem. A teacher can make a child feel capable and intelligent or stupid and not as good as others. A child who is happy with a success but doesn't feel loved could actually experience low self-esteem because the success still wasn't enough. It's actually quite sad that so many of us base our own internal happiness on how the world sees and values us.

Children (and adults) with low self-esteem become frustrated easily, think poorly of themselves, find challenges overwhelming, and reinforce their self-

critical, limiting thoughts: "No one loves me," "I can't succeed," "I'm no good,"
"I can't …"

Dr. Christina Hilbert uses a hierarchal
pyramid to achieve self-worth, and I think it
also represents quite well the key components
that contribute to healthy self-esteem. At the
foundation, you see self-awareness (who we
come to understand we are); next, there's
self-acceptance of that persona; and last (the
segment so many of us struggle with) is self-
love. Self-love is difficult for us because we

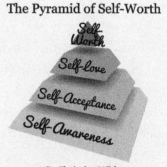

The Pyramid of Self-Worth

www.DrChristinaHibbert.com

often don't like who we are, and deep down inside, we don't want to accept that
view as truth. This causes a great deal of sadness. When we can look back, see the
false sense of self that we've created, and change that view to one that we openly
embrace, then we can experience self-love. When we love ourselves in a healthy
way, our self-worth (or self-esteem) empowers us to be openly authentic to the
world. Understanding the origin of why you're thinking, acting, and feeling a
certain way is the first step to starting your inner healing process.

When you know your truth, you become empowered.
When you accept and love yourself, you become invincible.

You might be recalling memories of your own early years, both good and
the bad. Regardless of which memories arise, accept the inner wisdom that is
being presented without judgment. However you feel your past impacted you,
you don't have to be a victim and accept those belief patterns from years gone by.
Every child internalizes information through impressions and perceptions, but
sometimes certain events occur that can have an even greater impact.

Here are a few examples:

- Traumatic experience
- Family dynamics, parent(s)
- Illness or death

- Puberty, peer pressure, bullying
- Physical looks, limitations, handicaps
- Difficulty in school, career, social situations

Did you know that one out of three adults has low self-esteem? Where do you place your self-esteem (right now, *not* where you want it to be)? (Scale of 1–10; 1 is low, 10 is high.) _____

Here are some questions that can reveal behaviors that children and adults might exhibit because they have low self-esteem or poor self-awareness.

- Do you argue and want to be right, or be heard?
- Do you need to control, or are you subservient?
- Do you defend, bully, and/or find fault with others?
- Do you get physical, yell, swear, or succumb to vices to feel better?
- Does your behavior change depending on environment and people?
- Do you have reservations, doubts, and/or regrets during and after events?
- Do you have a narcissistic personality and make others feel small and inconsequential?

Understanding the origin of why you're
thinking, acting, and feeling a certain way
begins the healing process within.

M.C.'s Story: the Lack of Beauty

M.C.'s family was very poor. There was rarely extra money for pretty clothes, new shoes, or anything other than basic essentials. Love was very much present in her household, but the perceptions she internalized (from others and herself) created deep emotional wounds that would follow her much of her life. M.C. was embarrassed by her old, tattered clothes, and she started to have self-confidence issues as she compared herself to the other kids in school. Her mother had premature greying hair, and when she attended functions at her daughter's school, her classmates would ask her why her grandmother had come to the event instead of her mother.

As an adult, M.C. found herself constantly evaluating others' worth by their appearance. Her grown children often wore T-shirts and jeans, had long hair, and didn't fit the image that she felt they should depict. Of course she loved them, but found herself thinking, "Why don't they dress and present themselves differently?"

M.C. took great pride in her appearance. She was always well put together, with perfect hair and makeup and fashionable clothes. As a widow, she struggled with accepting men who pursued her because there was always something deficient. When she would go on a date, she felt vulnerable because she thought the man may not *like her* because of her appearance. Furthermore, she would judge *them* as well. She found great dissatisfaction with the whole dating process because she never realized that her childlike inner critique (her *perception*) was continuing to affect her and create so much sadness in her life.

MC works at an elderly complex and focuses on trying to groom the residents. This is wonderful and caring, but notice where, even in her adult life, she places the emphasis: on appearance.

One day, when M.C. and I were working on actionable steps for growth and learning, I suggested that she had to walk outside, down to the mailbox pick-up station, with unmatched clothes and no makeup. Allowing herself to be vulnerable—letting others see her not perfectly put together—was extremely difficult and challenging for her, but she needed to learn to embrace imperfection. Accepting others (and herself) in order to see the beauty within: could this be M.C.'s Soul lesson?

After attending my class, she was able to see the impact that her innocent, early emotional pain continued to have on her life. She had never put the pieces together until then, and when she started to address the root cause, her life totally transformed. She experienced inner freedom and much more joy from the people in her life.

Think of M.C.'s schoolmates; at first glance, you may blame those young students for being rude, unthoughtful, and uncaring, but what do you think their lessons may have been? Maybe theirs were exactly the same as M.C.'s: to learn to look at everyone's Soul's beauty—who they are, not what they physically look like—to determine their worth. In reality, wasn't it M.C.'s *perception* of the situation that created her hurt, embarrassment, and resentment? If self-love and nonjudgment of others and self is a Soul lesson for M.C., then it's no surprise that it followed her throughout her life. Until we actually *"get it,"* the Universe continues to provide us ample opportunities to *learn* it.

Remember, everyone you meet in your life is there for a specific reason: as a support, a challenge, or an opportunity. That relationship or interaction is always double-sided; there are challenges for each of us to learn and grow from.

Let's Explore and Try to Understand!

Here are three powerful tools to help you to see and appreciate your truth. As you continue on, your understanding, growth, and appreciation for *self* will grow, so be honest and write from where you are now.

Understanding is trying to come up with a greater wisdom about how specific events impact your life.

As you begin, start with the memories that are most vivid and that you are most comfortable with initially exploring.

1. **Powerful Beyond Measure:** Journal Recall

   Continue to write in your journal daily (fifteen to twenty minutes) as you explore your past. Start with images and memories that come to your mind through your *Memory Recall*, letting your intuition guide you. Allow yourself the freedom to release the events, emotions, and energy around them. The sentences do not have to be perfectly written; just allow your Soul's voice to direct you to the wisdom it wants to share. You'll be surprised at what you write!

2. **Personal Beyond Measure:** Understand your story from a different perspective

Use this template to help shift your past experience to a position from *now*. Replace your previous viewpoint and limiting understanding by applying a positive, unemotional correction today. The questions below ask you to focus on key words: *think*, *perceive*, *feel*, *believe*, and *understand*. Each one is really a different experience and should help provide you with greater insight. You can use this powerful template over and over again, with current or past events; see if you can uncover a common theme. You are teaching yourself to shift your perception, emotional response, and understanding from the past to the present and to empower your choices, behavior, and beliefs.

Remember: Small steps lead to big changes, so keep it simple, relaxed, and fun!

(To download a printable version of this template, go to: www. PowerfulBeyondMeasureBook.com/forms.)

Journey Along: Own Your Own Story

Event date (e.g., four years old or last week): _____

Today's date: _____

Event: describe briefly.

_____

_____

_____

What did you *think* then, and what do you think now, looking back?

_____

_____

_____

What did you *perceive* then, and what do you perceive now, looking back?

_____

_____

_____

What did you *feel* then, and what do you feel now, looking back?

———————————————————————————————

———————————————————————————————

———————————————————————————————

What did you *believe* then, and what do you believe now, looking back?

———————————————————————————————

———————————————————————————————

———————————————————————————————

What did you *understand* then, and what do you understand now, looking back?

———————————————————————————————

———————————————————————————————

———————————————————————————————

3. **Heart's Home of Healing**: Meditation

I would love to share with you a powerful meditation tool called ***Heart's Home of Healing* Meditation** which will cleanse your internal house of emotional pain. Understanding how powerful your mind can be is quite liberating—and encouraging. Have you ever heard teachers or healers talk about the importance of letting go and wondered, "*Okay, but how? It's not that easy!*" See if this guided meditation doesn't do the letting go for you. It's certainly worked for me and many others.

This guided meditation uses the power of your mind to transfer suppressed or trapped emotional pain to a very special organ in your body: the heart. In your heart, the pain can be experienced, released, and replaced with love, light, and joy. Please don't doubt that your pain, whether from many years ago or just yesterday, is having detrimental effects on your happiness, health and harmony. That emotional pain must go—and it *can* with this simple and powerful technique!

Since your heart is ***the seat of your Soul*** and the organ that is capable of emotional feeling, we must engage it to: 1) release your suppressed emotional pain, 2) initiate healing, 3) reestablish your energy flow, and 4) fill in the void with love and light. I created Heart's Home of

Healing Meditation to do just this and to provide what I call "steps of release and love to heal your pain." I invite you to use this meditation often and enjoy profound relief from your old, accumulated pain, along with freedom from new pain. To participate, either listen to the audio version of this meditation at www.PowerfulBeyondMeasureBook.com/HeartHomeOfHealingMeditation or follow the guided steps found below.

For your beautiful healing and release:

- Sit or lie comfortably with legs uncrossed in a quiet and secluded space.
- Close your eyes and take three to five deep, slow, cleansing breaths (in through the nose, out through the mouth) emphasizing the exhalations. With each exhalation, release any stress, anger, or frustration, and with each inhalation, breathe in peace, happiness, and healing.
- Identify **one** element—a belief, memory, emotion, symptom/illness—that you want to focus on during this meditation.
- When you think of this element, where in the body do you feel it as a discomfort? This area is your House of Emotional Pain.
- Assign a number to indicate the intensity of your symptom in that area now (1 low, 10 high).
- Bring your attention to moving the discomfort from its current location into your heart.
- Assign a number to indicate the discomfort you are experiencing now in the heart (1 low, 10 high). Often the number can change between the two locations.
- Envision your heart, which has four chambers and four valves, as a house with four rooms, a central hub and four doors leading into those rooms.
- Step into the central hub of your heart space through the front door. This area is the *seat of your Soul*.
  - **A:** Enter the first room, notice the feeling within the room, and express that emotion with a word. Then gather up whatever

is in the room that you know does not serve you well—such as emotions, objects, or people—and place them outside the window.

B: Turn and observe the room and notice if anything is still present that doesn't feel good. Gather it up and once again place it outside the window.

- Walk through the door into the second room and repeat steps **A** and **B** in this room.

- Enter the third and fourth rooms and repeat steps **A** and **B** in these rooms.

- Now that you have cleansed the four chambers of your heart, move into the inner sanctum, the core, the *seat of your Soul*.

- Rest in this space, hear your beautiful heartbeat and notice how your pain has been greatly reduced or eliminated.

- Standing in this central space, the core of your existence, allow the winds from the north to enter through the north window, the east winds from the east window, south winds from the south, and west winds from the west. Let them all converge in your inner sanctum where you experience the clean, purified air and hold your intentions of health, harmony and happiness.

- The Heavenly Source (north) enters your crown chakra from the top of the head, filling you with abundant grace, love and peace.

- Feel the warmth under your feet or supported body from Mother Earth, (south) as her nurturing and healing energies cascade upward into your heart.

- Imagine these two energies from Heaven and Earth joining together to form a divine pillar of healing light that permeates the chambers of your heart and your whole body with every beat of your heart.

- Observe how all energies merge and flow effortlessly throughout your being, completely filling your heart with love and healing light.

- Rest and observe this inner space you hold, your heart space, and give gratitude for the release of all the emotional, mental, physical, and spiritual pain that you have removed from your physical body, and your divine being.
- Return to the rooms, starting with the last room and moving counter-clockwise until you end up in the first room, shutting each of their respective windows as you go.
- Your body and Soul are abundantly full, and only health, harmony, and happiness reside within you.
- You may now leave your **Heart's Home**, feeling refreshed and knowing you can return as often as you would like, to be replenished and restored with love and light whenever you feel the need.
- Take three to five slow, relaxed breaths and allow your attention to return to the present moment, moving your body parts and opening your eyes as you feel ready.
- Observe the original pain location and once again assign a number. You most likely will see that the number has been greatly reduced or is zero.

The **Heart's Home of Healing** has proven to be so powerful for my clients that many have immediately experienced a profound shift, or even a complete release. But it's not a one-time practice. This meditation is a tool for healing the *past and present*, and should be used as often as needed until your emotional pain, mental limitation, and energetic connection have been resolved. As you rehabilitate one element of concern, be aware that others may become evident and applaud yourself for your continued healing and release.

You have just taken another important step in unlocking your Power Within to reveal how Powerful Beyond Measure you are!

Well Done!

WOUNDS AND SELF-LIMITING BELIEFS
The weight of untruths

Your mind is more powerful that you can even imagine.

As we learned in the previous chapter, what we take on during our youngest years—when we are innocent, vulnerable, and influenced by so many—can in fact be inaccurate and counterproductive. Often it's our perception, based on that time, which is internalized (and even fossilized) so that we see everything through that same limited vision. The weight of these repressed, harmful memories can hold you captive, negatively impacting you both internally and externally. This is why the work you are doing in this section of the book is so pivotal and life changing. As you move forward, keep in mind that the resources within this book are not meant to replace traditional medical attention, but can be a valuable supplement to your inner healing.

Some information that we experienced as youngsters is critical and helpful to our survival. It's how we learn rules, expectations, laws, morals, and ways to stay safe. We've learned not to touch a hot stove, or a lit match, and to look both ways before we cross a street.

Did you know that there are five different brain waves: Alpha, Delta, Beta, Theta, and Gamma? Scientific studies tell us that until the age of six, children primarily use Theta brain waves. These are the same brain waves that are affected under hypnosis. These types of brain waves are receptive, where there is no judgement, no ability to filter or screen information. Around the age of six, when your brain starts to mature, your brain wave patterns shift, and you can start to filter information: stimuli is being absorbed and embedded somewhere in your mind.

Three Minds

The mind is divided into three components: the conscious mind, the subconscious mind, and the unconscious mind.

- **The conscious mind** is your present-day awareness of everything that is happening with you and around you (e.g., your clothing, actions, etc.).
- **The subconscious mind** is where you hold information that you can access once you bring your attention to it (e.g., memories, recalling phone numbers and birthdates, etc.).
- **The unconscious mind** is where the primitive, instinctual information that we cannot access on our own resides (e.g., the memory of a previous life, present-day life experience that you can't remember but you know that it still exists, [i.e., your birth]).

I think we all recognize the **conscious mind** as our understanding of all events, feelings, and actions that occur in the present moment. We are able to experience these using our five senses as well as our intuition. Our current awareness and processing includes the expression of thoughts, sensation, perception, memories, emotion, and volition. Whether the stimuli is seen or perceived is irrelevant; it's our conscious and subconscious minds that take in the information. Much of the information you're totally unaware of retaining and processing.

The **subconscious mind** is part of your conscious mind. You are not necessarily aware of it, but it can influence you nonetheless. For example, say you're in a group. You notice the individuals (four women and two men) who spoke, but you might not believe you noticed the clothes they wore. In fact, though, your subconscious mind did take in that information and can retrieve it if you bring your attention to it. The information is accessible if you make a deliberate effort to recall it. We touched on this in the previous chapter when I had you do an exercise on **Mental Recall** that accessed information you had stored in your subconscious mind. In *The Biology of Belief*, Dr. Bruce Lipton states that the subconscious mind works five hundred times faster than the conscious mind. Can you even conceive the vast amount of information that the subconscious mind has to integrate and process?

Our subconscious, repressed memories (including feelings, thoughts, urges, and emotions) are integrated with current-day situations and affect our actions, behaviors, feelings, and how we react or respond. This mental process can cause us to feel fearful, embarrassed, intimidated, angry, depressed, or sad. Can you see how our subconscious mind has created the self-limiting beliefs which have a strong power over how we act day to day, how we work toward our goals, and even affect our health? Talk about our earliest years continuing to influence our lives!

The **unconscious mind** (a term coined by Freud) refers to the part of the mind that is *not* known by the consciousness. This includes primitive ideas, thought processes, memory, affect, motivation, traumatic memories, desires, and even deeply repressed, painful emotions. Freud also believed that our memories influence our behaviors and beliefs in our present lives.

Sometimes experiences can be so profoundly troubling at the time of the event that, in an attempt to protect you, your mind places those memories where you cannot retrieve them easily, but that doesn't mean the energy associated with those memories doesn't still negatively impact you.

It is possible to access the unconscious mind through hypnosis, dreams, and various energy techniques. With hypnosis, the conscious mind is bypassed and we are more open and susceptible to suggestions that allow us access into the unconscious mind. Dreams often shed light on unconscious aspects that are trying to come into your consciousness to be dealt with. Keeping a dream journal can often be extremely helpful in resolving these conflicts.

In addition, the unconscious mind is responsible for many, if not all, of your basic physical functions (like breathing, heart function, and the immune system), and it is primarily concerned with your survival. Therefore, what lies in your unconsciousness becomes the comparison template for all your current experiences.

Look at these amazing statistics on how powerful your mind is:

- **We have 60,000 thoughts per day.**
- **80% of those thoughts are negative.**
- **95% of them are the same thoughts we had the day before.**
- **95% of our behavior is ruled by the unconscious mind.**

Ask yourself: what thoughts are present in my daily life, and what role do they play?

Many people believe that what has been locked in our unconscious mind can move into the subconscious, and then to consciousness, without traditional psychological intervention. Maybe you feel the same way and have experienced it yourself. For example, has a long-forgotten childhood memory suddenly come into your consciousness after many decades? Usually there is a specific trigger that opens up the pathway to reveal something that your mind wants you to discover, address, and resolve.

Wounds

Emotional wounds can hurt more than physical ones.

Traumatic experiences can threaten your life and cause you physical harm. Stressful events can also cause emotional and psychological trauma, making you feel helpless, unsafe, unloved, and vulnerable. No matter what trauma or negative events you've experienced, their emotional impact can be much more harmful than the actual physical circumstances. Your emotions become embedded, creating and fueling subconscious and even false beliefs. The more frightened, helpless, and emotionally affected you are, the greater the impact the traumatizing event is likely to have.

Our greatest desires are to be loved, wanted, and valued. When those values are in jeopardy, we try to understand why they are not present, often personalizing our *deficits* as the reason. Many traumatic situations can cause you to develop negative, self-limiting beliefs that have the potential to impact you throughout your life. Intentionally or not, significant people have caused you emotional pain. Your perception of those wounds and events has contributed to your own belief system. There is no right and wrong; life happens, and our bodies are wired for survival. What one perceives as a threat, another may not. That is why it's so important not to make this all about *you*, where you become the victim once again. Below, I've listed some general categories of events that can create our emotional wounds. Some of these examples may have occurred in your life, and you may have even accepted them as the norm.

• Family dynamics (divorce, absent or deceased parent(s), siblings, birth order)	• Trauma or significant event (e.g., illness or accident)
• Parent in harm's way (e.g., military service, dangerous occupation)	• Abuse (mental, physical, emotional)
• Financial dynamics: poverty or wealth (both have their own unique problems)	• Lack of nutrition and medical resources
• Environment and housing (safety and support)	• Mental illness (e.g., anxiety, PTSD, depression)
• Fear of death (e.g., dangerous neighborhood with killings, gangs, drugs)	• Dependency or addictions (e.g., alcohol, drugs, sex, gambling)
• Cultural and religious rules	• Punishment and guilt
• Value system: honesty, trust, order, community, country	• Education (availability, success, and expectations)

We carry our childhood wounds into adulthood.

Our youngest years have such profound implications for our emotional and mental health because our brains haven't matured enough to draw accurate inferences about the stimuli we receive. When we experience wounds as children, we create defense mechanisms in an attempt to respond to the pain—walls of protection that stop us from hurting. These are the walls that we eventually have to disassemble in order to address the root causes of our pain. Avoidance, withdrawal, and retaliation are not viable solutions that promote health and happiness.

Childhood wounds often have long-lasting effects on who we become as adults. I've listed several of them below. As you read along, pay close attention to the ones that resonate most for you. This will help you identify the areas you need to concentrate on as you journey toward healing your own childhood wounds—the ones that keep you stuck in an endless cycle of self-limiting beliefs and untruths.

Childhood wounds that may be impacting you:

• Feeling unloved, that you don't belong	• Relationship/intimacy problems
• Feeling devalued, disrespected, persecuted, and victimized	• Overly sensitive or unable to express emotions
• Abandonment, isolation, and loneliness	• Inability to trust (self and others)
• Lack of health/illness	• Demanding and unable to forgive
• Anger and resentment	• Irresponsible behavior/unsafe lifestyle
• Depression	• Shame, self-hate, and self-harm
• Anxiety and fear	• Unhealthy body image
• Frustration	• Identity crisis/gender conflict
• Hopelessness and despair: your desires, purpose, and goals are unattainable	• Perfectionism

Self-Limiting Beliefs and the Weight of Untruths

I love the metaphor of an iceberg to represent both the unconscious and the conscious mind. Our conscious thought (the voice inside our head in the present moment) is just the tip of the iceberg, floating above the surface. It is visible for all to see, judge, and respond to. Our subconscious and unconscious mind however, represent the lower 80% of the iceberg—the part that lies below the water's surface. This portion of the iceberg remains hidden to everyone, including ourselves, but it continues to affect how the visible section (our conscious mind) interacts with the world.

The most dangerous part of an iceberg is the submerged part. The same is true of our subconscious and unconscious minds if they hold unresolved, negative beliefs, behaviors, and emotional energy from earlier years. Learning how to navigate these uncharted waters—your subconscious and unconscious memories—is essential in creating a positive change in your life.

The subconscious and unconscious mind serves as our foundation, holding the past experiences (both positive and negative) that guide our present-day thoughts. We must be careful how much power we

Photo Credit: http://en.wikipedia.org/ wiki/Iceberg -Tip of the Iceberg

give to our unconscious, submerged memories if they are not serving our greater good.

Our unconscious beliefs exist under the surface, and they play a significant role in our behavior, perceptions, expectations, thoughts, habits, reactions, desires, emotions, and the self-limiting beliefs that we come to see as truth. The only problem with this unconscious memory mechanism, though, is understanding what is true and what is false. How do we know when it's something that benefits or hinders us? The easiest way is to ask, "Do I need this information because I am in danger or my survival is at risk?" Depending on the answer, you can ascertain whether it is tied to the memory of a time when you were in danger. You may even realize, now that you're stronger and older, that the environment may not be the same.

In the first chapter of Part II, Power of Your Authentic Self, you'll learn a specific process that works extremely well when negative thoughts, doubts, fears, and self-limiting beliefs arise, but first, before you can resolve and heal them, you need to understand *what they are* and *where they come from*. Then you will be able to reverse those self-limiting beliefs and remove the energetic charge of those wounds. This is what will bring about change within yourself and your life.

Lou Ann's Story: the Power of Touch

Lou Ann was a very loving child who wanted to be touched and to touch others. She lovingly embraced everything she came into contact with, whether it was a pebble, a feather, a flower, or another person. She loved to hold hands and make physical contact, but during her youth, her family members weren't receptive to her attempts to reach out. She began to feel that that something was wrong with her that caused people to be repulsed by her. She felt unloved and unlovable, and she actually started to avoid physical contact. Of course, these were all her perceptions of not feeling *loved enough*, and this heartbreaking loss led her to erect a protective wall to keep out the pain. She was saying, "I will no longer reach out to others, since they'll not reach out or be there for me."

Lou Ann's defensive mechanism resulted in isolation, loneliness, unworthiness, and feeling disconnected. The saddest part was that she had denied herself her greatest joy: the gift of touch, the energy and love that comes from a physical connection between people. She had robbed herself of what brought her the greatest pleasure. Can you see how her learned behavior, based on her perception and self-limiting beliefs, was in direct opposition to the unique spiritual gifts that brought her pleasure, passion, and the purpose that she was meant to share with the world? What could her Soul lesson(s) be? Possibly that the gifts you offer to others don't have to be returned to you? That loving through touch is very powerful, but there are also many other ways to demonstrate love?

As Lou Ann worked with me, she started to realize how her young perceptions had taught her to avoid the single thing that brought her the greatest joy. After months of unlearning untruths, awakening her desires, and doing her own individual healing work, she now has a thriving massage practice, embracing her unique spiritual gift of touch and bringing joy to herself and others. She now honors her purpose work, which has allowed her to open up and receive love in every area of her life. She has wonderful, nurturing friends, and she has learned to be grateful and appreciate that we all share our love in many different ways.

Just like Lou Ann, you can reframe your struggles and wounds as life lessons so they become divine opportunities for Soul growth. Knowing more of the details from an adult perspective can help you see how you've been trapped in that child's mindset, where victimization and emotional wounding occurred.

Being able to accept and release all parts of the event and the pain that you experienced is how you can break free from the weight of the experience. At this moment, identifying your emotional pains, self-limiting beliefs, and the untruths which keep you small, unhappy, and trapped is what is important. You cannot heal what you aren't aware of.

Releasing Your Untruths and Self-Limiting Beliefs

To help you explore your self-awareness, self-esteem, and Soul lessons, I encourage you to complete the **Journey Along: Getting to Know You** exercise below. This exercise, along with the information you started to reveal in previous chapters, will help you reveal the weight of the untruths and self-limiting beliefs that you took on so long ago. This is how your inner work continues and real healing begins. For a printed copy of this exercise, go to www.PowerfulBeyondMeasureBook.com/forms.

Continue to journal about the untruths you believe and the self-limiting beliefs you took on and are experiencing day to day. As you do this, you may begin to feel sad and sorry for yourself. It's very important that you *don't do that*! That negative energy will reinforce the *lacking* that you perceived as an experience in the past and present and make you become the victim once again. What happened then, happened then, and we are trying to put those events to bed and let you wake up to a life that isn't filled with false limitations and emotional pain.

Journey Along: Getting to Know You

Date: _____

1. Reflecting on your childhood, what were your overall feelings about yourself?

   _____

2. What were your family dynamics like?

   _____

3. Where did you fall within the family? How do you feel this affected you?

_____

4. What are your most accessible memories during these years and the associated feelings for each memory? List as many, or as few as you want.
   a. Memory:
      Feelings:_____,_____,_____
   b. Memory:
      Feelings:_____,_____,_____
   c. Memory:
      Feelings:_____,_____,_____
   d. Memory:
      Feelings:_____,_____,_____
   e. Memory:
      Feelings:_____,_____,_____

5. Reflecting back on these childhood memories, what lessons/themes do you feel that your childhood provided you to learn? They relate back to the memories in #4 (4a and 5a are about the same memory).
   a.
   b.
   c.
   d.
   e.

6. Do you feel that you have worked on any of these lessons/themes that you identified in #5? In what ways you have struggled with or been fearful of addressing them?
   a. For 6a.
   b. For 6b.
   c. For 6c.
   d. For 6d.
   e. For 6e.

7. Summary: What conclusions have you been able to take away from this exercise? Were you able to identify areas you may struggle with (e.g.,

independence, courage, perseverance, forgiveness, gentleness, giving, judgment, acceptance, love, self-love, faith)?

Be *excited* if you have been able to discern *any* areas which may become some of the Soul lessons that you'll want to learn, embrace, and value. If you feel you haven't been able to articulate your thoughts and feelings well at this point, that's okay, too. Your attempt at this exercise was the first step on your journey of understanding and growth—one I'm very proud that you've taken.

Don't be surprised if, when you walk away from this exercise, memories start to become more visible; your body and Soul want you to achieve peace, happiness, and growth, and your inner self is supporting your efforts. Please take a couple of moments right now to be your own cheerleader; tell yourself how proud you are of opening up to your own inner healing and love of yourself!

Your mind is so very, very powerful, and it has no limitations—
except the ones you superimpose upon it.

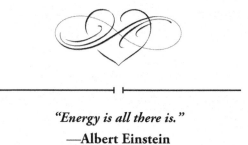

ENERGY AND EMOTIONAL PAIN
Everything is connected

Not all physical symptoms have physical origins.

If you've ever taken a chemistry class, you probably remember that everything is made up of atoms, with protons, neutrons, and electrons which are in a constant state of motion. Depending on the speed of this motion, things appear in a solid, liquid, or gaseous state. Most atoms on the periodical chart can't be seen with the naked eye, but that doesn't mean they don't exist.

The Laws of Nature state that everything is made up of energy, and energy is vibration. Every atom vibrates, and within the molecular structure, negative and positive polarities exist. Even sounds and colors have a vibrational component. Your thoughts, emotions, and environment are made of energetic vibrations as well. As you've been exploring your past, memories, beliefs, behaviors, and emotions have probably surfaced, causing a variety of feelings which also have an energy attached to them. Even though those memories are from months and years in the past, their energy is still at work in your mind and body. It's time to release the negative energy that is connected to them.

As we discussed earlier, when your body was developing in utero, neural pathways were created, forming connections between your brain and your extremities and organs by way of nerves. Your nervous, circulatory, cardiac, digestive, reproductive, respiratory, lymphatic, muscular, skeletal, and autonomic systems (to name a few) grew from only two tiny cells of creation: the egg and the sperm, and they are all interconnected.

As your cells divided, multiplied, and eventually took on their intended structure, *energetic pathways* were created among them. Think of these as superhighways where, depending on the need, *energy* can travel slowly, steadily, or move at lightning speed. Acupuncture refers to these pathways as *meridians* and uses them to treat the body for all types of conditions and symptoms. By working on different points within specific meridians, you can affect the different parts of the body that are tied to those energetic pathways. Releasing and improving the energy flow within a meridian relieves symptoms, and can also release the energy that is tied to events, thoughts, beliefs, and emotions.

The energy you hold within yourself has an attachment to your self-awareness, self-esteem, happiness, beliefs, perceptions—everything. An emotional, energetic imprint has been integrated into your mind (unconscious, subconscious, and conscious), and it interacts with you mentally, physically, spiritually, and emotionally. Learning to see how this repressed energy from your past may be hindering you, and quite possibly even making you ill, can be eye-opening.

Energy is always moving and interactive; it rarely becomes static. When energy does become stagnant, it can create an unhealthy environment where you feel depressed, withdrawn, exhausted, and ill. Our energy can be affected by many external factors like toxins, chemicals, radiation, diet, pesticide, steroids, medicines, chemicals, and sugar, but it can also be impacted by our emotions, thoughts, unconscious beliefs, and expectations, too!

Energy can become stuck, trapped, inflamed, over-reactive, irritated, and oversensitive. Think of a tea kettle on a stove: as it heats the energy that is occurring on the inside, the water molecules expand and there is a rise in temperature, the creation of steam in a gaseous state, and evaporation. Your own energy is quite similar: it can also be manipulated, transformed, expanded, or contracted by what you are thinking, feeling, and experiencing.

Let me give you a brief example of how your own energy can be changed and impact how you feel. Say you're at work, and you're pleased with yourself for completing a project. Your personal satisfaction creates an energy that supports feelings of success, expansion, respect, and value. Then you overhear a coworker gossiping about how slow you were to finish the project. Hearing this person speak behind your back negates your feeling of accomplishment and changes the energy within you, as well as the environment between you and your coworkers, and may even have negative impacts on future projects.

When you understand that your energy is in a dance with the energy that surrounds you, I think you can see why it is so difficult to feel well inside. We are constantly being bombarded by energies that come from outside ourselves as well as our continued struggle within, and they all affect us.

"Everything in life is vibration."
—Albert Einstein

If Einstein was right, that means that every event, action, thought, feeling, spoken word, and touch is composed of energetic vibration. When our bodies deviate from their normal, ideal vibration—whether it is due to our own thoughts, emotions, and stress or external factors like the environment, pollution, and the energy of other people—disease and dysfunction can occur.

Although metaphysics, quantum physics, and some progressive medical practitioners continue to explore energy and vibration with respect to health and disease, traditional science still needs to be able to see, quantify, and validate in order to understand and attempt to resolve problems. Western medicine relies on concrete, tangible, measureable, results-oriented tests, and doctors have difficulty understanding the more transient, subtle, alternative Eastern medical interventions like meditation, Reiki, and acupuncture. Physicians, for the most part, rely on tests results to make diagnoses and treat symptoms. Rarely do you see doctors trying to find the root cause of the condition, a reason which may not be physical.

Don't get me wrong; I've worked in the medical arena as a physical therapist for more than twenty-five years, and I've seen many wonderful medical advancements in diagnosis and treatment, but I believe that we can enhance our quality of patient care by looking deeper for the underlying cause and using a variety of treatments that work, even though we may not be able to explain why.

Many doctors will share stories with you of unexplained healings and even miracles. Many, if not most, cancer hospitals now offer Reiki treatments to patients (as well as their family members) to aid in comfort and relaxation and to promote additional healing. Even returning veterans who suffer from Post-Traumatic Stress Disorder now have access to Reiki. I believe there are many resources and treatment protocols that can benefit patients, and I'm excited to see the medical world become more transparent and receptive to other alternatives.

What would you think if a doctor sent you home with a prescription to laugh a hundred times a day or to sit or walk outside for an hour each day? What if he/she told you not to ingest any refined sugars? That doctor is putting your medical treatment back in your hands, giving you the power to create your own solution. No pills are given to mask your symptoms; instead, you are responsible for promoting and creating your own health. Most people would rather take a pill than have to take personal responsibility for their own healing. How sad, really. We have become a pharmacological-dependent society.

Maria's Story: Conflict with Confrontation

I met a young woman in her twenties named Maria, who had been diagnosed with a kidney disease (hydronephrosis—literally "water inside the kidney) at the age of four, when she was required to have surgery to prevent the backflow of urine from her bladder into her kidneys. The doctors had to open up the width of the tube to allow the urine to flow more easily into her bladder.

As we talked about her condition, I started to ask her details about her childhood. She recalled that her parents were always arguing. The environment was very combative, but she loved and was close to both of them. Sometimes she would cuddle with one and sometimes the other, often leaving her feeling that she was hurting the other parent. Maria found herself "*struggling*," trying to "*filter*" or "*balance*" who was right or wrong. She hated the dissension and found herself starting to *"contract,"* to be *"small"* so it wouldn't hurt as much. These were her words (in italics), and they're integral because they also described exactly what was going on with her kidneys.

During our conversation, she started to experience a discomfort in the area of her kidneys. Just recalling the memories, emotional pain, and energy from her childhood caused stress, and that stress was definitely tied to her kidneys. As a toddler, Maria had tried desperately to *filter* out the angry words between her parents and didn't know *which side* to take.

Can you see how, as a young child, her inability to *filter out* and protect herself from stress actually affected her kidneys, which actually perform the same function—*cleaning and filtering toxins and impurities within the body*? Interesting, no? Of course, the doctors probably wouldn't confirm this link, but I have found time and time again that we often hold our pains in different regions of our bodies, which ultimately produce physical symptoms. When you reduce or eliminate the root cause and emotional energetic pain, the physical symptoms often improve or disappear.

Continuing on, I asked Maria how she deals with conflict between people in her life today. She admitted that she struggles and finds herself trying to *balance, support*, and help them *resolve their conflicts*. She said that she finds it difficult to remove herself from their problems, always trying to *buffer and filter* out what she sees as their problem in order to help them find balance and harmony.

As a young child, this beautiful little girl took on the role of being a *filter between conflicts*, and she continued to use this unconscious behavior, even as an adult, in order to *feel love and valued*. To what end? We worked together to free her from this energetic imprint of ownership and resolution of problems, focusing on staying out of other people's conflicts. In time, she found that she no longer experienced discomfort in her kidney region, and she was more at peace within herself and became happier in her relationships. She even noticed that fewer conflicts were presenting themselves in her life. She had addressed one of her Soul lessons: other people's problems were not hers, and she wasn't responsible for solving, filtering, and resolving them. Freedom at last!

Amid's Story: Avoidance

I had another client whose parents argued too, but he was affected in a much different way. Amid, an Afghani man is in his thirties, struggles in many aspects of his life. He isolates himself and describes himself as depressed. He left his job as a document translator ten months ago and is currently separating from his wife. I could hear his sadness as he told his story; his life appeared filled with difficulty and an internal rift that he couldn't understand.

When I asked him what he felt caused this inner pain, sadness, and isolation, Amid said that he figured it was from his childhood but couldn't identify how and why. He was quick to say that he had read many well-known books by authors like Tony Robbins and Jack Canfield that promise to bring success into your life, but for him, the results were elusive and only left him feeling more isolated and unsuccessful. Many of you, I know, may have felt the same way. Often transformational teachers present how to achieve success but don't know how to effectively remove the emotional painful charge we hold within ourselves that keeps us from experiencing joy, abundance, and good fortune.

Amid was able to identify some key aspects that affected him as a young child. In retrospect, he could begin to see the things that had been negatively influencing him his entire life. Amid spoke about how his parents *argued* a *lot*. His mom was angry with her own family; his father married three times, and Amid was *afraid* of everything.

He recalled that, as a little seven-year-old, he felt very much *alone, unhappy,* and *fearful.* Amid found reading aloud in a classroom setting very difficult, and expressing himself was a huge challenge. He said that his other siblings also had similar problems, but not as bad as his.

When I asked if he had any physical problems, he stated that he has a lot of stomach and esophageal issues and was extremely thin and underweight. At that point, the light bulb went off for me, and I started to see the elements of what had been holding him back. I could connect his personal struggles, pains, and learned behaviors with how they energetically affected his stomach area, which is where your power station is. His throat, energetically, was affected because he learned that he had no voice and fear communication.

Any good coach will agree that it's always better to help the individual see their own issues and find their own "A-ha!" moments than for you to tell them. I would make one little comment that would seem to connect for him, but he still struggled to see the wisdom that was waiting to be revealed to him. In some ways, he was avoiding the confrontation of actually seeing what was right in front of his eyes, both in the present day and throughout his life.

I asked him, "As this little seven-year-old boy, when your parents were arguing, what did you *feel*? What did you *experience*? What did you *do*?" His answer was quite simply, "I would run away." The noise, the confusion, the arguing was so *upsetting*. Can you begin to see how this scared, lonely little child felt unloved and created a behavior of *avoidance* in order to survive? He learned that survival meant avoiding confrontation and removing himself, and that *communication* was a threatening event which only resulted in unrest. *Wow!*

Be an investigator and see if you can connect any words or parts of the story together and how it could be impacting his life. Certain words may have already jumped out at you: for example, *communication*. He is a *document translator*; why would he have picked that career? If he could stay in a room by himself where he could perform the translations, that would be one thing, but his difficulty reading aloud continued even as an adult; talking in groups was so uncomfortable that he found himself avoiding interaction, which resulted in him having to leave his job. The energetic connection to his pain affected his verbal expression and lack of power. The fear he'd felt as a child—the pain that led him to run away from conflict and challenges—had continued throughout his life. The pain of isolation continued to haunt him.

Amid's children and mother currently live with him. He finds himself constantly arguing with his older son, who is somewhat of a bully. Amid has become the "arguer" to his son, which is exactly what his parents were to him. His perceptions and behavior are so ingrained that he can't see the aspects that hold him back. He just knows that he is unhappy with all aspects of his life, and he doesn't know how to resolve any of it. He doesn't understand what goes into a loving relationship—one that is built on trust, commitment, and unconditional love, and that includes within himself. He even avoids that inner, intimate knowledge and runs away from the internal conflict that exists.

Don't forget how his emotional pains have actually affected him physically. You can see that he is very unhappy within himself and has a lot of buried emotional hurt that he holds within his esophagus and stomach area. His physical symptoms most likely will continue to grow in severity unless the root cause and energetic emotional painful imprint are released and resolved.

You might say that it was his parent's fault: they weren't supportive or loving enough, and his troubles were all their fault, but what good does that do? In the blink of an eye, you've cast him in the role of the victim and taken away his ownership, responsibility, and power over his past and present situations. How can he experience the feelings and behaviors that he must rise above and find his inner power, see his greatness, and use his gifts?

Until he realizes that his adult behavior is parroting his learned, scared, seven-year-old behavior and that he'll have to embrace what he fears the most, lasting healing will most likely remain elusive. If he continues to do nothing; he will continue to get the same results: isolation, the inability to freely express himself verbally, and avoidance of all physical and loving relationships with others. Is this a life anyone would want to live?

Children with combative parents can respond in very different ways.

You can clearly see how two children were affected so differently by combative parents. Maybe you grew up in a similar environment, so you can relate and see how that interaction impacted you. Without doubt, your childhood had unique dynamics which impacted you a certain way. How were your perceptions, behaviors, and beliefs created?

I believe that revealed untruths are actually Soul lessons to be learned. What I love about doing this work is that, when the elements come together, you can identify your Soul lessons and understand what you must take on.

In the previous **Journey Along** exercises, you identified significant memories and started to explore how the details may still be impacting you. After reading these two stories about arguing parents and the toll it took on their children, I invite you to dig even deeper to reveal what behaviors you used to try and cope and minimize the hurt/pain. Ask yourself if you're still using them in your life now.

Here is another tool that you can use to gain further clarity into your Soul Lessons and how your past continues to play a role in your life even today. Your written words will have *key words* like we found in the stories above that will really connect, if you can just open your eyes and see them. To download this form, go to www.PowerfulBeyondMeasureBook.com/forms.

<u>Journey Along: Digging Deeper</u>

Looking back, choose the memory that you feel was the catalyst—the one that is the most emotional, the one that you know hurts the most. If you are not ready to take on this one just yet, pick a less consuming and painful event or emotion.

1. When this happened: _____,
    I felt _____
    and did _____.

2. When I think about those times, I feel it in my (body location)

    _____,

    and these symptoms have increased or decreased over time.

    _____.

3. When similar situations occur in the present (identify the theme/situation/struggle)

    _____,

    I feel _____
    and do _____.

4. I can see a connection between how I felt as a child and how my same behavior, belief, and perception continues to be the template I use today. (Write it down here, and be as specific as you can):

    _____

    _____

    _____

5. I accept and have the desire to change this old mindset of (lack/avoidance/
    isolation/ … write in your own word) _____, to
    learn my Soul Lesson, to grow, and to love myself.

Congratulations! I hope you're feeling good about drawing conclusions
about why you felt, acted, and thought the way you did (or do) and realize that
you are no longer that child. You are a wonderful, resourceful *adult* who can
change how you behave, think, and feel. In the next part of the book, you'll find
specific tools and strategies that you can participate in that will empower you to
accomplish just that.

> *"Those who have failed to work toward the truth*
> *have missed the purpose of living."*
> **—Buddha**

"You can't connect the dots looking forward; you can only connect them looking backwards. So you have to trust that the dots will somehow connect in your future."
—**Steve Jobs**

REPETITIOUS PATTERNS
Connecting the dots in your life

You are so much more than any of the untruths you've come to believe.

Your self-awareness, learned behaviors, and limiting beliefs contribute to how you interact with people and respond to events in your life. On many levels, you're aware of where you fall short, what you desire in life, and the discontent that resides within. You've probably spoken these words silently to yourself many times: "Is this all there is? Why do I feel so lost, alone, frustrated, afraid …? Why does this keep happening to me?"

Our past is full of *redundant* experiences that continue to present themselves so we can learn and grow from them. The sad news is that we often do *not* absorb those lessons, which causes the need for the events to repeat themselves in order to provide us with *another* opportunity to develop. It can become a vicious cycle: in an attempt to prevent pain, our brain recalls the past and tries to direct and predict expected outcomes by drawing on the set of familiar, repeated responses we've created during our lives. Even though they haven't worked in the past, we return to these repetitious patterns because they're all we know. We have a limited understanding of how the same old responses don't serve our best interests.

What Holds Us Back?

If our past memories are filled with feelings of doubt, fear, unworthiness, isolation, and failure, then our decisions will often follow the path that feels the safest and provides comfort and security, even if our heart tries to tell us something different. I have found that many people are actually more comfortable with being *uncomfortable*—tolerating the preexisting patterns that continue to exist in their lives—than really being able to move into the unknown, where freedom and joy awaits. Addressing our emotional pains and issues can be challenging and even frightening, but continuing to do the same things in the same way can only provide you with the same undesirable results.

Do you ever feel that your responses are automatically generated, happening quickly and often without thought? Do you ask yourself, "Why the heck did I *do* that?" It's almost like your mental computer is stuck in default mode, programmed to react with only a single course of action. In an effort to handle all the crap that life may be handing out, we often respond in ways that simply enable us to survive and get by. They're *not* the best choices, but your action or reaction just occurred. Your body (or should I say your mind) does anything and everything to protect and defend you—to keep you safe. In many ways, this primal need for self-preservation becomes the distorted filter through which we see and the template for the ineffective behaviors we continue to use.

Over the years, you've developed *defensive behavior mechanisms* that cause you to continue to *believe in the persona* that you grew up understanding and accepting as truth. You've erected *protective walls* in an attempt to hide the pain, feel safe, and avoid things you don't want to deal with. You built those walls as your sanctuary, but instead they've become your prison. They confine you, keep you from interacting with your world in a joyful way, and limit your Soul's expansion.

Let me explain this with an example:

As a young child, Carol was very angry. Her anger stemmed in large part from the feeling that she was being ignored and unheard. She learned that the only time people took her seriously was when she overreacted, screamed, and lost control, which usually resulted in her getting her own way. Her mind took on these learned behavioral mechanisms—overreacting and throwing temper tantrums—to release the anger she held inside. These were the protective walls Carol built so she wouldn't have to reveal her true emotions (even, or perhaps especially, to herself) in certain situations and with other people.

Of course, Carol's protective walls, expressed in outburst and fits, only served to push people farther away, removing what she longed for the most. It's no surprise that her feelings of being ignored and unheard continued to grow. Carol had learned that people would respond when she lost control, but with that came the most painful outcome of all: rejection, isolation, disrespect, and avoidance. Her anger and emotional pain were holding her captive and alone. Throughout her life, Carol struggled and blamed others for the sadness and anger she held towards life, people, and circumstances. She could see no way out.

What are Your Repetitious Patterns?

Maybe you've always felt like the scapegoat or the rebel in the family. Or do you feel like you're the go-to person whenever there is a problem, but no one is there when *you* need help? What about being the smart one—well respected and independent but lacking long-lasting, close friends?

Answer these questions and try to pinpoint your own repetitious patterns.

(If you prefer to print or download the form, go to

www.PowerfulBeyondMeasureBook.com/forms.)

Repetitious Patterns, Behaviors, and Outcomes

1. What patterns have held you back, kept you stuck, and been repeated?

2. If you had to qualify the difficulties in your life, what would they be about?

3. How did you respond to them and what results were obtained?

4. Do you feel your struggles brought you to a better place, the same scenario, or something/somewhere worse?

5. Looking back on these events can you see the opportunity that presented itself?

6. How did you interact with those opportunities, did you move forward into that the unknown, or turn and retreat back into the same old pattern and behavior?

In Part I, Explore Your Past and Ease Your Pain, you have been using your investigative skills to identify the emotional pain, negative behavior, and beliefs, and you've started to identify your Soul lesson(s). This entire first part of Powerful Beyond Measure is so critical because this is where all your introspection starts to gel and you're able to really identify the areas you need to focus on. As you read and completed the exercises in the previous chapters, you recalled memories, explored what beliefs you took on, and examined how you felt in the past (and today). This helped you gain an inner wisdom into the events, emotions, and reactions that have repeated themselves over and over again throughout your life. In summary, what repetitious patterns have you identified that are still present today?

Connecting the Dots

Steve Jobs had many low points in his life: developing the first computer in his parents' garage, being fired from the revolutionary company he had created and led to astounding success, fathering a child that he rebuked for years, and, of course, his fight with cancer. In his now-famous 2005 commencement address at Stanford University, he spoke movingly about the many difficult times he'd had throughout his life when he felt angry, lost, and unsure about what to do or which way to go. He said that although he wasn't able to understand the purpose of his struggles while they were happening, later in his life, he could see how each one had helped him or at least offered him an opportunity to grow.

When he was going through those troubled times, it was not pleasant; he often felt like a victim, but later, when he connected the dots, it all made sense. They were part of his path and contributed to who he became. When he looked back, he saw the value in each of those difficulties and how they became the catalyst for new adventures. What was it that he needed to learn?

That is the critical question that we each have to ask ourselves.

The late Dr. Wayne Dyer, best-selling author and profound spiritual and transformational leader, agreed with Jobs's philosophy. In his inspiring memoir, *I Can See Clearly Now*, Dyer wrote:

> I wasn't aware of all of the future implications that these early experiences were to offer me. Now, from a position of being able to *see much more clearly*, I know that every single encounter, every challenge, and every situation are all spectacular threads in the tapestry that represents and defines my life, and I am deeply grateful for all of it.

Steve Jobs, Wayne Dyer, and I have found that when you're able to connect the dots, your world opens up in a way that you could never have imagined. You *can* see more clearly when you gain a richer understanding of the past and realize it all has been there to help you fulfill your life and goals in the present. It offers you a new starting point with a fresh view of the kaleidoscope of possibilities and wonder that are just ahead—your path for the future and the purpose you feel driven to fulfill.

Let's try and connect the dots between your past and present. Think of it like a child's book: you draw a line between the first two points (dots), and then another two, and so on until the final end point, when the complete image is revealed. At first glance, all you saw were dots with numbers on the page, and you had no idea what the final image or message would be. That's exactly how life is: you've taken many steps and experienced a great deal, but when you connect these events, you can reveal the message—the final vision of who you are and what your unfulfilled purpose is.

That's the goal of this chapter. You're connecting the events in your life to see the larger picture—what awaits you as you choose the direction you need, desire, and want to take—with greater clarity. Your Soul wants to grow and expand. When you're able to see how your protective walls have in fact limited you in so many ways, you can take positive, actionable steps to disassemble it and embrace and engage in life in a fresh and renewed way. The limitations which once held you back will become the challenges you're eager to take on!

Connect Your Dots and Reveal Your Truth!

Can you relate to the idea that your protective walls may in fact be limiting you from the things you desire the most? If so, how?

- What is it that you truly desire?

- What protective walls have you constructed over the years that you believe offer you shelter and safety, helping you to avoid feeling and being hurt?

- What, in fact, are you avoiding?

- What lesson(s) would you learn if you could lower your protective wall?

- Are you willing to seek your freedom, to grow and expand in ways that you never thought possible?

What is the truth that you were able to reveal after answering these questions?

_____

_____

For a printed copy of this exercise, go to
www.PowerfulBeyondMeasureBook.com/forms.

It's difficult to find the words to express what it feels like to be at peace within, to allow that inner healing to occur and experience life in a much more rewarding way. To be free, to feel, and to learn to love your authentic self instead of the lies, the limitations, and self-doubts you've been carrying for most of your life, but let me tell you it's so worth working towards your life changes in ways you cannot fathom.

You're beginning to really understand how your negative emotional memories hold you hostage and prevent you from reaching your full potential. You now see the repetitious patterns of circumstances and behavior that have been present in your life. You've identified the defensive behavior mechanisms that you've employed, and you realize that your protective walls have prevented you from experiencing complete happiness and joy.

It is my hope that as we conclude Part I, Explore Your Past and Ease Your Pain, and move into Part II, Empower Your Present and Embrace Your Self, that you have identified many integral parts where growth can occur on a personal and even spiritual level.

Your inner voice is trying to get your attention and assist you to resolve, heal, and grow so your life can be filled with happiness, abundance, and success. I know you long for this. We all do!

The past can no longer hurt you unless you give it the power to!

"There are only two days in the year that nothing can be done.
One is called yesterday and the other is called tomorrow.
Today is the right day to love, believe, and live."
— Dalai Lama

Part II

Empower Your Present and Embrace Your *Self*

In Part I, I shared stories that illustrate how the pain of past memories can affect every part of our lives, including our physical health. I'd like to share another personal experience with you to show you not only how deeply the past can impact us, but also how much our lives can change when we choose to become **Powerful Beyond Measure**. This story was quite literally a huge wake-up call for me.

I loved my husband very much, but he found it hard to sleep with me, and it was breaking my heart.

It all started with snoring—mine! I'd been experiencing severe bouts of it for many months, and even had scary times when I'd stop breathing completely, followed by a startling wakeup event that initiated my breathing pattern again—and usually woke up my husband. This often forced Tom out of our bed, which robbed us both of the intimacy we desired. I was embarrassed, hurt, and deeply alone.

I finally mentioned these issues to my doctor, who scheduled a sleep study for me. The results were scary: I had a condition called sleep apnea which prevented me from getting enough oxygen. I had a 50 percent sleep-efficiency rate, no REM (deep restorative sleep), and I was experiencing thirty-five apnea-hypopnea events per hour (>30 is considered severe). I was also sixty pounds overweight and had high blood pressure, so my health was becoming a life-threatening situation.

"Good news!" they told me. There's a machine that would help me sleep normally! A few nights later, I put on the clunky paraphernalia that came with what I called "the breathing machine" and thought, "This is worse!" I had felt bad before about keeping my husband up at night, but now I was mortified to even be seen! A mask covered my nose and was connected by a hose to a machine that generated a continuous flow of air pressure to keep my airway open. Very feminine and attractive—not in the least!

Once I was hooked up, snuggling was awkward—and forget about kissing. I found myself turning away from Tom so he wouldn't see me like that. Yes, my quality of sleep was better and I was feeling more rested, but my emotional well-being was deteriorating. I felt like a failure, and although Tom never said anything, I knew he was feeling the strain too.

Then one night, fed up and frustrated, I tried something different. I went to bed quite late to let Tom get some undisturbed sleep, and then I tried to sleep without using the breathing machine. I placed pillows around me to try to keep myself from lying on my back and fell asleep. It didn't work; I woke up many times gasping for air, and after a bit, I felt Tom get up and retreat to our spare bedroom.

In that moment, the memory of my father walking out of my life came crushing down on me like a lead weight, and I felt like I couldn't breathe. This wasn't a new memory, but my repressed emotional pain welled up and made me wonder once again, "How could he just walk away and leave my four sisters, my mother, and me?" I had worked on these issues of abandonment and lack of male support and affirmation for much of my adult life, but in that moment, I felt like I hadn't made any progress at all.

As I explored my feelings in my lonely bed that night, I realized that, even though I thought I'd resolved those memories, the emotional pain was still there, and it still continued to play a significant role in my life. The emotional wounds from my parent's divorce were still undermining my self-image and self-confidence, and now even my physical health. An intuitive feeling came over me: by wearing the breathing machine, I was creating a justification for my husband to abandon me. Would my new fear become my reality? I became determined to heal my emotional wounds permanently and turn my self-limiting beliefs around so I could heal my body and enjoy all the closeness I wanted with my husband.

I am excited to share with you the powerful steps I used that can free you from the emotional pain that I had carried for so long. I lost sixty pounds, regained my health and happiness, and, oh *yes*, eliminated my sleep apnea. Hallelujah, no more breathing machine, and my bed partner was able to stay the entire night!

The day I returned the breathing machine to my doctor, he said, "You look like a different person! How'd you do it?"

"Oh, just some internal housecleaning," I said with a chuckle.

Now let's get started on *your* housecleaning!

You've come so far. Are you ready to go even further?

You accomplished some very important work in the first part of this book, revealing the past wounds that you experienced or took on and how they may have impacted (or continue to impact) your life even today. Through your investigative work, you have identified trigger words or sentences that describe how you feel emotionally, and you've even uncovered some behavior mechanisms that you took on to protect yourself from further pain in the future. These mechanisms often become the walls that you must now disassemble in order to allow yourself to feel and love yourself again, be open to trust and receive from others, and permit your heart to express your passion and purpose.

If you're still not completely confident or you don't feel that you have a really good understanding of how your past has impacted you emotionally (and your resulting behavior), that's okay: whatever you took away from the first part of the Powerful Beyond Measure Process is perfect and appropriate for where you are in your spiritual journey. Be open and express gratitude that you're exploring, growing, and healing. Many people (including you) will repeat this process again and again, and each time, you'll be able to reveal more wisdom and interconnectedness with your lessons. Enlightenment, wisdom, and self-empowerment are processes that take time; they don't occur with a flip of a switch. You're exactly where you're supposed to be—there are no mistakes in our Universe.

In this next section, you will take the personal information that you were able to understand from your past, integrate it with lessons on how to release those trapped, suppressed emotions and pains, and create powerful transformations that will impact every aspect of your life. During this next part of the book, our focus is on the *present*. By understanding how we live in the ***now***, you'll understand that any resolution can occur only in *this moment*. Freedom, peace, love, abundance, health, and joy await you, and I promise that you'll learn many ways to positively impact your life.

Not everyone learns the same way. By trying the various techniques and tools within this book, you will create your very own personal **First Aid Toolbox to Health and Happiness**. Since we all learn differently and have various areas we need to focus on, obtaining tools that are perfect for you will help you be more successful. As you continue on with these next chapters, write down or print out the various techniques that seem perfect just for you. You can find some useful forms on my website at www.PowerfulBeyondMeasureBook.com/forms.

Emotions and Our Health

Many books, including those by Deepak Chopra, Ann Louise Hay, Barbara Ann Brennan, Dr. Wayne Dyer, and so many others, talk about how thoughts and emotions impact our health. Our emotions are a reaction to how we feel. For example, if someone pinches you, first there is a sensation of touch, along with pain. This triggers an emotional response (possibly anger, fear, or confusion), which is then connected to that sensation of being pinched. Often the original feeling is never acknowledged, but our emotions become the barometer for the pain or feeling that we experience.

Your brain ties the two together: a neural connection is formed between the event and your perception, emotion, and response. Often these neural pathways become the highways that we continue to use, leading to the same destination with the same results. Implementing the techniques in this section will facilitate changes in your internal environment and how you interact with the external world, creating new neural pathways with improved, present-day shortcuts that yield better results and greater satisfaction.

Your mind is always trying to protect you, helping you to avoid feeling painful emotion or physical discomfort. Regardless of the stimuli, if it's repeated and reinforced, it becomes the framework against which other situations are judged and compared. Returning to the pinching example, you may create a framework that includes not trusting people to get too close or the idea that touching can be offensive and should be avoided.

Of course, this is a simple example, but what if this behavior was repeated often (you'll probably identify with this if you grew up with siblings), leaving you feeling completely unsafe and afraid of the looming potential threat? Can you see how your emotional responses can create your mental understanding, where trust, intimacy, and belonging may be negatively impacted?

So often our emotions become heightened or amplified because of our memories and their connections with what we felt at that time. Your early years, as you have come to understand, can fossilize the emotional responses that became tied to how you *felt* during those experiences, so a synergistic reaction can also occur when you have those same emotions. These things happen because your past is a living energetic force that creates your reality—and you. Your feelings and mental understandings from those early experiences can become incorporated in a new experience, one in which you might feel untrustworthy, isolate yourself, and view yourself as being "picked on."

We usually find it easier to discredit, bury, or misinterpret our emotions, which only adds to our internal confusion and leads to feeling unheard, not cared for, and somewhat of a fraud. It is often uncomfortable sharing and exposing our true emotions for fear of judgment, retaliation, and our own inner struggle.

In some way, we don't know how to integrate these emotions and understand where they're coming from. We may want to blame someone or something else for making us feel this way—or, better yet, ignore them and not even have to deal with the emotions or events that created them. In a way, we are becoming more like robots, revealing a *self-programmed* behavior—acting and responding to imprints that have been passed on through previous lives, cultural patterning, and our own experiences during this lifetime.

I'm sure you remember the Tin Man from the *Wizard of Oz*: he searched for a *heart* so he could be able to *feel*, only to discover that having a heart also meant understanding how heartbreak feels, too. In this section of the book, we will be exploring in detail the **Emotional Fitness Program,** through which you'll learn to have (and express) a wide range of emotions without judgment and disconnect from the past experiential pains and wounds that you continue to carry forward.

This does *not* mean that you'll be encouraged to express only happy, positive emotions. What it *does* mean is that you'll learn tools to understand, accept, and express your emotions openly and freely without allowing your mind to make you contract, think less of yourself, and repeat negative self-defeating behaviors. It's learning to be imperfect and express your vulnerability openly.

> *"Emotions are vibrational interpreters."*
> **—Hicks**

Everything in the Universe has a specific energetic vibration. Our bodies, organs, thoughts, actions, and even our emotions have their own energy. What this means is that what we feel, think, eat, drink, touch, act, and do all have a direct impact on our health. When you worry, you create more to worry about. If your emotions are filled with trepidation and unrest, then your actions and your results will resonate at that same frequency. This is the Law of Attraction.

By changing your emotional attitude to one filled with higher vibratory sensations, you can completely change how you experience your life, what you bring into it, and the joy you take from your life and give back to the world. You can invite miracles into your life through thoughts, feelings, and emotions that support that vibration. You can literally transform yourself and the world you touch. Collectively, we can actually change the vibration of the Universe.

As we know, energy is in all creation, and even our emotions hold an energetic charge that affects not only ourselves but others as well. Because emotional energy cannot be seen, measured, or quantified, emotions are often discounted and devalued. With all the medical equipment available to us, there is not one instrument that can measure the emotional pain level that you hold within yourself. An X-ray couldn't show that you have five pounds of grief from a parent's death that occurred ten years ago, and an echocardiogram can't show that the congestion around your heart might be attributed to the unexpressed sorrow from years of profound sadness, pain, and despair.

Our bodies are constantly experiencing various chemical and hormonal reactions, many of which are in response to our emotions that positively or negatively affect our health. When we engage in activities that bring us pleasure, the body relaxes, and there is a decrease in heart rate and an increase in endorphins and serotonin. When we experience stress or become angry, our heart rate, breathing, and testosterone production increases, and cortisol (the stress hormone) decreases. There are also profound changes in the autonomic nervous system, which controls the cardiovascular response and the endocrine system.

Feelings, mental and verbal expressions, and emotions all have an energy associated with them. When you understand how your own energy is impacted (as well as the energy of others), you will begin to understand the effect this may have on your physical body and how it can actually create symptoms and disease. Your symptoms may be an expression of your emotional wounds. The mind-body-spirit connection is so powerful, but it's missing an integral component: emotions. No field of science would disagree that each of us can affect our bodies, often in ways that result in unexplained improvements in health that astound even the medical profession.

I believe that our Soul knows our path and tries to communicate and support us in our journey and growth here on Earth. The problem is that we are seldom quiet enough or able to be inwardly reflective and hear the wisdom that is shared. I personally believe that we each have Soul lesson(s) that we have been incarnated to learn, but we have no recollection and avoid the challenges where potential growth can occur.

If we continue to hold unhealed childhood wounds, or even additional emotional pain that has occurred more recently, how do we resolve those issues and find that inner peace we all ultimately seek? The unhealed childhood wounds that make us feel insecure, alone, scared, powerless, frightened, helpless, angry, and unloved become inflamed and cause us to react like we did as children; we often use the same tools we learned then to protect ourselves from further pain and hurt. It's actually quite amazing how our body tries to protect us from further harm. We develop defense mechanisms, construct walls of protection, and accept false senses of self that hamper the actual growth our Souls want us to achieve and learn.

As we continue to perpetuate this behavior, belief, and response, we allow the emotional imprints from our earlier days to continue to affect us even today. This primitive survival response actually holds us captive to a time, understanding, and perception that we took on many years ago.

Taking Control

If you were told that you had only six hours to live, how would you spend that remaining time? Wouldn't you treasure every moment, connect in a very sincere and heartfelt way, and savor all the sensory and emotional stimuli that you could experience? Why should we have to be given a death sentence to enjoy our lives? It's actually quite sad to think that most, if not all of us are awake fourteen to sixteen hours a day, but we seldom enjoy that time. The good news is that you have the ability to create the changes that will powerfully impact your own happiness, health, relationships, successes, and abundance. I will show not only how your own self-inflicted limitations, false beliefs, energy, and emotional blocks are holding you back, but also tools and techniques that you can implement with powerful and lasting results.

What if I told you that the past exists *only* in your mind? Wow, just think about that for a minute! *You* are the one who continues to fuel the past and the impact it has on yourself and your life. Did you ever realize that *you* are the one who allows the **past** to continue to exist in the **present** and actually permeate into your **future**?

Taking personal ownership—realizing that *you* have created a protective internal world that only serves to continue the cycle of so much, if not all, of your unhappiness—can be overwhelming, but that's the **good news**! This means that if you've played a role in creating your unhappiness, pain, and sadness, then you can *uncreate* it, too! How powerful is that idea—to know that *you* hold the keys to your own happiness, health, and harmony?

> *"I cannot always control what goes on outside.*
> *But I can always control what goes on inside."*
> **—Dr. Wayne Dyer**

You have to be willing to continue to do the internal work and healing, and you have to realize that there are *no* quick fixes. For most of us, our pains, wounds, and hurts have become so deeply integrated that it will take work, conscious thought, and a shift of emotional impact to alter those beliefs. I am here to tell you it *is* attainable and you *can* achieve it all.

Let's continue together as you take this next powerful step toward resolution, healing, and transformation. As you continue to work in this next section, remember that you always have a choice: happiness over sadness, peacefulness over anger, love over hatred, and health over disease.

If you would like to reach out to me to gain greater clarity before moving on to the next part on empowerment, clearing, and healing, I encourage you to contact me at www.PowerfulBeyondMeasureBook.com/contact to schedule a personal call. This call will help you connect the dots and gain clarity on what you may want to focus on during the next section of this book. Remember: your Soul knows everything, and it wants to support and love you, help eliminate your pain, learn your lessons, and fulfill your destiny.

> *"The strongest principle of growth lies in human choice."*
> **—George Eliot**

POWER OF YOUR AUTHENTIC SELF
Revealing your own brilliance

*The more you connect to your Power Within—
who you truly are—the more your truth is revealed.*

L oving yourself must start at home, within *you*! Healing can only occur from the *inside out*. When you can see and love yourself without judgment, criticism, or guilt, then you can look upon others with the same vision of acceptance, forgiveness, and love. When you stop hurting within, you can stop hurting others and, even more importantly, love and enjoy life from a state of peace and abundance.

If our true existence could be expressed from a place of self-love, there would be no want, no war, no terror, no stress, no disease, no condemnation, and no starvation. The energy emitted from all living beings would be one of harmony, emotional freedom, and the capacity to use our inner gifts to positively touch the world. What could be greater than that?

So how can you experience and live from your true Soul's essence and fall in love with yourself again? Taking responsibility for your own creation and how you interact with yourself and the world is the first step. How you view each moment (your thoughts and actions, which only you control) impacts your emotions and your level of happiness. It truly is that easy.

We talked about self-awareness earlier and how you created a persona that was based on the information you received at a very young age. The protective walls you built and fortified over the years to reduce the potential of additional emotional pain are in fact the same walls that are preventing you from learning your Soul lessons. In this chapter, you will explore how to turn self-condemnation and doubt into self-love and compassion.

What if I told you that any negative thoughts you have about yourself are completely a lie—an untruth? Does your mind immediately want to defend your position and come up with various reasons for why you aren't great, why people don't like you, or why you don't even like yourself? You're living a subconscious pattern that you took on from a very young age. You are no longer that age, and it's time to release those embedded memories that no longer serve you and replace them with new positive, supportive, and loving images of self. To be able to self-love, you must be authentic and transparent and embrace who you are.

Id, Ego, and Superego

Sigmund Freud's psychoanalytic model of the psyche contains the **id**, the **ego**, and the **superego**. The **id** is the only component of the personality that is present at birth; it is unconscious and includes instinctive and primitive behaviors. The id is driven by the pleasure principle, which strives for pleasure and immediate gratification of all it desires. The id is the strongest in infancy and often expresses the basic needs of hunger, comfort, and self-protection.

The **ego**, according to Freud, develops from the id. It is responsible for dealing with reality and understands that behaviors have consequences. It exists in the conscious and unconscious mind. The ego attempts to satisfy the id's desires in socially acceptable ways while satisfying the constraints placed on it by the superego.

The **superego** aspect of personality is the last to fully mature. It begins to develop around the age of five and provides guidelines for making judgments, using moral ideals that are learned from parents and society. The superego occurs in our consciousness and gives us our sense of right and wrong. The superego acts upon idealistic standards rather than realistic principles; this creates a conflict with the ego.

On one end of the spectrum you have the id, which only cares about your needs and desires, and the superego, which wants perfection and civilized behavior. The ego is constantly in struggle with the other two, and this can often lead to feelings of pride, value, and accomplishment or punishment, guilt, and remorse. You either win or you lose; therefore, you often compare others against yourself to determine your measurement of success.

The conflict among the id, the superego, and the ego creates anxiety that leads to defense mechanisms. The ego is associated with an inflated feeling of pride or superiority in relation to others. It sees you as better and places an increased value (qualitative or quantitative) on yourself. The ego is usually satisfied through the id: possessions, dominations, attachment, power, position, accomplishments, and expectations. The ego occurs in the present, while the superego tries to confine and limit the ego's reality. The ego, if not kept in check, is never satisfied, and it's only trying to fill a void that lives within.

Here are a few examples of egotism or self-importance:

- No one can do this job better than I can
- All of my fans adore me.
- If I can accomplish this _____, I will excel at _____.

All of these examples demonstrate a person's inner need to fill herself up. In fact, though, she doesn't feel capable, loved, and worthy, it's the ego's attempt at using the conscious mind to make her better and fill that inner void.

Not to worry; during these exercises, you'll *not* be feeding your ego, which represents *self* and contrasts or judges one with another in the world. Personal power comes from inner balance—when you claim who you are and the joy that you experience.

Let's not be confused—as you go forward to reawaken your authentic inner self and embrace who you truly are, you're seeking the truth within. When you live in a space of inner peace, self-acceptance, and self-love within *all* of you—the imperfections as well as your uniqueness—then you learn to live from a place of inner harmony and balance. Being better than someone else becomes irrelevant and inconsequential, since you are completely at home within.

I think this quote by Sigmund Freud (from "A Difficulty in the Path of Psycho-Analysis") says it quite well:

"The ego is not master in its own house."

And, might I add, *unless it is allowed to be.*

Contrary to what we may have been taught about being selfish and that taking care of others is the most important thing to do, the way we think about ourselves has a direct relationship with how we treat others and the happiness we experience in life.

Learning to Love Yourself

There are powerful ways to reprogram the old self-defamatory impressions of self into new empowering beliefs that support your health and happiness. Here are four powerful tools to awaken your inner brilliance and unlock the doorway to self-love. You hold the keys to your inner happiness, joy, and harmony. When your inner self is *full*, you'll not seek others to fill a void that no longer exists within. Shifting the energy towards believing in your Soul's beautiful essence is paramount to creating the harmony within. For a printed copy of this exercise, go to www.PowerfulBeyondMeasureBook.com/forms.

1. **I Can See Clearly Now!**
   a. *Mirror, Mirror on the Wall*

This is a simple but powerful way to begin to look at yourself in a more loving manner. Each morning as you start your day, begin looking more compassionately at yourself. Don't focus on your wrinkles, pimples, skin hanging down, baggy eyes, bad hair day, etc., but on the goodness that lies deep within. We need to see the truth that is not skin deep and change the internal way you see yourself.

A friend of mine, Robert Allen Drake, once said, "We only judge ourselves, for we are mirror images of one another. Judge not lest you be judged. For by which measure you judge, so shall you be judged."

b. ***Self-loving Post-its***

Using colorful note cards or Post-its, place key words on the mirror and around your home describing the inner beauty that represents your true essence. When you look in *any* mirror, say beautiful, loving comments to yourself. Look into your eyes—the windows to your Soul—and see the magnificence within. This practice is a fabulous way to heal your heart! What you start to believe and see, others will as well. Likewise, what you see and judge in others reflects the same in you. If you don't like the way someone speaks to another, that could be a reflection how you too may speak at times. The Universe loves to provide us with scenarios that help us see our truth so that we may grow.

We are all one—mere reflections of one another.

What you see in me, I see in you.

If one sees courage, it's their own courage they see.

Here are a few examples of comments to post:

- I am giving and compassionate.
- I have a loving heart towards myself and others.
- I embrace my divine essence.
- I am in perfect health and listen to my heart.

What words should you write on your **Self-loving Post-its**?

_____

_____

c. ***Self-Loving Theme for the Year***

I encourage you to create a Power Within theme to focus on for the entire year. Try and choose one or two words that indicate where you want to place your inner attention. Here are a few suggestions to consider, but I encourage you to find your own words that resonate with you: inner peace, freedom, expression, joy, happiness, self-approval, self-acceptance, love, and divine essence.

My theme for the year when I was writing this book was "Joyful Completion." I wanted to create and live in a space where I was experiencing **joy** in all that I did while **completing** projects. I wanted to be happy in the process, but I also wanted to complete the project. Focusing on these two words helped me approach completing my book with joy and inner happiness instead of feeling overwhelmed and stressed.

I believe we all use a ***Scale of Inequity*** to judge and evaluate ourselves. We compare ourselves to others—to a standard that we each have created and come to believe as a norm—and none of us share the same baseline image. We all measure our worth by different parameters that we have imposed upon ourselves. Why do we even *feel* that we need to be similar to others or different from our true selves to be more valued? You often hear people (including yourself) say or think, "I wish I was funnier, more outgoing, more athletic, skinnier, courageous, intelligent …" The list never ends. We have stopped experiencing who we uniquely are and have found ourselves in a state of constant flux, trying to fix, repair, and shift what we're unhappy with at the moment. We often become our own worst critics. Belonging and fitting in seem essential for our survival and happiness, but in fact they become our demise. We have lost our individuality and appreciation of **self**. We continue to search for what really lies within, but we have no idea how to get there.

Harmony and inner peace no longer exist if we cannot see, love, and accept our true selves. Actually, I believe that is why so many people are unhappy and discontent with life. It is from this place of **lack**—the sense that there is not enough of _____(fill in the blank)_____—that we come from, where fullness and completeness eludes us.

2. **The Past No Longer Controls My Present (*or* My Presence)**

    This powerful two-step process creates a shift in negative emotions, thoughts, and action that may have ties from your past or have originated here in the present. Either way, changing the energy, frequency, and belief within yourself is integral in creating health and happiness.

    a. *First step*

    Any time you have a negative thought or find yourself engaging in a past behavior that makes you feel small, angry, or unhappy, ask yourself one powerful question:

    Is this emotion, thought, or action one that originates in the *present* or one that has roots in the *past*?

    Be honest with yourself. Understanding the past emotional wounds and self-limiting beliefs that you identified in the first part of the book, answering this question should be much easier.

    b. *Second step*

    If your answer was "No" to the question above, meaning that your negative emotion, thought, or action *originates in the past*, then create a declaratory statement that reinforces to yourself the truth as you **see** or **desire** it in the *present*.

    I am _____ and _____ here and now, in the present, and I no longer need to act, believe, or feel the way I did previously. I am safe, loved, and believe in myself.

    Here are some words to consider as you fill in the blanks: capable, free, able, patient, strong, peaceful, loving, kind, healthy, worthy, deserving, loving, interactive, hopeful, forgiving, creative, confident, conscientious, hardworking, successful, dedicated.

    If your answer was "Yes, this negative thought/feeling/action originates in the *present*," then create a declaratory statement, positively acknowledging your personal growth and expansion *now*. Reinforcing your action to respond differently in the present is a **huge** step forward.

> **I acknowledge my thoughts and feelings here, in the present, and I am excited to overcome my _____ and _____ to learn, grow, and succeed in the present. I support and follow my intuition and know this experience is serving my greatest good, and I actively step forward into this situation while experiencing joy, grace, and trust in myself.**

Here are some words to consider as you fill in the blanks: fear, doubts, anger, hatred, lack of forgiveness, frustrations, trepidation, isolation, loneliness, hopelessness, struggle, pain, limitations, handicaps, self-limiting beliefs.

This particular exercise has two objectives: to *identify the origin* of negative thoughts/feelings/actions and to actively *create a shift* in your conscious mind that promotes personal growth and opportunity in the present moment.

To produce change, one must first understand what needs to be changed. You no longer need to repeat the patterning from your past. You are positively responding to the Universe, which is providing you with this experience to grow, evolve, and find your higher wisdom. Remember, you are not who you were in the past, and your response to the present is creating the new **you** that you want and choose to be in the **now**.

3. **Create Your Inner Sanctuary**

Find fifteen to thirty minutes each day when you can go inward and find a place of unconditional peace, acceptance, and love. During this time, the goal is to connect with your inner self. Allow yourself to empty your daily stresses or negative feedback that you may have been experiencing. This is **your** time. If you say you can't find time for yourself, then this specific exercise is even more important. Think about it: a typical day is twenty-four hours long, and you're saying you can't find fifteen minutes? Maybe there needs to be a shift in your schedule and priorities?

a. ***Rest in a quiet, nourishing space*** that brings you comfort, peace, and joy. This can be your bedroom, bathtub, park, porch, ocean, lake, garden, forest, church, etc., and the location can change from day to day. The goal is to realize that you need to center yourself and quiet your mind, allowing yourself to go inside, listen to your higher self (Soul), and restore (heal) within.

   Meditation and yoga are a couple of extremely effective tools you can use to achieve this. Science confirms that meditating for just ten minutes a day has been proven to have health benefits. Another popular technique, mindfulness, which Merriam-Webster defines as "maintaining a nonjudgmental state of heightened or complete awareness of one's thoughts, emotions, or experiences on a moment-to-moment basis" can achieve similar results.

   Wherever and however you can connect lovingly with your inner self is what's important.

b. ***Acknowledge your wins for the day and your heart's desires***

   Expressing gratitude for your accomplishments, successes, and even miracles is the greatest way to create inner strength, wisdom, and additional support from the Universe or the divine which allows you to remain open to receive additional blessings. Listening to your heart's desire and Soul's intentions is a big step in living and creating the harmony within yourself. Connecting with your inner self allows you to be in flow with your true essence. You may find that keeping a record or writing in a journal will help you express thankfulness and recognize the growth, ideas, and feelings that come to your mind or heart.

   Think of this exercise as becoming your own cheerleader. This means that you cheer on any growth, no matter how small, even if you fall short. Growth takes time, and it is worth every step along the way.

Scientific results continue to show that when you help people to love every aspect of themselves, there is a decrease in suffering, mental anxiety, shame, inferiority, and submissive behavior, as well as, an increase in joy, health, and happiness.

"Find the love you seek by first finding the love within yourself.
Learn to rest in that place within you as that is your true home."
—**Sri Sri Ravi Shankar**

4. **Nurture Yourself**

To nurture yourself, you must partake in self-care, self-compassion, and self-forgiveness.

a. *Self-care*

Taking care of yourself acknowledges the need to maintain a healthy body, mind, and spirit that supports your Soul's life here on Earth. There are many ways to care for yourself. Find activities that promote health, emotional happiness, and inner peace.

A fabulous question to ask yourself daily is:

If I could do one thing today that brings me joy and happiness, what would that be?

Try and honor that answer and facilitate ways to make it come true. Why shouldn't you be filled with joy and happiness each and every day?

b. *Self-compassion*

Offering compassion, kindness, and gentleness allows you to feel love within. Many of us find it much easier to offer compassion and love to others than we do to ourselves. Why do we feel the need to always be strong, emotionally protected, and guard against judgment? Creating a space within that allows you to feel loved, compassionate, and vulnerable quiets the crazy demands that we place upon ourselves.

When we can live from an inner space of harmony, peace, and love, the actions, words, and thoughts we give to the world will be filled with compassion, kindness, and gentleness. You'll find that you're not giving love outwardly in hopes of receiving love in return (to fill your inner void); instead, you'll be sharing love with others because that is who you are within. We can only give off to the world that which is actively present within us.

c. *Self-forgiveness*

Understanding that we were created with imperfections and that your Source/God loves you unconditionally should provide solace and enable you to provide forgiveness towards yourself and others. I have asked thousands of people what is the hardest thing to forgive, and the results overwhelmingly point to self-forgiveness. We can be so hard on ourselves, judging our actions unmercifully. We typically live in a state of continuous judgment and ridicule and rarely reflect on the goodness in our lives, others, and ourselves.

One of the greatest gifts you can give yourself is the **gift of imperfection**. Accepting this as a truth, you immediately understand that perfection is *not* attainable, nor is it a virtue that ever needs to be attained. None of us are perfect, and you must be willing to forgive yourself.

> *Loving that you have made (and will make continue to make) mistakes allows true healing to occur from the inside out.*

When you can live and experience the gift of imperfection, you can see that others are imperfect too and that they also need forgiveness and understanding. The inner pains that we each hold against others and our own wrongdoings lock us energetically to them, which negatively impacts our health and inner peace. It's so easy to cast or shift the blame onto another, but the truth of the matter is that you both contributed to the event and therefore both need to be forgiven. It's really that simple, although we make forgiveness something that seems so monumental. Now is the time to begin self-forgiveness and let go of those energetic imprints that prevent us from loving.

Some of you may be familiar with the Ho'oponopono Prayer for Forgiveness, an ancient Hawaiian Kahuna practice of reconciliation and forgiveness. Morrnah Nalamaku Simeona taught this self-transformational forgiveness and healing in Hawaii around 1980. Thousands of people have reported miraculous results and recovery just by reciting these four simple but powerful statements. I encourage you to say the Ho'oponopono Prayer of Forgiveness daily in your life if there are areas/people that need healing and forgiveness.

Ho'oponopono Prayer for Forgiveness
"I'm Sorry.
Please forgive me.
Thank You.
I love you."

Here is another beautiful little prayer I created to nurture your loving Soul. I recommend that you recite this prayer, or another that is special to you, to create the inner space for your Power Within to grow and thrive.

A Prayer to Nurture Your Loving Soul
Dear One (God/Source), please care for my physical and spiritual body to enable my Soul's work to be present in my life and touch others in the world. I ask for your support, compassion, and kindness that allow me to feel your unconditional love and acceptance. Remove all harmful and negative thoughts and feelings that do not serve my greatest good and help me to live from a space of inner harmony and love. Please help me forgive those who have wronged me or I have wronged, and be ever-present to

help me express my true divine essence. Please and Thank you. Amen.

In the last chapter of Part II, "Release Fears and Limitations," I will address forgiveness more with respect to our fears and limitations. It is my hope you realize that your mere existence is a gift not only to yourself but to the world. Love needs to begin within our hearts, because it already resides within our Souls. As you continue along in this book, let your inner love become more transparent and an integral part of your daily existence, both internally and externally.

"Yesterday is history; tomorrow is a mystery.
Today is a gift; that is why it's called the present."
—Alice Morse Earle

"Life at its best is a series of challenges. A big enough challenge will bring out strengths and abilities you never knew you had. Take on challenges and you will bring yourself to life."
—**Ralph Marston, Jr.**

OVERCOME THE "DIS- CYCLE OF SELF"

"Dis-satisfaction," "dis-ease," and "dis (dys)-function"

Discover how you can stop the "Dis- Cycle of Self"

Most people will confess that they have no idea what to do to change their lives, or even what needs to be changed. They don't know how to intercept and change those internal emotional and mental negative feelings of conflict and heal the internal pain that is always there, even subliminally. The harder you try, the angrier you become, and the more invisible and isolated you feel. It turns into a vicious cycle of "**dis**-satisfaction," "**dis**-ease," and "**dis (dys)**-function." That is not to say that you didn't have every right to believe and feel the way you did or even to create the behavior mechanisms and walls of protections that you built to protect yourself.

Any word that begins with "dis," also contributes and becomes part of the **"Dis- Cycle of Self"**: discouragement, disappointment, disillusionment, disbelief, disastrous, discern (-ment), discipline (-un), discomfort, discredit, discount, discriminate, disgrace, disguise, dishonest, disinterest, dismal, disorder, dismiss, disrespect, disqualified, dissonance, distance, distress, disturbance, distrust ...

Any of these words could represent where your inability within exists—the inability that becomes part of your "Dis- Cycle of Self." Is there any doubt why one often remains stuck, afraid to follow through, or start anew? If we allow ourselves to live in this space of internal discourse, our inner biology, emotions, and happiness are all negatively affected.

Your defense mechanisms and protective walls have protected you for so long that your brain doesn't want you to try and move forward into the unknown. But now is the time to understand that you cannot allow the past to dictate and control your present life any longer. You can use lessons from the past and present and grow from them.

Let's begin to look at the "Dis- Cycle of Self" and how it impacts each of us. Don't be intimidated by the challenge of wanting something different and allow your inner self to come alive.

So how does one overcome **dissatisfaction**? We live in a world in which we aspire to and desire more things in our lives which give us a false sense of value. Of course, this is the fuel that we need to feed our ego, satisfying the craving to fill the void within. When we're able to eliminate or release the aspect that has us believing that we are "less," we no longer have the need to satisfy that craving. Dissatisfaction means, quite simply, not being satisfied. If you are dissatisfied or experience "lack," then the energy associated with your belief is transmitted into you, both individually and throughout your life.

When you understand and accept that your self-limiting beliefs and memories leave you with a "sense of lacking something," you could deduce that you're dissatisfied with some aspect of the past. Thoughts like you weren't loved enough, smart enough, pretty enough, supported, liked, seen, safe, inferior, etc. all contribute to feeling dissatisfied. If you allow these feelings and emotional wounds to continue to grow and impact your life, dissatisfaction can turn into disease and dysfunction.

Here is a brief example: Joe was negatively impacted because his older brother excelled at sports and was enthusiastically cheered and loved by his family and town. He could do no wrong. Joe's personal dissatisfaction with his *perceived* inability to compete left him feeling incapable, unloved, and a failure because he "*feared*" competition.

His personal dissatisfaction created a feeling of "un-ease" ("**dis-ease**") within him. Both of these words ("un-ease" and "dis-ease") refer to a state of unrest within oneself. When you experience "un-ease," or "dis- ease," for a prolonged time, I believe that it may contribute to the creation of a disease. If you do not address the "dis-ease"—the original root of the problem—how can you really affect the disease that results?

Not all physical symptoms have physical origins.

Continuing on with the example, Joe started to experience headaches and stomach pains, and he outwardly expressed anger, especially towards his brother, which then resulted in guilt. The physical and mental symptoms continued to grow in severity and started to impact his life in other ways, too. He avoided all physical activities and any type of competition, had trouble with relationships, and no longer communicated with his brother.

Can you see how "**dis (dys)-function**" impacted his life? The original dissatisfaction created "dis-ease" within him, which resulted in dysfunction. The longer or greater the dissatisfaction that we experience, the greater the dysfunction occurs in our lives.

The **"Dis- Cycle of Self"** can be ever-present in our lives unless we choose to change and disrupt this perpetual cycle.

I have seen many patients whose physical symptoms had an emotional or psychological component. Unfortunately, the underlying root cause was never addressed, and therefore the outward symptom(s) were never truly eliminated.

Western medicine tends to treat our symptoms but often doesn't determine the underlying catalyst.

With the personal reflection that you accomplished in Part I and the identified areas of focus that you're resolving and healing in Part II, you are on your way to disrupting your "Dis- Cycle of Self," which doesn't support your health and happiness.

Which "dis" words are part of your Dis-Cycle of Self?

_____,_____,_____

What are you dis-satisfied with or about?

_____

Where is the dis-ease (disease) that you experience?

_____

How does dis (dys)-function impact your life?

_____

Honesty and vulnerability are key ingredients.

I do want to point out that doesn't mean you can't experience disappointment, sadness, loneliness, grief, etc., but what is important is what you do when you have those emotions. We have all seen a sad person (for whatever reason) and can literally see their energy as negatively being affected.

It is impossible to be sad and happy at the same time. What needs to occur is separation of the actual event from you personally. We tend to internalize the event or disappointment and make it *personal*. This is how we become wounded. We connect the event and find a relationship or reason as to what we or others could or should have done differently.

Let me give you an example. You're unhappy that you burned your dinner. You're disappointed with yourself and your performance. Immediately, the self-criticism begins—you're not being good enough, smart enough, and capable. Sound familiar? Let's **stop** right there.

The dinner might have burned because you were managing too many things or an emergency came up. Remember: *you* are not perfect! It is okay that the dinner burned; that is not a personal discredit of you. Remembering to forgive and be compassionate with yourself is critical to interrupting the "Dis- Cycle of Self."

Let's look at the actual situation. What is the potential lesson you could take away from this experience? Instead of looking at what you didn't do well, look at what you were doing. "I was bathing two children, putting the wash into the dryer, letting the dog out, taking two phone calls, and, oh yeah, I had to go to the bathroom.

I accomplished it all in forty-five minutes, but dinner was supposed to be done in thirty minutes." Maybe the synchronicity of events is trying to demonstrate that you are taking on too much and that you need to slow down and let some things go. I think we all can see that the tasks **you** placed on yourself may have been excessive. Self-reflection might help you see why you are overworking and feeling stressed and how this experience is leaving you feeling, both internally and outwardly (physically). Listening to your inner self—your intuition—can provide much insight into the situation.

I created a super-simple phrase that I use to help individuals assess negative thoughts, emotions, or actions:

STOP, LOOK, and LISTEN!

Do you recall Smokey the Bear's life-saving advice to "Stop, Drop, and Roll" when you're on fire? I created a three-word **First Aid Rescue Phrase**—"**Stop, Look, and Listen**"—for any time you're becoming enraged, feeling conflicted, or "on fire" within. Use this simple but conscious tool throughout your day when you're starting to take on negative emotions or thoughts—from the past or present, from yourself or others.

What you're doing is putting out your internal fire of anger, resentment, and frustration by no longer adding logs (negative thoughts and beliefs), thus eliminating the fuel (emotional energetic preprogrammed response) and smothering the old embers that lie waiting to burst once again into flames.

STOP PHASE

Using the "Stop, Look, and Listen" technique, whenever you have a negative thought, emotion, or action you literally **STOP** yourself. You might literally even say, "Stop!" out loud. I know that I do. This simple but powerful word STOPS the negativity and allows you to assess what to do next.

LOOK PHASE

During the Look phase, you actually are looking and seeing the truth of the situation. You're trying to eliminate the personal victimization and emotional response that is trying to be tied to the event.

If you go back to my example of the burned dinner, you'll see that in fact I implemented this **First Aid Rescue Phrase** to help you *not* personalize the situation and make yourself out to be the victim. As a mother, I'm sympathetic to this plausible scenario, and here are some questions we might want to consider during the **Look** phase:

- Why did everything have to occur within this time frame?
- Was that even a reasonable request?
- Why did I feel that I had to do it **all** myself?
- Could I have asked for help (assistance)?
- What quality of time did I really spend with my children, and how did they feel?
- Did I find any joy or pleasure in the tasks that I performed?

These are just some aspects that one may need to contemplate. Remember: your actions and how you're impacted are crucial components to consider but you're not the only one being affected.

For example, your children's' perceptions might have been any of the following: they felt rushed during bath time ("Mom has no time for me"), you may have raised your voice ("I did something wrong"), or they were told to go watch TV or read a book afterwards while you did the next task ("Mom doesn't love me"). Can you see how, when we live and act out of stress, frustration, and anxiety, we create more within the environment? Is that the type of environment that you and your family are living in?

The way we participate in our activities becomes a by-product of our results. We could say you were "burning the candle at both ends," and guess what happened? Your dinner got burned, too! The magic occurs when you see the wisdom from the experience so you can make the necessary changes and adjustments.

LISTEN PHASE

Let's look at the final step: Listen. It's during this phase that you listen to what your inner wisdom is saying, not necessarily what your brain (mind) is screaming at you. Your inner voice knows the truth in this moment, stopping the brain from relying on those repetitive neural preprogrammed responses is critical.

What could be some of the positive takeaway(s) during the **Listen** phase?

- The demands **I ask** of myself were unfair, unnecessary, and self-imposed.
- I need to feel relaxed and enjoy time with my children.
- I need to create a schedule that is reasonable and attainable.
- Am I trying to do it all, or could I have asked for help?
- I need to let my partner/spouse know that we need to work together.
- I need to be grateful for this awareness and understanding.
- I'm repeating the same pattern my mom did, which I hated as a child.
- I need to have a healthy attitude and enjoy the tasks I am capable of completing.
- Enjoying the moment is what it is **all** about.
- I am so capable and loved, I don't have to be perfect!

Using this First Aid Rescue Phrase ("**Stop, Look, and Listen**") allows you to create a positive change in self-perception, self-judgment, and self-awareness. What is great about this phrase is that you can use it anywhere to create an immediate shift in your thoughts and energy, and no one will ever know, except by the change in your unexpected behavior. The more you use this tool, the quicker you'll see a shift in the "Dis- Cycle of Self," recognize the self-criticism patterning, and understand the lessons of opportunity.

Who would have guessed that a burned dinner could have provided such nourishment?

I hope you found this exercise fun. I love helping my students and clients reveal messages in their synchronicities and life experiences. Remember: there are no coincidences. Everything happens for a reason. The more stuck we are in our ways, resistant to the lessons we need to learn, the more often the Universe will provide additional scenarios for us to grow. Enjoying life is a gift we all want to experience; let's be present in the moment so we can fulfill this desire.

"Realize deeply that the present moment is all you ever have. Make the Now the primary focus of your life."
—**Eckhart Tolle**

"What we achieve inwardly will change outer reality."
—Plutarch

WILLINGNESS TO TEAR DOWN YOUR WALLS OF PROTECTION
Lower your defenses

Empower yourself— find freedom and inner peace

E ach of us has created protective walls and developed defensive mechanisms in an attempt to defend and shield ourselves from impending danger or harm. Think about the beliefs and behaviors you took on when you were a child and wounded in some way. You may have done that consciously or unconsciously and continued to strengthen and solidified them as you matured. They became your shield and armor. You actually have become a master at creating a defensive structure to ward off all perceived danger, whether it is currently present or something that may occur in the future. In our attempt to protect ourselves from further harm, we actually reinforce and strengthen the reasons for why we need to defend our position. When do we ever say to ourselves, "It's safe? I can relax and express myself openly and honestly"? Like, never!

I have found that the protective walls we construct hold us back from the opportunity to grow, learn, and experience life more fully. Often these boundaries and defensive behaviors isolate and limit us in many ways. In fact, our own defensive mechanisms are the cause of so much of our sadness and misery.

Let me give you an example: Margot, a survivor of sexual, mental, and emotional abuse who never experienced a parent's loving embrace or any form of an expression of love, is incapable of asking for help from her son, grandchildren, or others. Instead, she isolates herself and experiences great sadness and loneliness, as well as many medical illnesses. When I asked her to draw an image of a place where she felt safe, she illustrated a circle (island) with a wide, expansive waterway that eventually met the mainland, but only on one side. This imagery represented exactly the life that she had created: she had become deserted and even destitute on her island of protection (and in life), where she only allowed people to cross the great water divide when she said so (and even then, only out of desperation). When I asked her what she wanted most in life, she said, "companionship, interaction, to belong and feel happy." Can you see how her walls of protection became, in fact, her walls of isolation?

I have found over and over again that our Soul lessons—the areas where we need to grow and expand—can only be learned when we lower our walls of protection, change our defensive-behavior mechanisms, and step into opportunities to transform our self-limiting beliefs into the awareness of our magnificent selves.

Now, you may be thinking "I don't want to risk getting hurt" or "I am comfortable in my life, even though I am unhappy." You may be afraid to step out of your space or your world for fear of rejection, hurt, and pain, or you may even be afraid of acceptance, love, and kindness. You might be asking, "What do you mean, afraid of acceptance, love and kindness?" Yes, in fact, I have found that many people are uncomfortable with receiving love. They feel it is untrustworthy, or that they don't deserve it, or that something is required in exchange. Can you see how this **"Dis- Cycle of Self"** can permeate all aspects of your life?

You need to see and be willing to accept that you are a contributing factor in your sadness; however, you also hold the keys to unlock the walls that have bound you. You need to be willing to step into the unknown, where your greatest reward can be received.

To conclude Margot's story, she was able to understand that she created her isolation—no one else—and when she started to allow neighbors and friends to actively come into her life, she was met with warmth, acts of kindness, and genuine interest. Margot continues to have to consciously be aware of not retreating into the safety of her island and learn to be comfortable when joy fills her heart. For Margot, living with a heart filled with love *inside*, as well as love offered by others, was the Soul lesson she needed to learn and grow from.

Fight-or-flight Response

Our survival mode, or "fight-or-flight" response, is organically built into our physiology. It's designed to do anything to ensure our existence, and it becomes activated when we experience a great perceived threat. This internal survival mechanism provides automatic, unconscious responses that help us during critical life-threatening experiences. I'm sure you've heard stories that illustrate the power of this built-in safety feature: an individual single-handedly flipped over a car to free a trapped passenger, or someone survived elements (temperature, time, disasters, and starvation) that were almost impossible to comprehend. Even though there was no obvious scientific explanation for their actions or the results, we cannot dismiss the actual outcomes. You might call them miracles, and maybe they are, but our body and spirit are miraculous creations too. They respond when our existence is threatened.

This survival system is unable to value and judge previous actions to see if the behaviors and emotions it produces are justified in all similar situations, so sometimes, unfortunately, you can remain stuck in an "overdrive" response mode, where any stimuli (even the nonthreatening kind) creates the same fight-or-flight, unconscious, programmed response. This fight-or-flight response is meant to be a short-fused reaction to the present threat and is not intended to be left engaged for long periods of time. Many who suffer from post-traumatic injuries will experience recurrences of events even when the threat is not present, as well as physical effects such as fibromyalgia (heightened nerve sensitivity) and autoimmune diseases because their systems are on overload, still responding to a potential threat that's perceived internally. Our bodies are simply unable to remain in this heightened state of fear and impending danger without experiencing serious repercussions.

Later, in the energy section of Part III, I will show you how to sedate your triple-warmer meridian, fight-or-flight response, releasing previously held emotional energetic charges and allowing this system to relax and be quieted. This usually is able to reduce or eliminate the physical symptoms.

To enable you to grow and create the inner and outer worlds that you desire, let's look at how we can lower your defenses and deconstruct the protective walls you've erected. You have choices: to facilitate newly formed positive emotions, thoughts, and behaviors, and to silence recurring negativism in all its forms. Remember, these are personal choices, and you are reading this book to create long-lasting changes that will bring you fabulous results.

Let me share with you a powerful, transformative, three-step process called **I *Choose* to, Because I *Can*.** The name implies that you are demonstrating your willingness to take responsibility and make the changes necessary to create something different while embracing your inner self. This process will enable you to create your own conscious mental shift, producing positive changes in your emotions, thoughts, behavior, expectations, and even how the world interacts with you. With this technique, you are *consciously* taking steps to communicate with yourself, change old patterns, and take purposeful action towards your success. You will be deconstructing the walls that actually held you captive and permit yourself to awaken to your Soul lessons, learn, and grow. This is an exciting time, and using this powerful technique will help you create and unleash your potential for happiness, joy, and freedom. For a printed copy of this exercise, go to www.PowerfulBeyondMeasureBook. com/forms.

I *Choose* to, Because I *Can*

1. **Mental Command** is the first step in stopping the repetitive chatter that fills your thoughts and prevents you from feeling alive, authentic, and even hopeful. This is where you consciously become aware of any negative thoughts, self-limiting beliefs, emotions, and behaviors.

    State this mental command to yourself: **I *choose* _____, because I *can*.**

    The blank is filled in with the opposite of the negative item; in many cases, this is also connected to your Soul lesson(s). By declaring what you *can* do, you consciously accept and open yourself up for growth, removing as many bricks from your protective wall as you are comfortable with.

    You are deleting the untruths and your self-imposed limitations.

    We have all said "no" to someone in our lives. Now is the time to say "no" to yourself: "No, I am not listening to that old belief"; "No, I am no longer that child who was hurt"; or "No, I choose not to still have those feelings, thoughts, beliefs or limitations that originated ____ years ago."

    You are consciously making a mental command to yourself!

    Here are a few *positive* declaratory mental commands you might say to yourself:
    -   **I *choose* to have a voice, because I *can*.**
    -   **I *choose* independence, because I *can*.**
    -   **I *choose* to be strong, confident, and courageous, because I *can*.**
    -   **I *choose* love over hatred, because I *can*.**

    Each of these statements is probably associated with a self-limiting belief you took on and are most likely connected to your Soul lesson(s). Connect the dots and find the link. Here are some plausible understandings for the four statements above:

- I *choose* **to have a voice, because I can**—the *realization* you have a voice and that your words are important, which may in fact become your gift to the world.

  Soul lesson: see the wisdom in your words, which originate from your Soul.

- I *choose* **independence, because I *can***—the *realization* that you are capable of doing things on your own because you are resourceful, you need to expand, and you no longer need to be dependent on others.

  Soul lesson: see that you have everything (strength) you need within yourself.

- I *choose* **to be strong, confident, and courageous, because I *can***—the *realization* that your strength comes from within.

  Soul lesson: connection between self and God (faith).

- I *choose* **love over hatred, because I *can***—the *realization* that love heals everything.

  Soul lesson: forgiveness is a form of unconditional love.

Now it's your turn. Pick one negative aspect that you *choose* to transform. It doesn't have to be huge—in fact, it's often best to start with something small. What one little thing comes to your mind right now?

Create a *Mental Command Statement* to correct it:

I *choose* _____,
because I *can*!

The *realization* is _____

The *Soul lesson* is _____

I hope you feel empowered just by seeing your declaration statement!

2. **Mental Command Acceptance** is the second step in this powerful transformation process. You have identified that you no longer want to be influenced by the negative element, and you've declared that in your statement. Congratulations! You are listening to your inner power, inner wisdom, and inner tuition (intuition = inner tuition = inner teaching).

Now comes the part that I can almost guarantee will occur: doubts, fears, and insecurities start to emerge within just moments of creating that statement. The old patterning starts to reemerge in hopes that you will retreat back into the old dissatisfied self and be less than who you really are. *Accept* those *subconscious* thoughts and say, "Not this time!" using your *conscious* (present) mind to create a change and become the victor. Remember that this is *your* lesson; if you don't embrace the opportunity to learn and grow, trust me, more opportunities will continue to appear. So let's take on your lesson right now. Regardless of the final outcome, you're creating new neural pathways to possibilities, outcomes, and results that are different from your past beliefs.

Create your ***Mental Command Acceptance Statement:***

I *accept* that I have this thought (doubt), but I can change and be/do _____.

It is important not to actually include the negative thought, doubt, or fear in your statement but just acknowledge that you sense it and then be very clear what you are changing and doing.

Using the four examples of statements from the previous section, you can fill in the blank with these words: *verbal, independent, strong,* and *love.* This step may seem simple, but making these statements is powerful because you are creating the foundation to the final step: action and success.

It's your turn. What doubt, fear, self-limiting thought, or emotion came to your mind?

Say to yourself, "I accept that I have this thought/feeling, but I can change and be/do _____.

Awesome job!

3. **Mental Command Action and Success** is the final step in creating action steps that will enable you to grow and succeed. The *final outcome* is not what is important. There is no finish line that you must cross to be the champion. You are in the preparation and "training phase" that is helping you learn your lesson(s). Applaud yourself for your attempts,

willingness, and growth. You have spent years reinforcing and living your negative self-limiting beliefs, and it is going to take time to reverse those thoughts, behaviors, and repressed emotions. Once you consistently use this technique, you will begin to see a shift; you'll catch yourself—your perceptions, behaviors, and thoughts. To create a change, you must first know that there is a need and then be willing to follow through. You've identified the behavior and you're willing, so what steps are you going to take?

Mental Command Action and Success is when you create actionable steps that support your mental command statement. What you are, in fact, doing is creating a doorway in the wall of protection that you've erected. You don't have to totally remove or disassemble the wall (just yet), but you have to be willing to walk through that door, go outside, and free yourself from those constraints.

Let's take the first example above and come up with actionable steps to success:

I choose to have a voice, because I can.

Identify *where, when,* and *with whom* you want to have a voice. Think about the ideal times to practice this step—at home or work, with parents, your spouse, friends, and coworkers.

Let's try a fictitious scenario for the purpose of demonstration:

Actionable Steps to Your Success:
- **I can speak openly at dinner with my family and share some stories about my day.**
- **I can encourage others to share their stories and actively interact in that conversation.**
- **I can approach my boss and offer an idea I've been thinking about for more than two weeks.**
- **I can speak up and tell my friend how her actions hurt me.**

Creating actionable steps already creates success, regardless of the results. Let me explain: you feel the need to speak—maybe because you don't feel heard, or you don't think you have value to add, or you were told not to talk. Regardless of the reason, you feel the need—the inner necessity—to speak. Trust that inner wisdom telling you that here is a growth opportunity or lesson to learn. Act on it.

Let's imagine a few ways the actionable steps in our scenario might play out. First, you shared a story about your day at dinnertime. You already succeeded because *you accomplished your goal*. No matter what someone else says or doesn't say, it doesn't change the fact that you went through the doorway in your wall of silence and verbally shared something that was important to you. That's a *win*!

Maybe your family didn't specifically react to your story, but it became the impetus for others to start to share their experiences. Lo and behold, *your* action created a spontaneous, increased communication within your family (the second actionable step). How awesome is that? Being brave and willing to listen to your higher wisdom has benefits that will be revealed, not only for yourself, but for others as well.

In the third actionable step, you approached your boss to share your idea, but maybe he was unable to take the time to listen. Initially, you felt rejected and hurt, and you thought, "He doesn't care what I have to say!" But you *stopped* yourself and changed that into a **mental command statement**: "I choose to share my idea, because I can." Then your new **acceptance statement** was, "I accept that he didn't have the time to hear my idea *at this moment*." You stopped yourself from making his inability to listen into your inability to speak. Awesome job!

Your boss calls you into his office a couple of days later and asks to hear your idea. Sounds like a win to me! It doesn't matter if he likes your idea or not. A comment like "Awesome idea!" would satisfy your ego, but that isn't what's important here. What came from this step is that you valued yourself enough to verbally express yourself—therein lies the success!

Sometimes we need to be patient to receive our rewards. Many also refer to this as "**Divine Timing**."

If your boss had listened to your idea when you *first* attempted to bring it to him, he might not have been as open to it and rejected it outright. By waiting a couple of days, when he was more relaxed and interested, he was better able to receive your *verbally* expressed idea. Can you see how the Universe wants to support and assist us in our journey?

This powerful **I *Choose* to, Because I *Can*** technique can even be used within the individual steps. Notice how, after approaching your boss, self-doubt crept in. In the narrative, you immediately *stopped* the negative mental chatter and created new ***mental command statements*** that prevented other self-defeating thoughts from being triggered again.

The fourth example allows you to share your emotions and express them verbally. Your friend may be very articulate—at times outspoken—and even make you feel intimidated. Can you see how the Universe may have placed this friend in your life so you can stand up against this force and use this lesson for potential growth?

You say to your friend, "I really wish you had asked me before committing that we would attend." Your friend says, "I didn't know you cared because you've always allowed me to speak up and make the decisions for us." If you didn't voice your opinion, nothing would change. No one can read your mind, and it is really unfair for you to ask them to. Your friend then says, "Sure, next time I'll ask you for your input."

Now it's your turn to create some actionable steps towards your success.

Take the ***Mental Command*** and ***Mental Command Acceptance Statements*** that you wrote above and generate steps towards achieving your goals. Start with easier steps that allow you to be successful without experiencing great stress or anxiety. In time, this technique will become second nature, and you'll be able to handle more challenging aspects as you feel you're ready. This is actually quite fun.

1.

2.

3.

4.

If you would like to download and print this powerful **I Choose to, Because I *Can*** tool as a printed form, go to <u>www. PowerfulBeyondMeasureBook.com/forms</u>.

Now that you've created a plan with actionable steps, I encourage you to put on the appropriate shoes (boots, high heels, or even go barefoot) for your specific task and **step** into your growth and success. Remember: you don't have to hold a trophy to actually be a winner! Often the journey can be more rewarding than reaching the finish line.

I hope you're feeling empowered and understand that *you* hold the keys that will unlock the door in the wall of protection you created. Understanding and enabling yourself to make these *conscious* thought modifications—ones that affect your belief patterns, emotions, thoughts, and actions—will totally transform your ability to express yourself, be authentic, and remain true to who you really are.

How awesome is that? The Power Within is that *you're* creating the change by understanding how your Soul lessons and growth potential exist in synergy with each other in your life. This experience can be so profound that you may find yourself in tears when you realize how you've limited yourself in so many ways.

Remember: that behavior was in the past. You're now living in the present, and I know you can continue to create the change that you want so badly. There will come a time when your wall of protection will cease to exist because you'll no longer have the need to shield yourself.

> *"Only you can take inner freedom away from yourself,*
> *or give it to yourself.*
> *Nobody else can."*
> **—Michael A. Singer**

Mind, body, spirit, and emotions are inseparable.

EMOTIONAL HEALTH AND FITNESS
Empowering Your Emotions

Learn how to get rid of your emotional baggage.

Emotions are a vital part of being human. We cannot consider being healthy and satisfied without having an emotionally honest relationship with ourselves. Often our emotions are repressed, ignored, and judged—both by ourselves and others. You might have felt you should have a "stiff upper lip," not allowing others to really know how you feel because they might feel uncomfortable or not be able to handle it. You may be more concerned with how others will judge you if you aren't acting consistently with the group's normal, accepted emotional response.

We are taught to silence our deepest feelings, especially if they express a sad, troubling, or painful emotion. Society, families, and most people in general are uncomfortable dealing with an emotional response that they believe they cannot "fix," so instead we negate, suppress, or simply ignore it and act like it doesn't matter or bother us. We're expected—by ourselves and others—to just put on a smile and move on, but trapped emotional pain within our bodies will resurface in some way. It could be through physical symptoms, negative thoughts and behaviors, pathology, or exaggerated emotions that spiral out of control, but it is only a matter of time before those repressed emotions ultimately resurface once again.

We have all heard the expression "mind-body-spirit," but I strongly believe there is a fourth component, **emotion**, that needs to be added. When one or more of these four pillars becomes cluttered, negative, or toxic, chemical, hormonal, and physiological changes start to occur that can lead to illness and disease. Emotions are the driving force that fuels all human experiences and helps us navigate our life's journey. Each emotion provides us with valuable information and creates biochemical and physiological responses within our bodies.

Our emotions become the key to unlocking everything about ourselves— our health, happiness, and the way we behave. As you explore your emotional responses, you need to ensure that your emotions are showing up appropriately for the *current* situation—with the correct intensity, at the right time, and specific to the present event. So often our emotional landscape from the past has been ingrained with a specific cause-and-effect mechanism that remains wired and translated into current situations. When you integrate and positively impact all four of these pillars (mind, body, spirit, and emotions), you achieve long-lasting energetic health and happiness. Learning to experience your emotions is the key to healing your broken heart and wounded Soul.

Scientists and medical professionals confirm that **stress** is the number-one cause of most illnesses and injuries, and I concur that our emotional stress seriously contributes to, and even causes, our diseases. Dr. Kim D'Eramo, practicing emergency room physician and author of *The Mind Body Tool Kit*, states, "All of our emotions are chemical responses." D'Eramo speaks of how certain emotions (like stress, anxiety, and anger) can cause diabetes, heart disease, obesity, cancer, adrenal fatigue, fibromyalgia, autoimmune disease, and long-term illness. She even states that "Cancer comes from some *expression* of life."

For example, anger is a primal emotional response to a threat, danger, or even death. The anger emotion triggers the amygdala, which changes our biochemistry and blocks the conscious mind from interceding, and we continue to have to deal with it emotionally. We need to understand the *origin* of the anger: is the threat or impending danger real, perceived, or a "dis-" cycle from our past? With anger, we become triggered, activating our fight-or-flight response in order to protect ourselves. This emotion (anger) becomes the fuel of our inner rage and can limit how we respond in a healthy way. There are appropriate times when danger is imminent and survival is essential, but when anger is present, it clouds how we perceive the information and therefore our reaction to it.

As Gene Monterastelli, author of *Comprehensive Anger Management*, says: "Anger is the information that the system (our body) perceives as being attacked and the emotion that shows up to keep us safe." Both individually and in our medical world, we often try to quiet and mask our symptoms, and we rarely explore *where* and *how* they came to be or recognize that there is an emotional component that may be the origin of our current signals.

We often ignore our emotional health and fitness and really have no idea how to achieve it, but, in actuality, it can be most fulfilling and rewarding, and it's something we all need to take seriously. The time is now to release the trapped emotional weight that has impacted us on the energetic and cellular levels.

Our emotions will always be present in our lives, giving us vital information about how we feel. It is important to remember that the emotional response in the present has an emotional component from the past (whether it's an hour or a decade ago), which influences both our emotion *during* the event and the emotion that is tied to our *future* actions in response. Emotions can never be removed from any of our experiences, but our oldest and unresolved emotions will continue to grow until we ultimately hear and release their voices. Our repressed emotions, and their messages, cannot stay buried forever.

Ample scientific evidence supports how our emotions affect our biology and our health. Until recently, traditional Western medicine treated the body as if the mind and emotions couldn't contribute to (or be an underlying cause of) the symptoms or diagnosis. When we're able to affect the underlying cause—which usually has an emotional and mental component—the physical symptoms often decrease or disappear completely.

Fortunately, most recently there has been a shift within the medical world that integrates alternative and complementary medicines into a care plan that *does* combine the total person: body, mind, *emotions*, and spirit. Results indicate that our minds and emotions are contributing factors in the care, treatment, and outcomes that relate to the health of our bodies. Our minds and emotions respond to our physical bodies, and our bodies react to the understandings and perceptions from our minds and emotions. There is a back-and-forth interplay among the mind, emotions, and the physical body; therefore, all four pillars need to be in harmony in order to achieve optimal health and well-being.

I think you would agree that society, families, schools, culture, and many institutions disregard emotional health, except in the context of psychology. Seeking psychological medical intervention carries a stigma: you have an emotional or mental problem. There is no mechanism or program available today that teaches us how to achieve emotional health—to be open, transparent, and vulnerable with our feelings while discovering the messages that are associated with them.

Normally, emotional personal assessment is often avoided, discouraged, and frowned upon, because to "feel" means to acknowledge the sensation, and sometimes that is just too painful or difficult to do. Sometimes the emotional toll is just too hard to bear. It's easier to repress, deny, hide, and keep secret the depths of your true emotions. You think that if you don't acknowledge them—or if you sugarcoat or discredit them—they can't affect you.

I believe this is the worst lie you can tell yourself. You attempt to numb yourself in order to stop the pain, but what really happens is that those raw, unexpressed emotions are intensified. Although this emotional behavior of avoidance is a learned pattern from our earliest years, pretending they're not there is like burying your emotions alive; trust me, with or without your knowledge, if these emotional hurts remain unresolved, they will continue to affect your life and health.

Within the pages of this book, you have spent considerable time and effort exploring your mind: your thoughts, recurring memories, and self-limiting beliefs. In addition, we have talked about your spirit, your Soul, and reawakening to your true essence. Now comes the time to understand the role that your emotions play in your life and health.

If you automatically say or think, "I don't need this" or you feel uncomfortable with the concepts in this chapter, that's all the more reason to be open and rest in the knowledge that these are *your emotions* and *they cannot hurt you.* Allowing ourselves to *feel* is what makes us human, and it's essential to creating a life of happiness. Within each one of us there lies a whole range of emotions, from loving, kind, and compassionate acts to the most destructive, evil, and hateful behaviors.

Emotions are energies that impact our motion.

Why does Western civilization frown upon having a healthy range of emotions that enables individuals to openly express how they feel and allows others to respond in a compassionate and supportive way? We often experience these emotional energies symptomatically in our bodies. Have you ever had "butterflies in your stomach" prior to speaking or performing on a stage? How about tension in your neck or head, or even indigestion or loose bowels? Could your physical symptoms be trying to tell you something emotionally?

Because the body, mind, spirit, and emotions are tied together, I believe our spirit/Soul also tries to communicate through our mind and bodies as well. For example, many people talk about having a feeling in their gut or their heart—an intuition. How do you describe those feelings? I see them as emotional, energetic vibrations that resonate within us, and we struggle to understand their meaning. Balancing our rational, conscious thoughts with emotional intuition can be quite challenging and often results in a struggle between the two forces.

I will share many techniques that will help you to release, let go, heal, forgive, and move on. These will enable you to live more openly in the present. Many of us have heard the advice to "live in the *now*," but we often find this extremely difficult, impractical, and unsatisfying.

In this chapter, we will be discussing how to **create a healthy "Range of E-motions,"** the importance of **responding vs reacting,** and how to **identify and de-emotionalize connections** that originated from your *past* and which may still be impacting you *today.*

Emotional health and fitness is a critical component to mental, physical, and spiritual health, and it's the foundation to living a life filled with love and happiness.

Creating a Healthy "Range of E-motions"

I like to refer to our emotions as "E-motions" because emotions have an energetic (E) component that affects our motion (m) (or action). In order to understand how your E-Motions play a vital role in your life, you may want to ask yourself these questions:

- Do you engage in behaviors like cigarettes, alcohol, drugs, food, and sex to avoid your emotions?
- Are you a workaholic, or do you exhibit other similar obsessive-compulsive behaviors?
- Do your emotional patterns support self-sabotage, depression, and limitation?
- Do your emotions affect your income, relationships, career, success, and happiness?
- Which emotions dominate your life, and what is their impact?

_____

_____

The emotional pain we carry is the cause of our pain.

We have all taken a trip at one time or another, but have you ever considered that your life is really a journey as well? When you decide to travel, you try to prepare ahead of time: you create an itinerary, decide on things to see, and—oh, yes—don't forget about the baggage necessary to carry all your essentials. So what would you take if you were going to travel: clothing, toiletries, money, documentation, food, and your camera or smart phone to recover the details of the trip and your memories?

How often do we take more than that we actually need? Our suitcases are stuffed to capacity, and we seldom have room to bring anything back from our adventures.

Do you realize that, during our journey of life, our emotional baggage is bursting at the seams, too? Unless we make room, nothing new can be added. We have stuffed so many events into memories that we often feel weighed down by our past experiences and unable to really live fully in the present moment. Our emotional and mental clutter is actually the heaviest weight that we bear—one which actually becomes the anchor that keeps us stuck, sometimes crippling or paralyzing us to the point that we are unable to move forward. Our baggage full of life's memories, emotions, thoughts, beliefs, and behaviors can be a burden of great proportions.

Maybe this is how you have felt at times. Maybe you're feeling that way right now?

When you allow your emotional weight to dissolve; you enable your body to be lighter, freer and happier; this then becomes a catalyst for growth and physical, mental, and emotional well-being. Emotional weight is like physically carrying the weight of all those trapped emotions within your body. It keeps you stuck and confines your perception of self. Every event, memory (and even your own perception) carries an emotional weight. Understanding how to change the weight of your emotions—transforming them into a vehicle for freedom, energy, and excitement—will totally liberate your life.

By decluttering, experiencing, and releasing our emotional pain, and developing a healthy **Range of E-motions**, you become mobile to experience life from a different vantage point—a new perspective. These concepts are essential for your health. Understanding why you're feeling a certain way can add great value and understanding when you decide on the motion or action that you want to take.

I find that most of us tend to be *reactive*, *defensive*, and *judgmental* with respect to what comes our way, how we feel, and even how we behave. I know we often struggle to understand *where* and *when;* we all have become so critical and unhappy with so many aspects of our lives. When we look at our world, most of us would agree there is too much unrest—globally, nationally, locally, and, quite often, even within ourselves.

As I stated above, emotions and memories energetically impact our bodies, minds, and spirits. They can be a blessing or a curse. It's impossible not to be affected by our emotions. We know that there is a physiological, psychological, spiritual, and subsequent emotional impact that occurs in response to our feelings. The question I pose is this: Can we choose what we feel? I believe that on many levels, we do have a choice as to our emotions and the impact they can have. Remember how our thoughts, beliefs, and perceptions interact and affect our bodies? So, too, do our emotions.

No one can make you feel happy unless you are *willing* to be happy. Someone can bring you your favorite dinner or take you out for a wonderful event, but if you choose not to enjoy it and be filled with happiness, all the goodness one offers you is for naught. It truly is up to you: how you perceive the experience, the impact you allow it to have, and the outcome you receive. You have a conscious choice to be filled with the present experience or to allow your past to dominate and control the outcome once again.

Your E-motion Quotient

So what prevents us from feeling emotionally happy, both inside and out? Often, past emotions that haven't been dealt with continue to have a direct impact on our emotional response in the present. The emotional functions of feeling are to experience, express, and empower. We often get stuck on the expression element and are therefore unable to let go or release the emotional charge/energy.

Typically, we try and hold onto everything, both good and bad: possessions, emotions, thoughts, doubts, anger, resentment, relationships, memories, and even love. At first glance, this may seem quite logical, protective, and reasonable, but the truth of the matter is that your brain has to store all this data, and at some point you and/or your mind has to assign the information/memory/emotion a level of importance. I refer to this as the **E-motion quotient.**

Let me explain.

An **E-motion quotient** is when you *divide* the Emotions (**Em**) by the Event (**E**), and come up with a *quotient* (the result), which is the **motion**. The motion is the response to both the emotions and the event. The motion component is the reaction, action, or movement that one takes. It could be wanting to flee, fight, avoid, defend, laugh, dance, speak, take on a belief or behavior—the list is endless. During this emotional process, the quotient (the motion or outcome), has been equated with a level or degree of importance.

$$\frac{\mathbf{Em}\ (\text{Emotion})}{\mathbf{E}\ (\text{Event})} = \mathbf{m}\ (\text{motion: action/behavior/understanding})$$

The *stronger* or more intense your **emotions** (numerator) are compared to the actual event (denominator), the more significant the E-motion quotient or motion (action) will be.

In nonmathematical terms, that means the *stronger, more intense your emotions* are, the more *dramatic, even forceful, your motion or action* will be. The emotion becomes the fuel for your response (action).

Think about an individual who really triggers you and how easily it is for you to become inflamed, agitated, and explosively reactive. You almost approach any interaction with that individual with your guns loaded and ready to fire. I believe our subconscious mind has learned responses and defensive mechanisms that all work collaboratively to protect, defend, and prevent us from being hurt again.

When a same (or similar) event or emotion occurs, your body/mind responds with the same preprogrammed motion (action) response (E-motion quotient).

This preprogrammed expectation and response may in fact not be appropriate for this new event, but your system responds in a similar pattern as a protective mechanism derived from learned behavior. Regardless of the cause and effect within the situation, the emotions need to be released and healed so they won't continue to cause internal strife and disharmony in other areas of your life.

We're never taught how to deal with and assimilate our emotions. We haven't learned to openly express our feelings, and we often have to disguise our truth. Often we try to avoid painful emotions (whether experienced by ourselves or expressed by others) by altering, hiding, or camouflaging them rather than acknowledging, understanding, and accepting them in a healthy way.

Because our bodies are made to protect ourselves, anything or anyone that has caused us harm becomes flagged and permanently stored for quick access in order to try to keep the same pain from occurring again. Understandably, no one wants or deserves to be wounded, but we become **hyper-alert, emotionally charged, and stand on guard** in case the situation or a similar event recurs.

In addition, we create our walls of armor that *protect* and behavior mechanisms that *defend*; at the same time, though, we can become ticking time bombs, waiting to explode and let out the painful stored emotions and memories.

I remember that, as a teenager, if I was in a disagreement, I would verbally unleash many past events, emotions, and situations that I had been storing within that had nothing to do with the current event, but that didn't matter. It was like my emotional volcano erupted and the red-hot lava (my inner emotional pain) was released. Over time, I was able to draw correlations between the experiences and how my emotions, and behavior were in response to a template that had been subconsciously archived. I needed to be able to discern that the detailed elements of the event and emotions, although similar, were, in fact, different. I had to stop holding on to the emotions (pain), be able to express them in the current situation, and let them go in a healthier, more productive way.

I learned that I needed to address my emotions when the event occurred and not let the past bias my present experience. This allowed me to release the negative energy associated with the event and the emotion. I believe the difficulty we all experience in releasing our emotional pain is one reason why we see so many individuals overreacting, erupting in unreasonable ways, and even causing harm to themselves or others. I know we are all shocked when we hear about these tragedies and wonder what could have been done to prevent them. We can only guess how those individuals must have been so emotionally unhealthy (unhappy) within. It's truly heartbreaking for everyone involved.

Of course, our happy memories are in storage too, and we can gain access to them whenever we choose, but since the body knows there is no threat associated with them, they are just archived with a low level of importance. How many times has your mind brought up a fabulous positive memory that supports past successes when you are facing a challenge in life now? Like, never! Quite often, the opposite occurs: the memories of pain, failure, fear, and doubt are presented with the E-motion quotient (motion) fully and energetically charged to guard and protect you.

Here are some questions for you to consider as we move into establishing a healthy **Range of E-Motions**:

- Is this the **E-motion** that you want to bring with you throughout your lifetime?
- How long can you stay mad or angry? Hours, days, months, years? Are you ready to let go?
- How long can you stay in a completely happy state, and what impact does it have on you? Are you comfortable being happy?
- Which state of being is easier to maintain, has a longer shelf life, and is one you want to inhabit: pain and suffering, or health and happiness?

We have all heard the adage "she/he carried it to their death." Let's decide *not* to be the one who's afraid to experience, express, and be empowered by our emotions. Isn't it time to change how we handle our emotions so we can have a wide Range of e-motions that support, embody, and promote health?

Have you ever experienced an ***emotional meltdown***, when you were completely torn, drained, and emotionally out of control, and the simplest gesture could send you over the edge? Reaching this emotional precipice is the culmination of many unexpressed emotions over a significant time frame, and you've arrived at the saturation point where total internal emotional confusion exists.

During this emotional turmoil, you most likely experienced one of more of these feelings: unworthy, unloved, unheard, unappreciated, and undervalued. You have already identified your roots of your emotional pains from the first part of this book. Now is the time to address them so you can finally move on and gain the inner freedom that we all seek. The hardest thing you may ever have to do may actually be the most rewarding.

Let's explore how to lose your emotional weight so you can gain your personal freedom and power.

When you're internally in balance and peaceful, your external world is as well, and the repressed emotional triggers and demons no longer negatively impact you. Understanding, releasing, and healing the inner emotional pain is the only way you can live a life with a healthy Range of E-motions that allow you to be authentic, expressive, and free.

E-motional Fitness Program

Let's explore my powerful, results-oriented, six-step **E-motional Fitness Program**, which facilitates harmony, happiness, and health within.

1. **Emotional Compass and Recalibrating your Emotional Set Point**

    You have created a direction, flow, and general predisposition with regard to your emotions that allow you to openly express yourself to others. Ironically, they may not even be authentic or truthful, but they can form the emotional framework and template that you use as a compass. Many of us are afraid of our feelings because there is a sense of vulnerability and being out of control, unable to stop. We deny our feelings and present a variation of our true emotional expression.

    The first way to assess your true emotion is to put a word to the feeling and ask these simple questions:

    - **Where is this emotion coming from: past, present, or future?**
    - **What is causing me to *react* or *respond* emotionally this way?**
    - **Is this emotion protecting or limiting me in some way?**

    Considering these questions during both quiet and emotional, stressful times can provide great insight into your inner compass and help you find your "true north."

    Let me provide a brief example. You're sitting quietly on the couch, with your husband and son in the room. Not a word is spoken, and everyone is engaged with their own activities. Suddenly, a feeling comes over you—the feeling of being alone, unheard, and even ignored. You actually even begin to feel discomfort in your lower back.

    The emotions you begin to experience are isolation, sadness, and even deep hurt. You wonder where this is coming from. No one is saying anything, so how can you necessarily blame your emotions on the other two people in the room? Are your feelings justified, or are they representative of a previous experience that had similar elements?

You might ordinarily react by saying something to get their attention, like "Why are you guys so interested in the television and ignoring me?" Can you see how this statement is most likely emotionally charged by an earlier event, originating from an earlier age when you felt ignored, hurt, and unsupported? Because the emotional need from the original incident was never addressed, it resides in your physiology and is expressed in the present situation.

In this example, you can see how to assess your feelings, understand that your husband and son are doing nothing wrong, and recognize that you can take ownership and shift your emotional response to say, "It feels so good to be here with my family and that they want to be near to me." You could tell them how much you enjoy being there together, and you could even communicate this with a physical action by snuggling up to one or both of them. This is a great example of how to use the First Aid Rescue Phrase, "Stop, Look, and Listen." See how powerfully it works?

Changing your perception by acknowledging your true emotions—discerning where they originate and then shifting the emotional energetic charge to be more aligned in the present moment—begins to recalibrate your **emotional set point**. When you make this conscious emotional correction, you are shifting what normally would have triggered you and allowing yourself to begin to release the root problem (more will be done with this issue as we continue).

Making this necessary adjustment in your emotional barometer can positively change your atmosphere and the climate that you choose to reside in, both internally and externally. Throughout the process, you're authentically open to experiencing your feelings, but you took the time to evaluate your emotions/thoughts and assess how to appropriately respond, instead of react.

By the way, the lower back pain was a physical symptom that corresponded to the emotional stress you were experiencing. I will speak at greater length about this connection between our physical bodies and our mental/emotional responses in Part III, but I will tell you now that the lower back is an area that is often associated with feelings such as a lack of support, stress, worry, fear, abandonment by a parent, and being on your own. As we continue to explore the mind/body/spirit/emotion connection, you may start to see areas in your own body that connect with your internal emotional stress or disharmony. This is great news and more information to help you heal and resolve.

Recalibrating your Emotional Set Point (ESP)

When I refer to ESP, I'm not talking about extrasensory perception. Rather, I'm talking about your **Emotional Set Point** (ESP)—a point that has been determined by you in response to your emotional environment. Our emotions dominate and determine the motion/action that we take in response to them.

We can all recall events when our emotions were inflamed and we regretted the words we used or actions we took. So what "*sets us off*"? Certain events create an internal emotional energy within you that creates an emotional response to those stimuli. Being able to name the original emotion that you are experiencing, along with assessing its appropriateness, can help you shift your emotional response in either direction from a conscious, authentic, truthful framework.

Ask yourself:

- **Is my emotional response appropriate, and is the intensity justified, for *this* situation?**
- **Can I move my emotional response slightly and adjust my ESP (Emotional Set Point) to one that feels more authentic (responsive rather than reactive)?**

Think of it in terms of a see-saw: your Emotional Set Point is the point of the fulcrum that connects with the see-saw bar, which holds the range of your emotions. If negative, sad emotions are on one side of the bar and positive, joyful emotions are on the other side, you can clearly see that whichever side is expressed emotionally will have the greatest weight. Each end has the most profound emotional responses: negativity and hopelessness on one end, positivity and love on the other.

There is a wide spectrum of emotions you can feel. A brief list can give you an idea of the emotional continuum, from the most negative and toxic to the most positive and nurturing: hopelessness, anger/rage, fear, guilt, grief, judgement, dis-/des- words (despair, discouragement, disempowerment, disappointment, discouragement, depression), empty, alone/lonely, agitation/frustration, sad, neutrality, peaceful, acceptance, happy, knowing, forgiveness, laughter, joy, splendor/awe, valued, hopefulness, grace, faithful, and love.

Rage/Anger

If you're experiencing, let's say, a lot of rage and anger, and that is your Emotional Set Point, it will take an enormous weight (of positivity) on the other side to bring you more aligned and in balance. Making a conscious effort to move incrementally along the emotional continuum towards a more positive, loving feeling will cause the emotional weight to shift so that you're no longer trapped in that intense, negative feeling of anger and hatred.

If you are feeling loved, valued, and spiritual, then the weight would be on the other side, and your life will be filled with this energetic vibration. It would require a great amount of energy to shift you from this state of elation to one that is negative.

Why don't you try it right now? Pick a current situation that you are dealing with. List the negative emotions that you're experiencing and ask yourself: "Can I move my emotional response (even a small degree) towards the positive side?" How would that feel if you did?

<u>Your Emotional Set Point Exercise</u>

Current situation: _____

Present emotion(s): _____

Recalibrating your ESP to: _____

How does that feel? _____

Did you notice an energetic shift in your perception towards the event, your emotions, and your response to it? Taking personal responsibility—changing the way you choose to feel—creates a different outcome, both inside and outside.

You are not necessarily trying to **fix** the problem, just assess and access the way you **feel** about it and emotionally respond differently.

This practice is strengthened and supported by the Law of Attraction, which says that where we place our attention is what we create. Simply shifting how you *feel* about something changes the energy, the expectation, and, ultimately, what is experienced.

2. **Emotional Calisthenics and a Healthy Range of E-motions**

Learning to stretch, bend, and expand your emotions freely, without limitation, creates relaxation, self-acceptance, and inner peace. Becoming emotionally fit allows you to assess a healthy, appropriate Range of E-motions. If your typical emotional response is of a quick, impulsive nature that is usually accompanied by an outburst which loses fuel and power in a short period of time, then you most likely are **reacting** rather than **responding**.

Reacting occurs when there is no given thought process to how you interact: it is an automatic, subconscious process. In contrast, *responding* is a conscious, thinking response to how you voluntarily decide to act. When you learn not to be triggered by the emotional weight of someone else's actions or words or past unresolved events in your life, then you won't take on their limitations, restrictions, and energy, and you can move emotionally with greater ease, comfort, and freedom.

Emotional Wheel of Health

I like to symbolically use a "wheel-and-spoke" configuration to depict our repertoire of emotional responses. The hub of the wheel represents you. Each spoke represents an emotion, and the outer rim represents the path that you travel. Some spokes (emotions) may be rigid, while others may be quite fragile or even broken. If our emotional spokes are not balanced (where we can openly experience all emotions), our wheel (range) of emotions can be disfigured and provide for a bumpy ride along our journey of life.

If you're a bike rider, you know exactly what I'm talking about. The individual spokes are integral to the integrity of the wheel and the type of ride that it provides. The same is true of our Emotional Wheel of Health. There will most likely be triggers along our path—maybe a pebble, a puddle, a hole in the road, or even a detour that we must take; if we are not careful, our emotional wheel can become dysfunctional and misshapen, and instability, rigidity, and even a complete lack of motion can result.

Let's look at how we can use emotional calisthenics to optimize a healthy Range of E-motions:

- **Can I express my emotion without taking on the role of a victim, feeling threatened, or needing to defend myself?**
- **Can I genuinely be true to my inner feelings: can I accept them, be vulnerable to experience them, and respond in a _loving_, forgiving, and compassionate way?**

You can see how these questions help you to stretch your ability to experience your true feelings, provide stability, and give you flexibility to take positive action that supports you in a more loving way. Learning to be authentically true to your emotions creates a peace and harmony within.

3. **Perception and Emotional Ergonomics**

Did you know that your perception is emotionally biased? Your perception of a situation will change based on your emotional position at that moment. If you are in a state of sadness, then your emotional response and perception of the situation will usually generate a lower energetic response. If you start from a happier state of well-being, your emotional response and perception of the event would tend to be perceived more positive.

In many ways, our emotional perception dictates and directs whether we have an emotional **reaction** (subconscious and impulsive) or an emotional **response** (conscious and deliberate). **Self-sabotaging tactics** and **guessing** what others are feeling, saying, or doing can impact how you emotionally feel and respond. Learning to be emotionally grounded within and listening to your inner self prevents you from riding an emotional roller coaster—one that has convoluted twists, turns, and climatic drops that cause drama, exhaustion, and fear and allows others to regulate the outcome.

Understanding the role that perception plays, let's examine the stressor(s) to our emotions. Ergonomics is the study that evaluates stress on the body, optimizes the environment and the individual, and strives to prevent or reduce personal injury. When you have an unsafe, counterproductive, and inefficient lifestyle, this can cause frustration, loss, fear, limitations, rejection, and health issues.

I have found that emotional ergonomics is critical in establishing a healthy emotional life. Being able to identify the triggers, stressors, and toxicity of the environment and/or individual(s) in it (including yourself) allows you to effectively alter your behavior, biology, and emotional response.

Let me explain that in more general terms. When you identify a stressor that sets you off emotionally, that creates a negative impact, both internally and externally, that can harm you as well as others. As an ergonomist, it is your job to identify the triggers that create the emotional stress. What impacts you may not impact others. Understanding and taking what you have learned from your past will help you to clarify the stressors that impact you emotionally.

Here are some valuable questions to help with your perception and emotional ergonomics:

- **Is my perception of this situation accurate, or am I shielded from the truth?**
- **What stress is stimulating this emotional response, and is it justified?**

- **What can I do to remove or minimize the emotional trigger(s) (stress) and experience greater peace, happiness, and freedom?**

When you reduce the emotional stress that you experience, everything energetically shifts in your life.

What are some emotional triggers in your life?

4. **Emotional Wardrobe and Facelift**

How we dress and what we wear often shed much light on how we feel. Your wardrobe makes an emotional statement. If you wore a dress to a court hearing that didn't end well, you can bet that the negative energy and emotional response from that event is still tied to that garment, which will be a reminder if worn again.

Bold colors, pastels, loud prints, loose- or tight-fitting clothes, formal or relaxed attire—all are an expression of how you feel on the inside and outside. Some people feel ugly and not attractive at all, often starting at a very young age. Women especially struggle with this, but it's not gender specific; men also suffer as well. You cannot run or hide from how you feel within: your emotions, energy, and natural rhythms all contribute to who you present to the world.

You can follow the newest, most expensive trends, but if you don't resonate with those fashion statements within, they just won't work. How many of you recall trying on a variety of outfits before finally deciding on one, leaving a barrage of clothing flung here or there. How is this practice self-serving? We're left feeling not good enough, not pretty enough, or our size and shape are wrong. Why are we so discontent when we go to put on our clothes?

Often we try on an outfit that may conflict with what we feel inside, hoping to achieve a different result. For example, a speaker will often wear the color red to express strength, confidence, and presence, but have you ever seen an individual wearing red who comes across as too bold, screaming, aggressive, and not to be trusted? Learning to wear clothes that reflect and are in harmony with who you are brings out your brilliance.

Carol Tuttle's book, *Dressing Your Truth*, speaks about the various types of energy and natural movements of an individual. It is her intention to "help people identify and honor their true natures, strengths, and gifts."

In her words, "Amazing things happen to people who honor their true natures."

Learning to love yourself—who you are on the inside—and being transparent and authentic will totally transform your life. You can wear clothes to try and present a different emotional response, but without the internal emotional shift, people often feel false and uncomfortable and don't get the results they had hoped for. When you change or disrobe the *emotional internal wardrobe*, you can make a profound, lasting change in how you truly view yourself. If you're not happy with your internal wardrobe, you'll never be happy with your external image, and it's time to make a change.

Size and shape most definitely can influence your wardrobe, but loving yourself is the single most important garment that you should own.

It is perfect for every occasion, and when you own that, nothing else matters (especially what's on the outside), because your radiance shines from the inside-out.

What does your face say?

We have talked about the external façade that we show to the world. Now think about this: what does your face illustrate with respect to your inner emotional status? Did you know that your face is the most expressive part of your body, as well as the most immediately visual aspect that the world sees? Your face has many small muscles that portray your emotional status at any given time. You can pretty easily discern if someone is upset, angry, tearful, afraid, happy, or melancholy, but did you realize that the face is also the mirror into the Soul? If you're upset emotionally, it would be impossible for your face to successfully express and radiate true happiness.

Your energetic odor, fragrance, and perspiration

I often talk about the essence, fragrance, and even perspiration that we emit. Think of Mother Teresa—a small, humble, elderly woman who radiated an essence of divine, unconditional love. Maybe you know someone who is vile, angry, and hostile; just being in their presence is enough to feel, smell, and taste their negative, toxic energy. I'm not talking about what they are wearing, but the energy they emit from themselves.

Learning how to positively impact the internal view of yourself with the various tools I have previously described will create the best facelift ever, without spending a dime. All the spa treatments in the world cannot affect the internal face that you wear. How often have we said to a mother-to-be that she "glows"? The nurturing, internal love that is ever-present during pregnancy can be seen on her face. The same is true when you nurture and love yourself. Healing, changing, and living an emotionally rich and authentic life is the best gift you can give yourself. Allow your inner radiance, glow, and true essence to be seen by everyone.

As you change your internal wardrobe and give yourself a much-needed internal face lift, your essence will also be transformed.

5. **Emotional Nutrition, Sleep, and Health**

What have you been feeding yourself for years? I'm not talking about the food you consume like fruits, vegetable, carbohydrates, and proteins, but the emotional nutrients that you have been ingesting. These are the emotions, feelings, and thoughts that you store in your inner pantry and use to fuel your life.

Have you been feeding yourself emotional nutrients like pain, grief, sadness, disrepair, regret, and unhappiness, or—on the other end of the spectrum—satisfaction, acceptance, love, and forgiveness?

Each of our emotions has a nutritional value that contributes to our health and well-being.

Some common "emotional foods" include self-pity, loathing, grief, discomfort, pain, shame, and guilt. If you've been feeding yourself toxic emotions, how can you expect your health to be optimal? When we consume ingredients that reinforce why we feel so poorly, it only provides us with fuel that continues that negative image of self, even if it is untrue.

What is your **emotional comfort food**? Can you name it?

LACK

The emotional nourishment we must feed ourselves belongs to these food groups: *love, acceptance, compassion* and *kindness*. I've chosen these words of sustenance on purpose; the first letters of each word combine to form the acronym **LACK**. Almost all humans feel that we *lack* something, but with **L**ove, **A**cceptance, **C**ompassion, and **K**indness, there can never truly be a lacking.

If you hear yourself (or someone else) say, "I *lack* confidence," think about the LACK acronym as a reminder to see **L**ove, **A**cceptance, **C**ompassion, and **K**indness, and you will have as much confidence as you need.

Tell yourself, **"I *love, accept,* am *compassionate,* and *kind* with my confidence."**

There is no **LACK** of confidence. Your whole being and energy will shift when you change the emotional food that you consume.

Sleep is another vital component of restoration which allows healing to occur. It is recommended that we get between seven and nine hours of sleep per night for optimal health. Many interesting research studies reveal the negative effects of sleep deprivation. Sleep researchers indicate that fifty-seven million US adults have a problem with sleep or wakefulness: only fifteen percent feel rested after sleep, and only ten percent report sleeping well.

The Centers for Disease Control and Prevention report a direct correlation between restful sleep and the level of happiness one experiences. In fact, they say that **the quality of your sleep has a greater impact on your happiness than your income or your marital status!**

In addition, a 2013 research study at the University of California at Berkley used brain scans of sleep-deprived people to show that higher-calorie foods increased activity in the areas that control your desire to eat. The research found that sleep-deficit subjects were seventeen percent more likely to be obese. Sleep deprivation and insomnia are like any other physical symptoms—outward representations of our inner emotional pain. My personal story of sleep apnea absolutely had a deeper origin that needed to be addressed and resolved. Remembering to get enough sleep each day will add years to your life.

As you strive for health, happiness, and harmony, start to embrace emotional nutrition, rest, and **LACK**, knowing they'll support and feed your Soul.

6. **Emotional Freedom and Loving Your Authentic Self**

Emotional freedom comes from loving and accepting yourself. That means all the parts you love, as well as your imperfections. Once you accept that *no one is perfect*, than what's *not* to love? If you try, every day, to live from a place of *love, acceptance, compassion,* and *kindness* (there's our LACK acronym again) towards yourself and others, the peace and happiness within will exceed all expectations, and true health and happiness will be abundantly present. I promise you this is so very true.

The most important elements for long-term, permanent emotional health are the ability to release toxic, trapped memories and emotions; a shift in your mind's perception of loss, hurt, and expectation (both past and present); and forgiveness of self and others. When you can turn away from feeling like a victim and look upon events and your emotions with a compassionate understanding, you're able to learn and grow.

Remember that you create your energetic vibration and you control what your magnetism attracts into your life. You are the creator of emotional health, life, and well-being. You might never be able to master anything, but *you* can most definitely be the master of your*self*. William Ernest Henley says it very poetically:

"I am the master of my fate: I am the captain of my Soul."

In the 2012 film, *Tales of Everyday Magic*, Dr. Wayne Dyer talks about how the venom we allow to flow within our body is what causes us harm: "A snakebite is just a bite, but it's the venom inside that circulates, attacks, and destroys within. Wisdom is communicated indirectly, metaphorically, to us, but many times we're not open to hearing and seeing it. What kills you is not the bite but the venom that stays within you, unless you learn to get it out of your system, release it, or—better yet—assimilate it. We need to transmute what was once toxic and turn it into our own medicine."

Your emotional pain is the venom that courses through your body and impacts your health and well-being. The key is to stop recalling the snakebite (the event) and use your emotional wound(s) as a teacher and friend, turning what was originally a toxin (emotional pain) into the internal medicine that you require to heal and grow.

Creating your own internal medicine will help you master your emotional health: write yourself a prescription that supports your personal growth and helps to create the happiness, love, and health that you deserve.

<u>Prescription for Emotional Health and Happiness</u>

Fill in the blanks:

To (name):_____

Date: _____Forever _____

Take _____, _____, and _____
out of my life and replace it with

_____, _____, and _____.
(e.g., Take anger, hostility, and regret out of my life and replace it with love,
peace, and acceptance.)
Consume emotional nutrients that support my health and well-being.
Loving thoughts of:

_____,_____,_____.
Get plenty of sleep and drink lots of water.
Frequency: Take as often as needed.
Signature: (yours) _____

For a printed copy of this form, go to
http://www.PowerfulBeyondMeasureBook.com/forms.

Change the way your life unfolds by changing the way you feel.

"Courage does not always roar. Sometimes courage is the quiet voice at the end of the day saying, 'I will try again tomorrow.'"
—Mary Anne Redmache

RELEASE FEARS AND LIMITATIONS
The Healing Power of Forgiveness

Start learning how to let go.

There are two remaining elements to the healing process: identifying and releasing your fears and limitations and showing more forgiveness. Your fears and limitations, as you already know, are usually created in your younger years. The inner work you've already done within this book has opened your heart and mind, and you can now see the constraints that hold you back today.

As you identified your self-limiting beliefs, Soul lessons, and triggers that impacted who you became, you probably discovered some aspects (and people) in your life that you may feel the need to forgive, including yourself. Some of us came from dysfunctional families or experienced a profound loss or significant pain, and we continue to carry these emotions, thoughts, and beliefs into the present.

If your mother *feared* your father or was terrified by her dad, then you may feel the inability to trust as well. If your parents struggled financially—feeling that no matter how hard they worked, they could only create enough wealth to get by—then you may also believe the same is true. It's almost like their emotions, thoughts, and beliefs became part of your DNA and, by extension, your expectations in life. The energy in which you grew up creates more of the same vibration until you change that frequency.

What you do today, at this moment, actually becomes the foundation for what will become tomorrow, and tomorrow will become an integral component of the past, which you just created at this very moment.

> ***The present moment is fleeting,***
> ***but it is the only thing that you actually have any control over.***

So, by living in this moment, the question you need to ask yourself is: "How do I want to think, feel, and act, right here and *now*?"

Who is in charge of your thoughts? You might think your mind is, and in a way you are correct, if that is the **power** you give it. But it doesn't have to be your subconscious mind that controls you; it can be your inner wisdom, your heart's desire—your Power Within—that guides and redirects your conscious mind to think, act, and feel the way you choose.

Of course, that doesn't mean that we don't have goals, expectations, or dreams, but how we think and feel about them *now* affects the energy and emotions we experience in the present time. Our fears and *self-sabotaging beliefs* often hinder our *potentiality* for *possibilities*.

> ***Our past tries to control the present.***

I love this quote from Louise Hay's book, *The Power is Within You*:

> ***"The point of power is always in the present moment."***

The present moment is truly the only time when your strength and power can be expressed.

So let's look at how to release our fears and self-limiting beliefs. Within Part II of this book, I have shared many tools that enable you to shift your controlling, subconscious, limiting beliefs and take conscious steps, inspired by your inner self, toward following your heart's truth for inner happiness and peace. The technique "**I** *Choose* **to, Because I** *Can*," along with the **Mental Command sequences**, is extremely effective in rehabilitating old patterns.

With anything that you've done for a lifetime, it takes time, effort, and determination to create a permanent change. You can accomplish this and so much more! Thousands of people transform their lives and live in ways they never knew could have existed, experiencing joy and happiness in the *now and so can you.*

Fears, Limitations, and Courage

Fear is defined as an **unpleasant emotion** caused by anticipation or awareness of danger; to be afraid and apprehensive. Some synonyms for fear are dread, fright, alarm, panic, terror, trepidation, anxiety, and wrath.

Fear can cripple, limit, and cause us to feel stuck, frustrated, desperate, and hopeless, so it's reasonable to wonder why anyone would try anything without confirming a desired outcome in advance. But fear is an emotion, one that is self-created. You can choose to experience fear in the moment. Often our fears have deep roots dating back to our childhoods and the perceptions and beliefs we took on.

You need to look at the origin of your fears. Where do they come from? Are they a learned behavior/belief, an expected result, or an inability to trust oneself?

Limitation has many definitions, but for our purposes, it is the act of limiting or the state of being limited; a shortcoming or defect. Where do our limitations come from? Of course, there are limitations—rules, orders, and expectations—that our society, government, and morals place upon us, but the self-limitations that we hold near and dear are much more controlling and, in some cases, more impactful than any other ones.

Our self-limiting beliefs were formulated during our earliest years. These limitations indicate the shortcomings and/or defects that we have come to believe about ourselves. If you believe you're not smart and lack intelligence, then your fear would raise its ugly head when a scenario or challenge presents itself where you need/should express your knowledge. The stronger your belief system is with respect to your limitations, the greater your fears will be.

Here are a few examples of limitations that you may accept and believe as true: I am not wanted, not loved (or lovable), not good enough, untrustworthy, inferior, a failure, or cursed. Address your limitations directly. Give them a voice. Put pen to paper and acknowledge them. If you can't see or hear your self-limiting beliefs, you'll never be able to change them or affect their control on your life.

Fear and Limitations Resolution

Here's a tool that will help you identify the root causes of your fears and limitations and learn how to gain the courage to overcome them.

Be honest here about what you are afraid of: relationships, intimacy, a move, career, belonging, abandonment, change, etc. Remember that **fears are only unpleasant emotions, ones that have been self-created and probably stored within you for quite some time**. Be willing to release the power that they have over you. For a printed copy of this exercise, go to www.PowerfulBeyondMeasureBook.com/forms.

Step 1

Write down the fear(s) and/or limitations you're experiencing right now. If you can't think of anything at the present moment, write down ones you've experienced in the past (e.g., I am not pretty enough).

1.
2.
3.
4.
5.

Wonderful!

Step 2

Now, for each numbered item above, write down whether the fear and/or limitation is a learned behavior or a belief, an unexpected result, or an inability to trust yourself. Also note how long you have believed this to be the truth (e.g., I am not pretty enough; learned belief; since five years old).

1.
2.
3.
4.
5.

Step 3

In the last part, write down what it would take to make you feel ***courageous enough to overcome that specific fear/limitation***. (Suggestions: confidence, strength, willpower, vision, support, knowledge, perseverance, determination, initiative, belief, vision, and acceptance.) Continuing with the example, I have to see myself as pretty; plan on changing behaviors that would make me feel prettier (e.g., beauty parlor, clothes selection, posture—try things that I wouldn't have in the past, and engage in activities that put me in the public eye).

1.
2.
3.
4.
5.

Congratulations! Seeing words on paper that describe your fear(s) should help you see that they don't physically exist; they are only fragments within your mind originating from an emotional stress/pain that you had or are experiencing.

Courage

Look at the list of courageous acts you identified to overcome your fears. Courage is the mental or moral strength to stand up to your fears or difficulties. This mental action, firmness of mind, resists the unpleasant emotional feeling (fear); it's persistent and willing to achieve your goal(s). You acknowledge the emotional aspect (which is important to do), assess where it's coming from, and then take action to create what you desire.

Sounds simple? It really is. If you have failed in the past, don't fret; it was a learning opportunity, and remember that the Universe will continue to present scenarios to help you grow and gain wisdom until you get it. When you can take action steps to vaporize your own self-imposed fears and limitations, your life abounds with exponential possibilities.

Now that you completed the above exercise, I want to share with you some fears that you may not have considered and how they may be impacting you.

FEARS	LIMITATIONS
Fear of failure	Keeps you from trying
Fear of success	Sabotages your every effort
Fear of outcome	Past dictates the future
Fear of speaking	No one cares what I have to say
Fear for your safety	Expect/deserve the same treatment/abuse
Fear of acknowledgement	Keeps you small and unseen
Fear of trust	Keeps you isolated, alone, and feeling hopeless
Fear of poverty	Familiar history dictates your lack of abundance
Fear of going out into the world	Keeps you safe, protected, and alone
Fear of not having knowledge	You think you're not smart enough, incapable
Fear of loneliness	Push others away
Fear of our passion/purpose	Stops us living our truth

When you're dealing with fears and limitations, ask yourself these questions:

- Where are my fears coming from?
- What am I going to do about them?
- When am I going to take action?

Without fear, one wouldn't need courage. You have *already* embraced courage—you're participating in the Power Within process to become Powerful Beyond Measure, and that took a lot of courage.

You didn't know what that outcome would be, but you responded to your inner calling to learn, grow, and heal.

Courage comes when you stop saying "I can't" and replace it with "I can"!

Of course, there are times when fear is justified. I'm not talking about those situations when there is a real potential of threat or harm, when you should do everything in your power to get away and find safety. If you are currently in a dangerous situation, *you* have the courage to seek refuge, and there are various resources that offer support. You deserve to be treated with respect, love, and compassion.

Fear of impending harm is justified, but tolerating it isn't acceptable. I once heard a phrase which actually didn't sit too well with me at first, but after further consideration, I had to agree: you can only be battered, abused, or physically harmed one time; if you stay, you become your own abuser.

I know it sounds harsh, unkind, and unfeeling; I felt that way at first as well, but it is the truth. You are the only one who can escape from the abuse. I understand that situations may be complicated and that, as much as you fear the abuser, **you fear the unknown even more**. The dreaded "What ifs" start to fill your mind: What if I leave—where will I stay? What if I leave—how will I eat? If I leave, will he/she retaliate?

All I can say is: be courageous enough to
seek the help that you need *and deserve.*

You'll find that courage is like a muscle: the more you use it, the stronger it gets, and action becomes effortless. When you remove the fear and stress, the courage muscle won't have to work as hard. This is an example of emotional ergonomics (which I discussed in the previous chapter). When you understand the things within yourself that stand in your way and eliminate the fears and limitations, success will follow, and you'll experience happiness and achieve personal growth. Sounds like a winning formula—one in which failure is not an option.

The Cherokee Tale of Two Wolves
(retrieved from unbelievableyou.com/a-native-american-cherokee-story-two-wolves/)

One evening, an old Cherokee Indian told his grandson about a battle that goes on inside people.

The grandfather said, "My son, the battle is between two 'wolves' inside us all. One is evil. It is anger, envy, jealousy, sorrow, regret, greed, arrogance, self-pity, guilt, resentment, inferiority, lies, false pride, superiority, and ego.

"The other is good. It is joy, peace, love, hope, serenity, humility, kindness, benevolence, empathy, generosity, truth, compassion and faith."

The grandson thought about it for a minute and then asked his grandfather: "Which wolf wins?"

The old Cherokee simply replied, "The one you feed."

Feed the wolf that you want to thrive.

I love this folk tale because it so simply depicts our internal struggle. This is especially true when it comes to fear. Each and every day, we choose which wolf we feed with our thoughts, actions or inactions, and the choices we make. Will you allow the evil wolf of fear to limit and paralyze you, keeping you from achieving the desires that serve not only you, but also the greater cause?

Courage is a food you choose to consume that nourishes you from within.

Here are ten action steps to release your fears and limitations:

1. Meditation

   I encourage you to use the **Heart's Home of Healing** meditation to help clear your negative energies, fears, and limitations. To refresh your memory, go back to Part I, Chapter 2 ("Own Your Own Story"). To listen to the audio of this powerful guided free meditation, go to <u>www. PowerfulBeyondMeasureBook.com/HeartHomeOfHealingMeditation</u>.

2. Choose not to be constrained by your fears and create action steps towards success. See the section on goal setting in Part III, Chapter 2 ("Own and Create Your Happiness").

3. Be your own cheerleader. Love and applaud yourself!

4. Use **"I *Choose* to, Because I *Can*"** to shift your fears and limitations.

5. Use the **Fear and Limitations Resolution** form to identify the strengths you need to work on to succeed.

6. Be with people who support and encourage you.

7. Choose optimism, capability, and excitement rather than pessimism, inability, and anxiety.

8. Journal about your thoughts, feelings, and action steps.

9. Sedate your Triple Warmer (Fight-or-Flight Response) Meridian (see Chapter 3, "Wellness and Health," in Part III for more details).

10. Use tapping to release the energy associated with your fears and limitations (see Chapter 3, "Wellness and Health," in Part III for more details).

When you eliminate your fears, or at least stop them from dictating your future, your life will totally change. You'll become more engaged and excited about things you normally would have avoided. Your life will be fuller with new and exciting opportunities.

Forgiveness

Another extremely important component that stands in the way of our freedom is the inability to forgive and let go. I briefly touched upon forgiveness in a previous chapter, but the impact of *not* forgiven is so limiting that I want to go over it in much greater detail.

> *Forgiveness is a vital, lifelong skill that's*
> *essential for a healthy, fulfilling life.*

We've talked about taking responsibility for yourself as an important step that allows healing, peace, and inner transformation to occur. No one can make you feel or think a certain way except yourself. Forgiveness, compassion, and unconditional love are integral components for releasing your fears and limitations.

For some of you, just thinking about forgiving yourself or someone else is beyond comprehension or even consideration. If this is the case for you, I need to ask you a few questions.

- How does the *inability* to forgive help you or the other individual?
- Does remaining angry at yourself or others change the outcome?
- How many years of built-up hatred, resentment, anger, guilt, blame, and shame will ever be enough to make you feel restored and justified—to bring resolution?
- How will holding onto these emotions, memories, and behaviors ever bring you peace?
- Can you change the events that happened?

Not one of us has figured out how to go back in time and reverse the order of events. It's literally impossible. When you're unable to forgive, that also means you're unwilling to let go of the past.

How will *not* forgiving someone ever change your emotional, physical, and mental health? No matter who is at fault (either yourself or someone else), holding onto these emotional pains, memories, and anger will *never* resolve your inner conflict. Ironically, through unforgiveness, those old wounds perpetuate themselves into the present moment. The hurt, unreleased emotional pain, and haunting memories continue to fuel the inner battle within you.

The definition of forgiveness by most dictionaries is an *intentional* and *voluntary* process by which the *victim* undergoes a *change in feeling and attitude regarding an offender*. I have a problem with this definition because it assumes that one person is a victor and one is a victim.

Can't both participants be contributing components? What if one person appears to be more at fault; shouldn't we still consider the contributing role of the other individual or the impact that comes from the experience? Where is the real damage, and what actually needs to be forgiven? It also doesn't clarify or qualify the type of change in feeling or attitude against the offender, who can even be yourself. I believe the two most important parts in the definition are "intentional" and "the victim undergoes a change." This means that you intentionally (consciously) decide to forgive. That's huge. The act of forgiving the other and yourself has a direct effect/change on your attitude. So the act of forgiving benefits you.

Many find forgiveness one of the hardest things to do because they equate forgiving someone with excusing their behavior, which means they can no longer be held responsible or accountable for the pain they caused. Neither of those statements is true.

Of course, there are many situations in which forgiveness is needed (e.g., a very specific physical assault, verbal statement(s), or a lack of response), but is that single event really *all* that we need to focus on? Shouldn't we deal with the events before and after the experience—the ones that, in fact, cause us even more pain? I often find that when we forgive, it is not usually for *one* very specific thing. The actual event, emotions, and thoughts become much more entangled and have even a longer-lasting impact. This adds to the complexity of forgiveness.

Mother Teresa often said,
"Forgive everyone *everything*. It makes you better ..."

I believe forgiveness means allowing room for error or weakness. If perfection is unattainable, then how can we *not* expect errors to occur? This statement in no way condones or accepts outrageous behaviors (murder, rape, and assault, etc..), but it does open the door to possibly considering why a person could've harmed you in such a way—or how you could have harmed them. Whether you forgive or not, everyone is always accountable for their action and inactions—legally, socially, morally, and spiritually.

Forgiveness is for the forgiver, not for the forgiven.

Have you ever heard a story about someone who forgave the person who killed their child? Did you think, "How could they?" The senseless, violent act—how horrific! I have struggled with this myself, and I wonder if I really could forgive in that situation. Holding onto anger and hatred towards an individual(s)/event and injustice ends up robbing and destroying your peace and joy. All you can do is relive the agony of the loss, so the act of forgiveness is often more important for the forgiver than the forgiven. Even if you could forgive the person who inflicted the harm, that doesn't mean he could ever forgive himself.

I asked this question on Facebook: "What is the hardest thing to forgive?" Hands down, most people said it was to forgive themselves! Why are we so unaccepting of our imperfection? Do we feel that if we continue to punish ourselves, then our errors are somehow atoned for, or that if we continue to hold them, then we'll never forget? Is there an aspect of self that doesn't want to release and let go? The painful event may not even be your story, but somehow you took it on. Forgiveness is really about healing *our* issue. If it wasn't our issue to heal, we wouldn't be holding the grudge.

I believe that, in order to truly heal and forgive someone (including yourself), there have to be *emotional* and *behavioral components*. The **emotional aspect** occurs on the *inside* and sometimes that can be the hardest to accomplish because no one can see the hurt, pain, and guilt. The **behavioral aspect** occurs on the *outside* and is usually a visual display or action that you perform. Both aspects, I believe, need to be incorporated to successfully forgive.

Emotional healing occurs on the inside
and behavioral healing occurs on the outside.

Let's consider a fictional scene that I think we can all relate to: there was an argument at the dinner table last night. Words were said by multiple people; everyone got heated, and by the end, no one was listening and everyone felt they were right. Egos were bruised, relationships strained, maybe trust was violated, and the verbal assault only added fuel to your self-limiting beliefs. So who is at fault?

Do we really know all the elements that actually precede this event? Maybe there was something extremely difficult that happened beforehand to one or more of the individuals which became the catalyst for the fiery exchange. Maybe you reacted to a reoccurrence of how you felt when you became the victim once again. Were you displaying defensive behaviors to protect yourself?

Why is it that we find forgiveness so difficult? Is it because someone has to be at fault (ideally not ourselves)? I am not saying in any way, shape, or form that horrific acts don't occur every minute of every day. I know that we'd never condone outrageous behavior, but by reliving it through our senses, we allow the egregious behavior, trapped anger, and emotional pain to continue to persist within; this allows that negative, toxic energy to hold us prisoner.

I have found these three elements to be essential for long-term, permanent healing within:

1. **Forgiveness** of self and others;
2. **Release** of harmful trapped memories and emotions around the event and individuals; and
3. A **shift** in your mind's perception of loss, hurt, and expectation—in the past, present and future.

When you can turn away from taking on the role of victim and instead look at the event(s) as just another place and time that you could learn and grow from, you can de-emotionalize, depersonalize, and desensitize the impact that it has on you. The events can never occur again, except in your mind, heart, and Soul.

The decision is yours; you can choose if you want them to be repeated again and again or let them go once and for all.

Here are a few of the top reasons for why it's so hard to forgive: judgement, pride, trust, deceit, lies, resentment, anger, self-pity, pain, ego, guilt, betrayal, hatred, and vengeance. Granting forgiveness for some can be quite challenging because they view it is a show of weakness, taking on blame or shame, being right or wrong, opening old wounds, or accepting the specified act.

As I have discussed before, forgiving yourself or someone else *never* takes away accountability and responsibility for that behavior, but it does allow you to move past, let go, and perhaps gain a greater understanding whereby the event or action doesn't define who you are.

You see, you could actually say to someone who is at fault, "I forgive you for (xyz)," but your words will fall by the wayside if the individual is unwilling to forgive himself. We are our own worst enemies; we often cast judgment and criticism so someone else is at fault, but internally, we *know* that we are not being truthful and now hold ourselves victim to our *own* lack of forgiveness.

It is a vicious cycle of disrepair that will continue unless we change the way we view the circumstances, the role we played, and learn to be more accepting, loving, and compassionate toward others, knowing we are all imperfect. Perfection does *not* exist in anything or anyone. It is our own perceptions that continue to contaminate and negatively impact ourselves, our happiness, and our health. When we are willing to start the forgiveness process, true healing can begin.

Studies have shown that just the *simple thought* of being willing to forgive yourself or someone else can have a profound, positive effect on your body. When you are able to forgive, you experience less stress, hurt, anger, and pain, and you experience more optimism, self-confidence, vitality, success, trust, freedom, joy, and love. You actually exist in a more peaceful state within, one that no longer is filled with inner turmoil, stress, and anxiety.

So how does one forgive? The Power Within *you* is governed and controlled by love, acceptance, compassion, and kindness (LACK acronym). It doesn't know anger, hatred, and retaliation. When you make a *conscious* decision not to be a victim of the past any longer, you free yourself to create a new life—one that is guided and supported by your divine Power Within. Anger and resentment originate in the mind; love and forgiveness originate from the heart and Soul. Which source do you choose to draw from?

In accepting and understanding that we each play an integral role in the creation of our own past, outcomes, reactions, you may start to experience an overwhelming need to blame yourself, and you might even want to take on self-pity. Taking responsibility is different than blaming yourself. The good news is that, by taking responsibility, you are *empowering* yourself to say "never again" and *enabling* yourself to make personal changes. Remember: *you* are the only one who can really affect your behavior, emotions, and thoughts.

The moment you start to take pity on yourself, you allow yourself to once again become a victim. Feeling empowered creates an inner strength and allows the wisdom you've obtained to assist you as you move forward with forgiveness, growth, and success.

> *Inner peace comes when you accept but no longer judge—*
> *even though you may never comprehend—*
> *and allow your feelings and emotions to be released.*
> *Their voices are heard but no longer can hurt you.*

By looking at your past as the richness of experiences that they are and knowing that you did the best you could do at that time, you allow yourself to accept what was (which cannot be changed), forgive, and *let go*.

> *Today is the perfect time to start to forgive.*
> *Forgiveness comes from the heart, bringing you inner peace,*
> *where the wrongdoing no longer exists.*
> *To forgive or not forgive—it's your choice.*

Part III

Envision Your Future and Expand Your Possibilities

In Part II, you explored various ways to empower yourself and really understand how you can make significant changes in your life here and now, in the present moment. You worked on finding and loving your authentic self and stopping the Dis-Cycle of Self that kept you feeling small, unfulfilled, frustrated, unhappy, and confused in so many areas of your life. You then continued on to address the emotional pain(s) that you've carried for so many years, saw how they were still impacting you, and took actionable steps to improve your Emotional Health and Fitness. Learning to be open to *feel* within yourself and share emotions in the Now were integral steps in honoring and valuing your heart and Soul. Lastly, we looked at the importance of lowering our defenses and tearing down the walls of protection that we erected so very long ago—walls which may have become our prisons. When we opened ourselves up, we were able to acknowledge and address our fears and limitations and embrace them for the lessons and growth potential they actually serve. Forgiveness and unconditional love towards ourselves, others, and events/situations became the foundation for letting go, wanting something different, and finding the inner peace that allows you to be open to hear your heart's desire and passions.

In Part III, you'll be learning to develop and strengthen your communication with your intuition and to use strategies to create happiness, health, and wellness in your future, which in turn becomes your present. You'll ignite your inner desires and reach for what your Soul is calling you to do while bringing abundance, success, and miracles into your life. You'll play an active role in creating a life filled with joy, love, happiness, and peace, and I know you're ready to begin the next part of your journey toward feeling alive, passionate, and Powerful Beyond Measure.

I would love to share a couple of personal stories about pivotal moments and life-changing opportunities that put me on the road I'm now on. These are events that I had never even dared to envision, but I now realize they were greater than what I could even have imagined was possible at the time. I know the same can be true for you. As you begin Part III, I am so very excited for you as you allow your passion and the seed(s) of desire to emerge and take form. This new path offers so much for you personally, but it will also touch many others in a very profound way.

A Father's Loving Words

The father I had always longed for came and spoke to me one night through a medium. Sitting in a beautifully adorned theatre with more than 1,500 people, we waited for James Van Praagh, a spiritual medium intuitive with a wonderful gift: the ability to channel and communicate with spirits and provide communication between the spiritual and physical worlds. Many audience members carried memorabilia of their loved ones, hoping to connect with someone who has passed on from this physical life. I had never been to anything remotely like this, but because my mother had lost her second husband to Alzheimer's disease nine months earlier, I purchased tickets in the hope that it might bring her some peace to know that our loved ones are around us and that, even though there was physical death, their spirits live on eternally. Unfortunately, my mother didn't feel up for the lengthy trip and wasn't able to attend, but my husband Tom, a friend, and I decided to attend anyway.

After Van Praagh took the stage, he shared with us how he had avoided his gift as a child because people made fun of him for his ability to speak to ghosts. But no matter how much he rejected his gift, the Universe always found ways to bring it back into his life. He finally decided to embrace his Soul's purpose when he realized that he could make a difference in the world.

James said that spirits present themselves to him and share facts that will only make sense to the person they need to communicate with. After an hour of hearing various exchanges and having audience members stand to hear their messages, I was impressed but still skeptical, and I had doubts about the accuracy and legitimacy of what I was seeing. I even thought, "These people had to be planted. There's no way he could know those kinds of details."

Just after those doubts ran through my head, James started to present a new scenario as a different spirit spoke to him. He was looking for someone with a father named Bill who had recently passed away, had a dog named Jazzmine who also had passed, and was an artist who had traveled to France recently.

I was stunned. Every one of those details—and more, as Van Praagh went on—described my mother's second husband perfectly. Wow! Could this really be for me? Bill was a very quiet man, and to think that he exerted enough presence with all those other spirits around was amazing to me. Although he was my mother's second husband, he hadn't really been a father to my sisters and me, since we were adult women when they married. Sitting in the fifth-to-last row of a sold-out amphitheater, I stood at my seat as an usher brought a microphone so I could speak to James.

At that time, my husband and I had been working on our marriage, and I was conflicted about who I should be and what I should do so that Tom would *love me* and *stay* in our marriage. I desperately didn't want another man who was supposed to love me walk out of my life. I was very torn and emotionally distraught, struggling with the question "Who am I?"

The next words James spoke to the audience and to me pierced my heart in a loving way, as if Bill was standing there himself: "I want you to know that I have no limitations. I can walk, hear, see, and understand without any difficulties." At the end of his physical life, Bill's disease was so severe that he had no recollection of his loved ones. He was totally deaf from his flying days, blind from macular degeneration, and his lack of physical capabilities greatly limited his mobility. Bill then went on to say that Jazzmine (my dog) was with him, as well as Fluffy, who had been my mom's and Bill's dog.

What came next took my breath away. Bill said (through James), "You are perfect exactly as you are, and you shouldn't change for anyone." Finally, a father who told me that I was wonderful and loved! My tears flow lovingly even as I'm writing this for you now. He proceeded to say, "You have enormous light around you, and your life has been in preparation for the teaching and healing work that you'll do in this part of your life. You'll write, teach, heal, and reach the masses and show people how powerful they are." I stood there, mesmerized. It was as if there was no one else in that huge auditorium as his fatherly words offered comfort, love, and guidance, telling me that I had a destiny to fulfill. Little old me! Yes, I had been talking about writing a book for years, but to hear that it would have this kind of scope and really be transformative and healing for others was another thing entirely.

I was blessed by this spiritual communication with a man that I had never referred to as a father but who made it known through Mr. Van Praagh that he had to speak to me. This went on for half an hour with many other messages, but these in particular were so potent and appropriate that I wanted to share them with you to show how we all have a calling—a destiny—and that shaping (or should I say following) our path and our passion is where our truth lies.

I was filled with so much awe, peace, and grace by the gift I had just received. I realized that I needed to stop trying to be everything to everyone, quit changing to fit what I or other people thought I should be, and focus on finding and loving myself. To see my beauty, gifts, and purpose. I had always known from a very young age that my hands were very special and that they would play an important role in this life, but that realization was unfolding before my eyes.

Almost a year later to the day, I was in such a better place, Tom's and my relationship had greatly improved and he supported the work I was doing with teaching spiritual and empowerment classes and healing work. The Universe/God/angels continued to bring opportunities that enriched my new path and passion. I was finally at peace within myself and realized that my true power, the spiritual gifts that were unique to me, would allow me to fulfill my destiny whatever that was, and where ever that would take me; I was open to follow and trust all that was brought to me.

A Gift from the Universe

Would I open it or always wonder what was inside?
Miracles happen when you least expect them. Doors present themselves, waiting for you to turn the handle and enter. One day, I was at my computer working on a class I was giving on The Power Within. I loved what I was doing and the profound impact it was having on the students, who ranged from fifty to ninety-eight years young.

As I went through my inbox, I noticed a name I hadn't seen before, and opened a beautifully colorful, enticing email promoting a "Your Miraculous Life Mentoring Program" that was searching for eight lucky women to be mentored by Marci Shimoff. My immediate response was, "Who is Marci Shimoff, and why did I receive this email?"

I quickly Googled her name and learned that she is a #1 *New York Times* best-selling author, a world-renowned transformational teacher, and an expert on happiness, success, and unconditional love. Her books include the international best sellers *Love for No Reason and Happy for No Reason*. Marci is also the face of the biggest self-help book phenomenon in history as coauthor of six books in the *Chicken Soup for the Soul* series. With total book sales of more than fifteen million copies worldwide in thirty-three languages, she is one of the best-selling female nonfiction authors of all time. Once I read about Marci, I immediately knew who she was because I owned four of the six *Chicken Soup for the Soul* books she had coauthored. I was really perplexed now, wondering even more so why I had received this email.

In that instant, I knew on a deep, spiritual level that this email was sent *to* me, *for* me. I don't know how I knew, but my intuition was screaming at me to jump up and down and fill out the form. I found myself saying things like "Oh, my! I can't believe this is *it*!" God, Jesus, my angels, and the Universe had created another vehicle for me to jump aboard that would help me fulfill my life purpose. I pushed back from my desk, slightly winded and filled with anticipation, excitement, and awe. How did these events and scenarios just keep happening to me? Over the past year, I had been blessed with countless situations that had profound impacts on me and others.

I hadn't even applied yet, much less been selected, but on a deep spiritual level, I *knew* this program was destined for me and that Marci would be a huge source of support for my life calling—writing this book and impacting others in the world.

Well, that jubilation lasted all of three or four minutes, and I'm sure you can guess what came next. That's right, thoughts filled with trepidation, self-doubt, fear, and incompetence instantly flooded my mind. Boy, how the mind wants to make you second-guess, live with anxiety, and devalue yourself! My mind started to whirl with thoughts about the vastness of this opportunity, the anticipation of failure, and the belief that my message was not that important—who was *I*, after all? Why would she pick me out of the thousands of women who would submit an application? "Come on Cindy, you really think you have a chance at becoming one of those eight lucky women? Be realistic!" But at that instant, I had the "knowing": "Why *not* me?" During those minutes of internal conflict, I experienced almost every emotion possible, from excitement to terror, hope to fear, and joy to regret.

I wondered what would happen if I was chosen and what that would mean for the fulfillment of my life purpose. I was scared out of my wits, but at the same time, I was filled with pure adrenaline and excitement. As I rode that wonderfully thrilling, terrifying rollercoaster of emotion, I started to do some encouraging self-talk, expressing gratitude for this wonderful opportunity and telling myself that I *had* to apply because in my heart and Soul , I already *knew* I would be selected. That was both scary and exciting at the same time: it meant I would *have* to write this book instead of just talking about doing it someday.

How are we supposed to respond to these beckoning, searching, and enlightening experiences and opportunities? I say with open hands, heart, mind, and Soul , filled with gratitude and a knowing that this is *exactly* what you need and were meant to do!

I am not saying that this is easy to do, but we need to be our own cheerleaders—encouraging, self-loving, and supportive—and embrace what the Universe creates for us, so, with continuing reservations that I kept trying to deny, I completed the application. I answered each question honestly, letting my heart guide my responses. I wasn't sure where the words were flowing from, but after I wrote them, I'd say to myself, "Where did that come from? It's actually really good." Many of the questions called deeply to me, making me ponder and search my Soul for the answers that would speak my truth. I felt energized, hopeful, and excited. I even used a quote that I had shared in my classroom that very day: "When a student is ready, a teacher will appear." I also shared one of my own: "Your student is ready. Will you be my teacher?" I momentarily questioned whether or not to include that last quote because I didn't want it to sound too hokey, but it was *exactly* how I felt. Trusting myself, I decided to leave it in. I said a silent prayer, used my Reiki symbols to energize my application, pressed "Submit," and said, "Let it be so!"

What more could I do? The application had been sent. Doubting myself served no value; it would only cause more mental dysfunction: fear of rejection and disappointment, along with questioning my self-worth and the expectation of my life purpose. I *chose* not to go there. We always have this choice: to be filled with trepidation or love, fear or hope. I had to trust that what comes our way is integral for our higher learning, providing the platform for our spiritual life lessons and purpose.

Amazingly, the very next day, at 1:11 p.m., I received an email from Kim Forcina, the director of Marci's Miraculous Mentoring Program. She wanted to set up a personal telephone interview. Speechless is not a word I often use to describe myself, but it certainly did apply in this instance! I was breathless, completely in shock, and totally taken aback. I was in awe; in less than twenty-four hours, I had received an email advancing me to the next stage in the competition. Jubilation filled my weekend, and somehow I had this deep, peaceful "knowing" that all was well and exactly as it should be.

When Kim and I spoke a few days later, she said she had been impressed with how thorough my application was and that she was very drawn to my story and my passion. She told me that, as of that morning, there had been 1,111 applicants. For those of you who follow numerology, you'll understand why I recognized the significance of the fact that the number "1" had been appearing repeatedly. According to Doreen Virtue's book, *Angel Numbers 101*, 11 and 111 both represent staying positive: "your thoughts are manifesting instantly, so keep your mindset focused upon your desires. Give any fearful thoughts to Heaven for transmutation."

The process included several more interviews with Kim and then finally advanced to a scheduled video call with Marci. As that day approached, I remember thinking, "Why am I not nervous?" I kept positive thoughts about the outcome and envisioned that this whole program had been developed for *me* so that she could help me fulfill one of my life purposes— completing and publishing my book—as well as advancing my calling to engage in public speaking and teaching.

I thought our Skype interview went exceptionally well. Marci was so beautiful, expressing a sincere interest in my desires and trying to determine if I was a good fit, not only for the program, but also with the other seven women she'd be selecting. She said she had been deeply moved by my application, the dream of my work, and the impact it would have on the world. I believe there is no greater gift than to empower someone else, and I was hopeful that she would be that force for me. Empowerment of others is the absolute gift of *love*.

During our talk, Marci told me that they had received more than 1,600 applications and that I was among twenty-five women who had been chosen as finalists. That left me speechless all over again! I tried to hold fast to my belief that the Universe was directing me toward Marci. She let me know that they'd be narrowing the field down further to twelve women and that she would be conducting a second personal interview with all of us. She also asked for my birth details so her Vedic astrologer, Bill Levacy, could see what my chart indicated about my life cycle and the timing of what was to come.

The second interview and Bill's reading were simply over the top. The comments Bill shared about my chart predicted a royal presence—a power that would be brought to the world—and that the next ten years would be filled with expectations and outcomes *beyond my present understanding*.

Ultimately, I was selected as one of the eight women who would have the privilege of being mentored by this tremendous, heart-centered, loving woman. I was floating on top of the world, but at the same time, I was overwhelmed by the gigantic leap of faith and productivity that I had now committed to.

You might have thought, "What could be better than that," right? Well, a few days after our first group call of eight, I received a phone call from Marci. I remember her exact words to this day: "Cindy, I'm not sure this program is really right for you." Tears filled my eyes as all those negative thoughts and emotions welled up within me. I thought, "What did I do? How could this be happening?" I just knew deep in my Soul that I was supposed to be working with Marci. What had I done wrong? Her words pierced my heart, and I had a momentary flashback to yet another person walking out of my life.

Marci must have sensed my pain, because she immediately said, "No, Cindy, you're misunderstanding what I'm saying. I want to work with you one on one, become your mentor, and really help you fulfill your purpose." She told me the story of the day that Jack Canfield had become her mentor and how it changed her life and direction forever.

Starting then, in the fall of 2014, my life totally changed in so many amazing ways. Marci became my mentor, friend, and confidant. She has helped me spread my wings and follow the purpose that I was born to fulfill. If you haven't read the foreword to this book yet, please take a moment to do so. It's with great respect, love, and appreciation that Marci agreed to write it for me, and I feel forever blessed by her presence.

I shared the previous two stories (and trust me, there are so many more I could've added) because I wanted to demonstrate the power of *you*—your destiny, your gifts, your calling, and how you must listen and know what is true within. Being willing to grow, learn, and be receptive when the Universe provides new doorways to things that are for your greater good but often beyond your understanding is where your freedom and joy will be experienced. Know that your role in fulfilling your passions, purpose, and calling is being supported by the Universe—the God of your understanding—and you already have the ability within you to be Powerful Beyond Measure.

As you advance into Part III, allow yourself to come alive deep inside yourself. Ignite your fire and hear the inner wisdom that is always there as you search for meaning, purpose, and how to live your life to the fullest. Your life matters! You were born to make a difference and touch the world as only *you* know how!

Join me as we begin this final step on your journey: exploring the ways to Envision and Expand your Future.

"You are very powerful, provided you know how powerful you are."
—**Yogi Bhajan**

POWER OF INTUITION
The infinite resource of divine intelligence

Discover what you can do to shape and direct your future,
which ultimately will become your present.

We've all heard the word *intuition*, and most of us can come up with a vague definition of what it means. "Gut feeling," "the little voice inside my head," "something just told me"—no matter how you phrase it, you know what it's like when that elusive "feeling" comes over you, telling you the right choice to make or guiding you in a particular direction, even when it's the polar opposite of what your mind says. How often have you said, "Thank goodness I followed my heart instead of my head!"? Even though we can't see it, taste it, or smell it, we know how strong that "sense" can be.

We all have an inner divine intelligence that supports us and interacts with everything in our lives. That inner wisdom—our intuition—is always available, but how often do we proactively seek its advice and guidance? Many of us find it difficult to call upon our intuition whenever we'd like to, so how can we learn to connect with it and depend on the insight it brings? Intuition is like a muscle: the only way it becomes stronger is to use it on a regular basis. When you learn to consistently rely on it, you gain a trust and confidence that goes hand in hand with that communication from your inner self.

Intuition—the voice of your Soul—always knows your truth.

Merriam-Webster's dictionary defines intuition as "a natural ability or power that makes it possible to know something *without any proof or evidence*: a feeling that guides a person to act a certain way without fully understanding why." Notice that your intuition doesn't engage the mind in any way. There is no thought, analysis, or solution-driven decision making. Intuition is completely a "knowing" without "knowing": it isn't governed by mental processes.

Break down *intuition* into its two components, **in** and **tuition**, and consider their definitions. Tuition relates to teaching, training, schooling, instruction, guidance, and coaching. Our intuition becomes our teacher, our coach, offering us support, guidance, and instructions, but we need to be receptive and attentive to the lessons that are being presented. We are *in training*, and our lives are our playgrounds for that learning! Wow, what a powerful statement!

Where does this "inner knowing" come from?

What if I told you it was your Soul, your true essence, the voice of your Self? You are not your physical body. Your Spirit lives within that outer form which allows you to exist in this earthly plane. I believe that our Soul/Spirit was created by the One, which you can define as Almighty, God, or whatever word or phrase you use to identify the Creator of All. Each one of us is an extension of our Creator; we're not separate from that Source.

You are part of that creation, connected through eternity to that divinity, brilliance, and completeness of love. Your Soul knows everything there is to know about you—your past lives, why you came to live this life, your Soul lessons, your gifts, and the purpose or destiny that you're meant to fulfill. Understanding that your Soul holds all this wisdom, of course your "Self" wants to direct and guide you on the path you're meant to follow.

Steve Jobs once said, "Intuition is more powerful than intellect." I love this quote because it reinforces how *powerful* our intuition is. We must learn to listen, trust, and utilize this inner knowledge in all aspects of our lives. In Part II, I spoke about our inner compass, being our own GPS navigational system, and how we need to learn to find our true north and steer towards our divine path of spiritual growth and purpose.

Our minds are constantly making assessments, analyzing, judging, reflecting, and weighing the likelihood of success or failure. We already know how many times thoughts tell us not to do something, why we should be afraid, to be satisfied with complacency, and all the reasons why we can't succeed. What if it's actually the physical mind that's holding us back?

When there is a fork in the road, you contemplate which way you should go. You intellectualize the benefits, risks, and goals, but *when* do you stop and intentionally ask your higher self which path is the right one for you? Like never, right? But maybe you should! Who actually knows better than your *Self*, your Soul, what is best and in alignment for you? Our intuition is always trying to steer us in the right direction, but we turn a deaf ear, block out our gut feelings, and ignore the only way our Souls can communicate with our physical forms.

What if you could learn to develop a better way to communicate with your inner self and harness your higher wisdom? First, I want to tell you that you're already intuitive. We all are. Some of us are just more in tune with our inner selves, but we all need to learn to be open, listen, and trust that inner wisdom.

Intuition comes in many forms:

- Have you ever had a feeling that something was going to happen (like a surprise party was being scheduled) or had a sense about something (maybe you knew what was in a letter or package before you opened it)?

- Have you ever had a feeling that you knew someone was lying to you or couldn't be trusted, but you ignored that inner wisdom?
- Have you ever had a bad feeling about something which turned out to be right or had a vision which later proved to be uncannily familiar?
- Have you ever experienced a physical reaction like shivers or goose bumps (God Bumps)?
- Have you ever had dreams, signs, or synchronicities that seemed to indicate just what you needed to hear or experience?

These are all examples of intuition, when you're experiencing an understanding, a "knowing" that has no explanation or foundation in logic. It just occurs; it's simply present.

That Power Within is talking to us all the time, but we have to be open to really listening to the inner voice that calls from within.

How incredible would it be if you could seek counsel from your intuition, your*self*, when there are important decisions to be made, trouble is present, or you just need guidance and support? Why not turn to your best friend for the love, compassion, and wisdom you need?

When you learn how to develop and use your intuition, you will experience:

- Increased confidence
- Improved awareness and foresight
- Increased creativity and intelligence
- Enhanced sensory abilities
- Reduced fear of the unknown
- Greater wisdom from your inner self
- Connection to the higher realm/God/Universe

10 Ways to Follow Your Intuition

Intuition is your Soul's voice guiding you along the way.
Can you hear the message?

Here are ten powerful ways to develop a keen ear that enables you to listen to your inner voice and hear the wisdom that can not only totally transform your life but, even more importantly, steer you toward the path that is for your greatest good. For a printed copy of this exercise, go to www.PowerfulBeyondMeasureBook. com/forms.

1. **Be present in your *Self.***

   Learning to be present within your Self creates a sanctuary of rest, acceptance, and grace. In this space, you are in flow and rhythm; life is balanced, and you are able to enjoy and experience love in all areas of your life. Your ability to *sense* and *connect* is easy because your frequency, your vibration, is in harmony. For some of you, this may seem impossible, but trust me, utopia does exist within your being. You just have to find your way home to the stillness within.

2. **Allow your Self to *sense* (feel) without physicality.**

   To *feel* means to acknowledge. Often we try desperately to ignore our feelings, but that only makes us numb to the experience of sensing or knowing. I spent a lot of time in Part II talking about Emotional Health and having a healthy Range of E-motions; we have to allow ourselves to "feel" in order to understand.

   Our physical bodies have five senses: touch, smell, taste, sight, and hearing. I often refer to *intuition* as our sixth sense because it also provides valuable information to our physical forms. *Five nonphysical senses* feed into that intuition: vision (without sight), wisdom (without hearing), knowing (without thinking), spontaneous action (without conscious volition), and state of peace (where there is no need or want).

Using our intuition and tuning into these five subtle but powerful nonphysical senses can totally transform our decisions, interactions, relationships, decisions, goals, health, and our internal self-care needs.

3. **Look for symbols, synchronicity, déjà vu, and dreams.**

Your Soul is connected to the Universe, and it's capable of powerful things beyond your limited understanding. Your intuition often tries to communicate with you through symbols or signs. You may smell a certain aroma, hear a special song with the exact words of wisdom you need to hear, or see an image (a bird, a tree, a street sign) that holds special meaning for you.

> *"That power in the universe is talking to us all the time."*
> **—Dr. Wayne Dyer**

Synchronicity occurs when events or people come together and connect in an uncanny, unexplained way. I personally feel these are extremely important. It's as if that relationship or exchange is so paramount that the Universe, Souls, and angels create that opportunity. For example, I had a "knowing" that I had to complete the application to be selected by Marci Shimoff, even in the face of 1,600-to-one odds. Intuitively, I already knew that it was divinely created for me and I would be selected.

Déjà vu is slightly different but no less powerful. One example is when you're talking with someone and feel as though you've had the conversation before. The message served both participants and brought you together for your greater good. Déjà vu can also occur around a location: you believe you've been in a certain place before but you know that's impossible, at least in this life time. What could your Soul be trying to show you with this inner knowing?

Dreams can be very powerful and appear quite real. Some believe that as we dream, our spirits leave our bodies and stay tethered to our navels, giving us easier access to the spiritual realm, and that is why dreams can be quite prophetic. Our dreams can present us with clues, but it is more important to connect with our feelings in the dream than the actual physical objects. What one dream means to one individual can be quite different for someone else. Keeping a dream journal by your bedside to record your feelings as soon as you wake up can be very revealing when you contemplate them later.

Margot's Story: A Dream of Hope, Vision, and Love

Margot, a very special client of mine, suffered her whole life with various forms of abuse, along with a variety of serious illnesses. After I had been working with her for a couple of months, she experienced a profound dream one night that really resonated for her.

She recalls that in her dream she woke up to a raucous commotion. Outside, there were construction workers, all dressed in white, tearing up the pavement with jack hammers. White dust glistened on everything around them. Margot noticed that she was standing on a loveseat as she looked out her apartment window, and all the adjacent neighbors' windows had their curtains drawn tight, as if she was closed off to the world.

That dream was an expression of her inner wisdom. Margot analyzed her dream and realized she used the word "loveseat" because she knew she needed to experience love in her heart. The construction workers were angels tearing up the old roads she had traversed, and her new path was being divinely guided. The white glimmering dust from the broken pieces of her path represented all the tears she'd wept, but now the route glistened with hope. The windows with closed curtains were her attempt to shut out the world and protect herself from being hurt once again. From this viewpoint, though, her vision was clear: her future was bright, and she needed to reach out into the world.

I love this story because it represented her Soul offering hope, compassion, forgiveness, and direction. What more could we ever ask for? She knew that her path was divinely guided and that she was protected by angels.

4. **Ask if the knowledge brings growth, opportunity, and is for your greater good.**

   When we receive an intuition, we often want to dissect it, examine it, and pick it apart. Our minds are such eager participants, just wanting to get involved, and they often try to send us in a different direction, but sometimes our inner guidance pushes us into situations that are uncomfortable or difficult, always with a divine reason that serves us and, ultimately, even the others involved.

   Sometimes we need to just trust, accept, and receive those "intuitive hits." If you hear it from your *Self*, leave, and go do it! Don't question it; trust that your wisdom knows what's best. Do you recall the story I shared in the book's introduction about how my intuition told me to go and help my husband, who had just walked out on me, clean our lake house? Talk about trusting and following blind faith! Remember, our struggles bring us one step closer to our success. Avoidance often sends us in the wrong direction.

5. **Meditate, write, draw, sing, and dance! *Create* to allow your inner voice to be expressed and revealed.**

   Creativity is the expression of spirituality in its purest form. Your imagination and heart is the gateway to that expression, so let it run free and see where it takes you. There is an unbounded number of ways to express your Soul's essence. Dancing, singing, writing, drawing, painting, sculpting, or playing an instrument—whatever you're drawn to that lets your creativity flow with ease—are all vehicles for the expression of your Soul 's essence. All those creative forms that we participate in (or appreciate with love) resonate with us in a deep, profound way. What you imagine will eventually be achieved.

   When you can be free within—authentic and vulnerable—your creativity becomes an expression of your divine being. I've spoken about the importance and value of meditation in much greater detail already in this book, and I'll stress it once again: being "still" provides room for that connection to Self and allows you to be more readily available to receive your intuition, so take time each day to connect within (whether though meditation or just quiet self-reflection time), to give thanks, and to be open to receive.

6. **Demonstrate gratitude and appreciation for your relationship with *Self*.**

There is a higher intelligence in the Universe. You have access to it and the power within yourself. That divine intelligence is within each one of us, connecting us back to its original source. There is no separation.

Your divine intelligence will guide you to self-love and the deeper relationship with Self. Express gratitude, appreciate your gifts, and honor your path and divine essence. Understand that you are a beam of light and love, a beautiful part of the master plan. Your intuition will continue to support you on your journey. ·

7. **Test out your intuition on less important decisions.**

It can be fun to test what kind of results you can obtain on less important items. For example, let's imagine that you want to paint your bedroom and you can't decide on the right color. Place the paint samples face down. Move them around so you don't know which colors are where, and move your hand over them, asking your Soul to choose the color that would serve you and your partner as a safe haven that provides restful sleep and quality intimacy. Colors can have a powerful impact on our health and well-being, and asking your higher self may be just the perfect solution. Be clear about your question and what you hope to achieve.

Another simple way to develop and trust your intuition is to pick three objects and place them on a table. Place a blindfold over your eyes and have someone mix the placement of the objects. Without physically touching them, move closer to sense the physicality of the objects and their vibrations. Tune in to your intuition and identify which objects are where on the table. See how accurate your results turn out to be. Practice make perfect. Building trust in calling on your intuition when you need clarity is a very useful tool to rely upon.

8. **Grow to love the wisdom that you openly receive from *Self*.**

When you receive wisdom and guidance through your intuition, stop and recognize the value in that higher knowledge. Don't poo-poo it, discount it, or discredit it. If you do, you're only telling yourself, "I don't trust (myself), I'm not going to listen (to myself), I'm afraid (of myself and others), and unwilling." You're only hurting yourself by not following your intuition.

9. **Accept that your physical life is here for your spiritual growth.**

Your physical body is not really who *you* are, but instead a vessel that allows your spirit to exist in the physical realm. When you take care of your physical body, you're honoring your temple. By the same token, when your Soul is peaceful, your physical being is healthy.

Developing an improved communication with 'Self' is integral in being authentic and true to one's self.

10. **Seek answers from your higher *Self* through energy, pendulum, and body pendulum testing.**

Your Soul really knows all there is to know, and you can even ask questions of it directly in order to find guidance. I teach the following techniques in my class, and to my clients. Although they're much easier to explain in person, I'll do my best to make them as clear as possible here so you can use them effectively, too.

As you trust and explore using your intuition to guide and nurture, you'll come to understand that there really *is* something more than your physical body. Try the following exercises and be amazed at how responsive your body (Soul) is to your questions.

- *Finger Muscle (Energy) Testing:* Some of you may have had experience with physical therapy. First, your muscle strength is tested to determine a baseline, and then those results are used to develop a rehabilitation program that improves your strength. You can use similar muscle (energy) testing to determine if a certain body part holds *strongly* or *breaks*. The resistance that you apply is really checking the energy flow and not the actual muscle strength. Muscle strength doesn't change from moment to moment, but emotional responses and thoughts can impact the energy within your body.

To perform this test, you'll need a partner to help you.

Touch your thumb to your middle finger and maintain an approximately constant pressure. Have your partner place two of his fingers on your middle finger and two fingers from his other hand on your thumb. Verbally ask a yes-or-no question, or just think of one silently. Your partner holds the thumb and middle finger together while he is trying to see if the tension (contact) breaks. If the finger and thumb stay strong and maintain contact, the answer is "yes"; if the digits break apart, the answer is "no." There is a variety of ways to test and reveal energy-tested responses, but this is one the simplest versions you can use.

Always start with a question you know as true: for example, I might ask, "Is my name _____?" When you energy muscle test, the thumb and middle finger should maintain a *hold*. Next, ask yourself a false question, like "Am I one hundred years old?" When you energy muscle test your thumb and middle finger, they will appear *weak* and *break contact*. This signifies a "no" response. If these are reversed, your energies are scrambled and need to first be realigned. See Cook's Crossover, which is included in the forms page on my website at www.PowerfulBeyondMeasureBook.com/forms.

This is just one technique in which you pose a question to yourself that elicits a "yes" or "no" response.

- **Shoulder Muscle Energy Testing** is another way to test the energetic response and flow. You will need an additional person to test the client. First, confirm that client's shoulder that will be tested doesn't have an impediment/condition. Have client extend arm out to the side parallel to the ground. Have client state a positive statement (i.e., my name is ___ fill in the blank ___). As the tester individual applies gentle but firm and constant pressure on the client's wrist; the extended arm should hold firmly. Then have the client state a false statement and retest in the same fashion. The extended arm when gentle pressure is applied should fall down or as we refer to it as 'break', due to the inaccurate response energetically. If the client energetic tests are reversed, their energy flow patterns need to be re-established by using Cook's Crossover. To get directions for Cook's Crossover exercise, go to www.PowerfulBeyondMeasureBook.com/forms.

• *Pendulum Testing* is another tool you can use to test and ask your Soul for guidance and answers to your questions. First, find a pendulum—any object that hangs down freely. You can buy a specific pendulum for this purpose, or you can simply attach a paper clip to a string or use a necklace with a pointed pendant. You first need to program your pendulum by determining what motions will indicate "yes" and "no" responses. Let's say that a "yes" is a vertical, up-and-down motion (as if you're nodding your head) and a "no" is a horizontal or side-to-side motion. Start by hanging the pendulum over your open palm. Create the vertical movement and say, "This is a yes, this is a yes" a few times, then stop the pendulum, switch to the horizontal motion, and say, "This is a no, this is a no." Once you've done this initial programming of the pendulum, you *don't* have to repeat it again or each time you use your pendulum.

Now you're ready to ask your question. It's important to be very clear and ask only a yes-or-no question. Place the pendulum so it is dangling about one or two inches above your palm. Start with the pendulum at rest. Ask your question and wait; the pendulum will start to move in one of those directions. If the pendulum goes into a bizarre motion or moves in a way that's different than the movement you programmed, you may need to rephrase the question in order to obtain a clear answer.

• *Body Pendulum Testing* starts with standing comfortably and confirming that your energy is flowing correctly (north to south) so your responses will be accurate. Always begin by asking a question with a true answer, like "Is my name _____?" and wait. Your body should move, tilting in a forward direction in response to the "yes" answer. Next, test a "no" question: "Do I have one hundred children?" You should feel a backward sway or tilt a bit backwards to indicate a false statement. Once you have confirmed that the "yes" response goes forward and the "no" response has you leaning backwards, you can proceed with your next question.

If your "yes" questions cause you to lean backwards and your "no" questions have you tilting forward, this indicates that your energy flow is *not* north to south and that you need to reestablish normal healthy energy flow. The best way to do this is to use Cook's Crossover, which is included in the forms page on my website at <u>www.PowerfulBeyondMeasureBook.com/forms</u>.

Your feet never move when you pose any of these questions—you just notice a slight leaning forward or backward. For some people, this is very effective, while others have trouble sensing that subtle shift in movement. If you have balance issues, you may prefer to use one of the other methods listed above.

Try it and be amazed at how responsively your body (Soul) responds to your questions!

Your Soul and physical body are not separate entities; they coexist in your lifetime. *You* possess special, unique gifts, and there are infinite possibilities for accomplishment and experience just waiting for you. *You* can impact everything through the *Power* you hold *Within*.

Let your intuition become your loyal companion, one that will always have your back, lead you by the hand to exactly where you need to go, and support your Soul lessons of growth, opportunity, and success.

Soul Messages: Connecting to Intuition

In India, The Art of Living Foundation offers a two-day program that trains eight- to eighteen-year-olds to develop their intuition. Through various exercises, they learn to connect to their physical senses without actually using them. For example, while they are blindfolded, cards are placed in front of them; through intuition, they are able to "see" the colors, "taste" images of food, and draw pictures that match the ones on the cards without ever seeing them with their physical eyes. It's amazing how our intuition, if used and developed, can actually become one of our most powerful senses of all!

I have a powerful intuitive program that provides your Soul with another way to communicate: it's called *Soul Messages: Connecting to Your Intuition* (http://www.CynthiaMazzaferro.com/SoulMessages). With this program, you'll choose an image from a new collage every week that speaks to you. Intuitively, your Soul knows what message you need to hear and directs you to pick the image that speaks to you, revealing your own personal intuitive message that will help you focus on your Soulful lesson for that week. It's very powerful and insightful. In addition, there are monthly "Connect to Your Intuition" calls that allow you to gain greater wisdom about the decisions you struggle with and the direction you're are looking to take.

Your Soul is Powerful Beyond Measure, and that means you are, too!

*"Real happiness isn't based on what we have or achieve in life—
it's a physiological state of lasting inner peace and well-being
that isn't dependent on any conditions in our day-to-day lives."*
—**Marci Shimoff**

Own and Create
YOUR HAPPINESS

Happiness is a place where you choose to live.

Discover the courage and confidence to create everything you desire.

Who doesn't want to be happy? Everyone does, but sometimes when troubles or challenges arise, happiness is elusive and difficult to maintain. There are times when our inner being is unhappy and no matter what we do, happiness is short lived. Often when the state of happiness wears off, we are left feeling even worse than we did before.

We engage in so many activities to try and make ourselves happy—dance, laughter, movies, theatre, music, company, shopping, sex, eating—and reach for solace in things that numb us, like alcohol, drugs, pills, or smoking. But what happens when those activities don't provide the infusion of happiness that we're longing for? We revert back to those feelings of unhappiness—frustration, fatigue, sadness, anger, depression, victimization, and loneliness—with the flood of mental images that go along and support those negative images.

Throughout this book, you've learned so much about the power of your mind. You've started to resolve many of your past memories that prevented your health and happiness. In Part 2, you learned techniques to change how you live in the present moment, and I know that if you have implemented these tools, you're already seeing that shift in your life. How spectacular is that? Trust me, when I say it will only continue to improve!

Happiness is a state of being that you _choose_ to experience.

Now we need to look at how to live in a place of happiness all the time. I know you probably just said to yourself, "That's impossible!" If you did, take note: you just allowed that negative thought and doubt to enter your presence. Don't get me wrong; I'm not saying that every moment of your life is going to be Utopia. What I *am* saying is that you can feel blessed and happy inside no matter what's happening on the outside.

"When you're happy for no reason, it's not that your life always looks perfect—it's just that however it looks, you'll still be happy."
—**Marci Shimoff**

Many people refer to my dear friend Marci (who I spoke about in the introduction to Part III) as "The Happiness Expert." In 2009, she wrote a wonderful book about how to find happiness. *Happy for No Reason: 7 Steps to Being Happy from the Inside Out* explains in detail how true and lasting happiness cannot be dependent on external circumstances and that we make our happiness from the inside out.

You're going to have to go through all of life's ups and downs, no matter what, so why not look at that time from a place of happiness and enjoyment, creating the energy that supports you and your success? The processes, experiences, and outcomes will completely change when you are filled with a sense of happiness.

When your inner *self* is at rest and filled with love, compassion, and forgiveness, happiness is abundantly available to you.

Some folks—and we all know people who fall into this category—are just ornery and find every reason to be unhappy. There are many reasons for this kind of tragically miserable response to life. They may not feel entitled to happiness. They might be pessimistic about their future. Maybe they feel unloved, disconnected, and hopeless, holding on to the only things they know: pain, guilt, and anger. To be honest, this book is the best medicine you could give them: what greater gift could you offer than the chance to open up, heal, and welcome love, joy, and hope into their lives?

Overcoming Fear-based Adversity and Resistance

Happiness can't be achieved if we're living from a place of fear. We've talked a lot about the impact that fear can have in every part of our lives, and it most definitely applies to the search for happiness. I've urged you to step into the unknown and seek the knowledge and success that awaits you. You did that in Part I, when I asked you to examine your past and how it was affecting you and your life. I'm sure many of you were very unsure and even resistant, but you forged ahead. You didn't know what that process was going to open up—the painful memories, emotional hurt, or the results you were going to receive—but you trusted the path. Your intuition guided you along the **Powerful Beyond Measure** process, which has brought you here, envisioning your future to experience it in your Present. Talk about an exciting new beginning!

In the last chapter, I talked about the power of your intuition and listening to the wisdom that is revealed. But what if that inner voice is telling you to go where you're not comfortable? That can be really scary, and don't forget that your brain most likely will tell you to turn and run away. Fear is really just an old feeling raising its ugly head, trying to make you deal with it once again. The fear that you envision is really just your perception. Does it really exist, or is it only a figment of your imagination? What's one to do when fear is part of your life?

Fear is distressing. Negative feelings that you
perceive as a threat might not even be true.

Ask yourself these six simple but thought-provoking questions:

1. What is it that I'm really afraid of, and where is it coming from?
2. Have I seen this same fear before in my life?
3. Is my fear an inability to trust myself and others?
4. Is my (or others') physical safety at risk?
5. What if I stepped forward—what are the possible outcomes?
6. What do I have to lose if I don't try?

Super—now you know what's holding you back! Every struggle, difficulty, and fear is an opportunity for growth. Yeah! That's right, the Universe created this opportunity just for you. How special does that make you feel?

The bigger the challenge, the greater the opportunity for growth, which is success!

Feeling uncomfortable, scared, challenged, unsure ... none of these are reasons not to try. You've tried many things in your past and succeeded at all of them in some way. Look at all your vast knowledge. Even if you feel that it includes bad choices, lousy outcomes, failures to begin, and procrastination, all those experiences add value to this opportunity.

When your world seems like it's falling apart, that's when it's actually falling into place.

Fear: A Family's Soul Lesson

Elsie is a beautiful ten-year-old Mexican girl I met on vacation. She was there with her parents, her sixteen-year-old brother, her grandmother, and her uncle. I watched with amusement as Elsie's uncle tried to teach her fifty-two-year-old mother how to swim. After all of his attempts at instruction, she continued to fail. She moved her arms feverishly, but she couldn't stay afloat, much less propel herself forward. This went on for fifteen or twenty minutes as Elsie, wearing a white, wide-brimmed hat, floated nearby on an inner tube, watching intently but holding tightly to the stair railing. Elsie's brother, Jose, tried to offer support and advice, but nothing seemed to help. Even so, their mother was determined to learn, regardless of how exhausted she was from her many failed attempts.

My older son has always been a fabulous swimmer, and I had taught many children how to swim myself, so I decided to swim over, strike up a conversation, and see if I could offer some advice. I was delighted to be of service. Most people might have just minded their own business without getting involved, but I was being pulled in. There was a strong magnetism, a connection, an intuition that spoke to me, telling me to get involved. I've learned to trust my intuitive feelings even when I have no idea what they will bring.

Jose was the only member of the family who spoke English, so he had to translate everything I said. We worked together as the family watched in amazement. This woman was soon able to float without her buttocks heading south, then progressed to rhythmic freestyle (with her face in the water and reciprocal breathing), and even tried some backstroke. I too was amazed at her willingness and how quickly she learned.

Something drew me to Elsie. Even though she wore swim goggles atop her forehead as she floated on her tube, she never let go of the railing. She didn't smile, and she seemed extremely sad. When I asked if she knew how to swim, she simply replied, "No, I'm too afraid."

The next words out of my mouth were "You know, *fear* is like the *devil*," which Jose translated into Spanish. Their mother, who had joined us by that time, was watching our interaction but remained very quiet. I had no idea where those words came from or the impact they would have. Elsie looked at me and tears started to well in her eyes as her brother continued to translate our words to each other. Elsie said, "I don't want to fear, but I don't know what else to do." I explained to her that fear can be crippling if you allow it to be: "It can hold you stuck, just like you've been holding onto this railing the entire time. When you allow fear to control your life, you rob yourself of all the joy that life can offer."

With gentle reassurance and coaxing, I was able to persuade Elsie down off the tube and into the water while she remained on the stairs. Slowly but surely, she started to let me play with her. I even got her to wear the goggles and have her push off my thighs into her mother's waiting arms. Back and forth we went, and then I told her it was easier to swim underwater than on top. Before we knew it, she was swimming between the two of us underwater. She started to grin and laugh, wanting more. She had an unquenchable thirst—to do more, to learn more—that seemed insatiable. She was so *alive*, full of her child's sense of adventure and wonder at learning something brand new.

We continued to play, and once she realized that she could swim anywhere in that particular pool and stand up any time she felt fatigued, there was no stopping her. I was able to get Elsie to swim underwater everywhere. She was so proud of herself that she even asked to learn how to swim on top of the water, too. She took to it, literally, like a fish to water. The entire family seemed overwhelmed by Elsie's accomplishments. I was delighted that I could help and see such great personal growth for Elsie and her mom. As we parted, I encouraged them both to continue working on their swimming during their vacation. At the time, I had no clue about how significant this seemingly normal rite of passage was for Elsie and her family.

I didn't see Elsie and her family over the remaining week. I wondered how they were doing and was surprised that our paths hadn't crossed, but on the last day of our vacation, as my family and I set up near a remote section of the pool with deeper water, I was shocked to see Elsie and her family across the pool. They all came over, greeting us warmly, and they couldn't wait to show me what they could do. Filled with excitement, mother and daughter got into the pool. Tears filled my eyes as I watched Elsie's mom, wearing swim googles, swim almost forty feet from the edge of the pool. She was using rhythmic breathing without fatigue or interruption! Her strokes were graceful, effective, and effortless. The entire family was overjoyed. Elsie took my hand as Jose translated her message: "Watch me with excitement and a huge smile." She jumped into the water and proceeded to show me how well she could swim—no stairs or railing needed. She proudly showed me how she had mastered underwater breathing; she could hold it the entire length of the pool, and her rhythmic breathing was almost competition-level. Needless to say, I was in awe!

Jose then told me that I had no idea what a gift I had given them. When I asked what he meant, he explained that Elsie had been diagnosed with lupus as a very young child and had led a very sad, quiet life, centered on weekly trips to her doctors. She had very few friends, since she wasn't allowed to participate in many activities with the rest of the children. Jose started to choke up as he described how difficult his life had been, protecting and taking care of Elsie, and how sad he felt about her illness. He was crying by then, saying that his whole life—especially his ambitions for college and a career—would be unfulfilled because he needed to stay home and be with Elsie.

Elsie's mom soon joined us. With Jose's help, she shared her profound sadness about how severely their whole family had been impacted by Elsie's illness. She started to cry uncontrollably, explaining that when she became pregnant late in life (at the age of 42), she had been afraid for her unborn baby's health. She worried that her child would be ill or born with deformities. There were no complications, and she prayed constantly, but she had been intensely worried and fearful throughout the pregnancy. Standing there in the waist-deep water, sobbing with her son, she told me that she blamed herself for Elsie's illness.

So many questions ran through my mind. She had told me about her mental and emotional states of being while she was pregnant; had she lived her whole life filled with fear? Were her own parents fearful of what life had to bring? Was she a timid, scared individual with respect to life in general? Did these repetitive thoughts and behavior patterns continue in all aspects of her current life? Did her fearful feelings during the pregnancy transfer into Elsie's fetal cells), and could this have contributed to her illness? How did the mother's feelings affect the cellular environment which supported growth and development? Did the mother see herself in her daughter?

The outpouring of pain Elsie's mother shared was heart-wrenching, and we all embraced each other and wept together. Their entire family had lived every day in a state of constant belief that Elsie was sickly and that they needed to protect her to prevent the disease from getting worse. She hadn't been allowed to do anything, nor did she have the energy or desire. The combination of pain, guilt, and fear they all shared was a disease in itself.

Elsie's mother went on to tell me that she had found her daughter's private, tear-stained diary one day. It described in great detail the extreme sadness and hopelessness Elsie felt. Her mother struggled to find even one positive statement on those pages. How did this precious little girl learn to be so sad?

I beckoned Elsie over and asked Jose to translate the messages that came from deep within me. I asked Elsie what her happiness and energy levels were on a regular day before meeting me. She replied that her happiness level was very low (one or two), and her energy level was zero to one. I then asked her, "When you were learning to swim all week with your mom, how did you feel?" She answered that she had never felt tired, and could she pick a bigger number than ten because she was so happy? She pulled my head down close so I could hear and whispered, "*No fear anymore.*" Tears filled my eyes as Elsie just beamed at me. Anyone could see that she had been given the greatest gift: freedom and joy through living without fear.

So, a few simple swimming lessons ended up being a miraculous event for an entire family. Those seven short days literally changed every aspect of that family's life, individually and as a unit. I would have never guessed that my life would have been impacted so greatly—and I certainly wouldn't have predicted the kind of transformation Elsie's family experienced—by simply reaching out to teach someone to swim. I know that my intuition guided me over to them, and I was so happy that I had followed my inner voice.

This story has so many precious jewels of wisdom. Quite possibly, the most miraculous thing that occurred during that week was the family members' realization of the Soul Lesson they *all* needed to learn: to not allow *fear* to hold you back from living a life filled with joy, opportunities, and happiness.

Note: this story is lovingly dedicated to Elsie's mother, who was brave enough to overcome her fear of water (even at the age of fifty-two) and learn to swim. That single act of courage and desire became the catalyst that allowed Elsie to stop drowning in pain and sadness and take hold of the life preserver that's offered to each of us: life, health, and happiness.)

"Courage is resistance to fear, mastery of fear, not absence of fear."
—Mark Twain

With courage and confidence, you can defeat any foe, even (or especially) the ones that live within you. They're not exactly the same thing, but they're both necessary if we want to face our fears and the internal resistance they create. Courage means having the mental strength to keep moving forward even when you're unsure of the end results, while confidence is a "feeling," a "knowing" that you can reach your desired endpoint with favorable results. Can you see the subtle difference between these two words? One is not results oriented, while the other is rooted in the belief that something is attainable.

Courage is the mental or moral strength to venture out—to stand up against danger, fear, or difficulty. It is the ability to resist and meet opposition and hardship head-on in the pursuit of your goals. If you want to display courage in your life, you'll need willpower, desire, vision, belief, knowledge, strength, support, and confidence.

Courage truly comes down to believing in one's self. It really is that simple. No matter how many times someone says you can't (even if that person is you), the day you believe you can is the day you win the race.

Courage comes when you <u>stop</u> saying "I can't" and replace it with "I <u>can!</u>"

If you feel a lack of courage when it comes to reaching for your dreams, aspirations, and passions, then start the process with this affirmation:

I *am* Powerful Beyond Measure, and I *do* have the *courage* to move forward with _____**(write goal)**_____ _____ **and succeed!**

Confidence is a *feeling* or *belief* that you can do something well or succeed. It is having conviction, belief, trust and faith that a positive result will occur. There is a *knowing* that success or completion is achievable. Maybe it is your intuition speaking from within, but you believe that you can!

Since confidence comes from within and we had it when we were born, it's just a matter of finding it once again. If you *feel* you lack confidence use this affirmation to start the process of *believing*.

I *am* Powerful Beyond Measure, and I *do* have the *confidence* to move forward with _____goal_____ _____ and succeed!

Repeat these affirmations to yourself over and over again. You may not feel a huge increase in your courage and confidence after the first, or the tenth, or even the hundredth time you say them—that's your fear and resistance standing in the way. Don't give up! Be sure to recognize and give yourself kudos every time you take a tiny step out of your comfort zone. Every new chance you take, no matter how small, is evidence that you *can* build your courage and confidence.

You *will* feel more courageous. You *will* feel more confident. You *will* succeed!

We're going to be talking about success in a lot more detail later, but for now, let's focus on understanding how you can move forward with any project you want to take on, even when fear is present.

Strategic Happiness Intervention Tactic (S-H-I-T)

In addition to the fear-busting tools and techniques I shared in Part II, I'd like to offer you a simple but powerful strategy that can be used at any time and with any event that comes your way. It's all about acknowledging your apprehension but not allowing the resistance and fear to immobilize you. Focus on the outcome, the prize: the reward may come from simply trying, even if you don't ultimately reach your desired end point. In fact, you may even find that the prize you *think* you want is not really the most valuable reward at all.

When life presents you with situations that are demanding and difficult, you need to realize that you can handle *everything*. You've made it this far, right? It's about how you want to participate in your life. Remember how *powerful* you are: **Powerful Beyond Measure**! When life is challenging and scary—when you've been handed a pile of crap (aka shit), how can you move on and stay positive and happy, with a victor's mentality? The Strategic Happiness Intervention Tactic (S-H-I-T) is a tool that will help you reduce the stressors that you *believe* you

are experiencing in your life. For a printed copy of this exercise, go to www.
PowerfulBeyondMeasureBook.com/forms.

There are only two required steps to Strategic Happiness Intervention Tactic
(S-H-I-T):

1. Take a moment and **breathe out.** This is *very* important.

    The **outward** breath allows an exit for the *negative emotional energy*
    (fear, apprehension, sadness, etc.) that you were/are carrying about this
    experience. You're an expert now, and you know the importance of
    giving your emotions a way to be released.

2. Say the following:

    I am Powerful Beyond Measure, and **I can handle** ____, ____,
    ____, and ____ while filled with happiness, joy, and hope.

    Just stating this single, powerful phrase sets your intention on having
    everything you need, enjoying the experience, and being successful.
    What more could you want? You are strong, capable, and resourceful,
    and you can experience life with a positive, supportive, and loving mind
    and emotional framework.

Following Your Passion

"Believe it can be done. When you believe
something can be done, really believe,
your mind will find the ways to do it.
Believing in a solution paves the way to a solution."
—**David J. Schwartz**

Do you have a dream? A goal? A secret wish you'd love to fulfill? We all do. Passions
and desires are living energies that stir from within. Creating and believing in
your passion generates your perfectly-resonant harmonic vibration—the one
that's in tune with your inner- voice.

When you don't pay attention to your dreams (or even worse, ignore them),
you're telling yourself that you don't count, your dreams are unattainable, and

it's easier to be an observer than an active participant in your life. If you have found yourself feeling frustrated, unhappy, dissatisfied, and trapped, it's most likely because you're not being true to yourself and following your inner calling.

On April 3, 1968, Dr. Martin Luther King, Jr. gave his timeless "I've Been to the Mountaintop" speech in Memphis, Tennessee. The next day he was gone, taken from the earthly plane by an assassin's bullet.

Well, I don't know what will happen now. We've got some difficult days ahead. But it really doesn't matter with me now, because I've been to the mountaintop. And I don't mind. Like anybody, I would like to live a long life; longevity has its place. But I'm not concerned about that now. I just want to do God's will. And He's allowed me to go up to the mountain. And I've looked over. And I've seen the Promised Land. I may not get there with you. But I want you to know tonight, that we, as a people, will get to the Promised Land. So I'm happy, tonight. I'm not worried about anything. I'm not fearing any man. *Mine eyes have seen the glory of the coming of the Lord.*

Dr. King knew his life was in danger everywhere he went, but instead of giving in to fear, he rose up and faced it with courage and confidence. He was born to make a difference in our world, to bring the plight of a brutally oppressed people to the attention of a larger national and international audience. His fight for justice and love among all was a stirring that came from the depths of his Soul. He had a choice—free will. No one would have blamed him if he decided to put his safety first, but the voice within him was too strong. Where would we be now if Dr. King hadn't chosen to follow his inner guidance?

You, too, have something that stirs within you. Your gifts and your purpose are no less important.

Even though I had a burning passion and desire to write this book, it wasn't always easy. I had many days and months when fear and doubt were my constant companions. I devalued what my words would mean and minimized the impact they would have on people's lives, but when I stepped into true understanding,

I began to trust my inner voice. It woke me up on many nights with words that just seemed to flow through me onto these pages. I'm tempted to say that I have no idea where they came from, but that's not true. It came from my inner knowing: I *knew* this was my path, my purpose. I couldn't hide and remain small any longer. My entire life's journey was in preparation and training for this gift from above. I am humbled and see myself only as the scribe, recording the words the Creator wants me to write.

Once I accepted this inner calling, I was open to seeing the opportunities that presented themselves in abundance. Everything—and I mean *everything*—miraculously unfolded in front of me. This book was originally going to be called The Power Within, but the title morphed into something even *beyond* my capacity to see.

Dr. Wayne Dyer spoke quite eloquently on the importance of following your path and purpose: "… each Soul is driven by his or her own dharma. This dharma, or purpose for life, drives us to uphold our unique individuality." The more aware you are of your uniqueness and individuality, the closer you are to Source.

What is your *Dream, Goal,* and *Passion?*

Dreams, goals, and passions come in all shapes and sizes. Every one of them is precious, a part of our legacy of love that contributes to the greater good. I know with every fiber of my being that you have something very special that you're supposed to do. Ask yourself, "What is my deepest desire—the fire that burns within my Soul?" Listen, be observant, and pay close attention to the answers that appear. This is such an exciting time for you!

With all the personal work you've accomplished thus far, I know you've identified areas that you're already working on. Maybe your goals deal with personal development: forgiveness, compassion, self-love, inner peace, authenticity, confidence, strength, courage, faith, and trust. Others might be honesty, empathy, philanthropy, anger elimination, positivity and optimism, happiness, joy, and health.

Then there are goals that involve accomplishing tasks and following a dream, vision, or purpose. They could range from minimal tasks to larger endeavors: finishing a degree, seeking career opportunities, engaging in humanitarian work, expressing yourself creatively and artistically, starting a business, finding a life partner, and traveling are just a few examples of the infinite variety of choices you have available to you.

Goals take many forms, and all of them are important. If you're saying you're too old or asking yourself why you should bother, you're only making excuses for the failure to satisfy what stirs within. Trust me; the longer you live dissatisfied, the unhappier you will be, so what are your goals or desires?

Goal Creation
List five things you would love to create in your life:
1.
2.
3.
4.
5.
Now ask yourself the following questions:
1. "What's holding me back from achieving my goals?"
2. "What must I do to get from where I am now to where I want to be?"
3. "Am I willing to step into the unknown, follow my heart, and listen to my inner voice?"

> *"It's easy to make goals for yourself—*
> *and it's even easier to forget about them*
> *or give up when the going gets rough."*
> **—Jack Canfield**

Don't be the one who contracts and becomes small, dissatisfied, and unhappy. Be willing to work hard and create the energy that supports your vision.

Your Gift to the World is Living your Purpose!

Chris Attwood and Janet Bray Attwood are among the many good friends I've made on my journey. Together, they wrote the best-selling book, *The Passion Test—the Effortless Path to Discovering Your Life Purpose*, which helps you to discover and really begin to live your passions. I strongly encourage you to read their book if you're struggling to find your inner fire that stirs from within.

Believing is the missing link to achieving.

For every goal we take on, there is a time when we need to give it our **in**tention, **at**tention, and **no**-tension. As we know from the *Law of Attraction* (LOA), what and where you place your attention and energy on, whether positive or negative, is what you'll attract into your life.

Here are three steps toward mastering the LOA to become happier, healthier, and more abundant in your life.

1. **Set Your Intention**—be clear about what you want.

    Clarifying what you want to create is so very important. Be careful with your word choice, why you want it, and use positive words. For example, if I just said, "I want a new job," then I shouldn't be surprised if I get fired or laid off, forcing me to find another job that I may or may not be happy with. Instead, using a more precise statement like this is more likely to reflect what you really want: "I am delighted to secure a new job that brings me great happiness, increased responsibility, and financial security so that my family is well supported and our children can attend college."

    Notice how the last statement clearly states that you have secured the job, but it didn't indicate what it would be. It allows the Universe to direct the best scenario for you that will help you find happiness, success, and the financial freedom to support your family. You didn't say, "I want to find a job that pays $500,000." That statement may only serve you. Our goals become more powerful when they serve both us *and* the greater good.

2. **Focus Your Attention**—take steps that support your stated intention.

    By placing your *attention* on your *intention*, you lovingly believe that this goal will be for your greater good and see it benefiting others as well. It is very important that you don't allow your mind to focus on anticipated problems or resistance, because that creates an energy that supports additional conflict. Envision ease and perfect timing that brings the best results.

    Often people become impatient; you may feel that your intention will not appear when it doesn't happen in *your* time. Your timing is not necessarily the best timing, and it can often yield poor results. Believing and trusting that everything comes together exactly as it's supposed to is the best thing you can do.

    That doesn't mean that you're not going to be active in the attention stage. You most definitely will be. Using our example, looking within your current company to see if there are other opportunities, refining your resume, and searching for new job opportunities are just a few of the things you can do to take action steps and giving *attention* to your *intention*.

3. **Resting with No-Tension**—release the tension and allow the Universe to create.

    During this phase, it's about letting go, giving your dream—your intention—to the Universe and allowing its birth to come to be. Sometimes we struggle with being patient and forget to enjoy this time of creation. You can't rush a masterpiece.

    Sometimes it's during this quiet period when you need to do additional goal setting to prepare for your intention. Everything happens in divine timing, and if we can keep our thoughts and feelings positive, believe that all is exactly as it should be, and remain grateful for all that is, the Universe responds in infinite, magnificent ways that are beyond our comprehension.

    Continuing with our example, say you've applied to five jobs, taken additional training that provides greater value, and had three interviews. Now you have to wait. See the perfect job in your mind. How would it feel? What would change? Envision all that you hope this new opportunity will present and realize that, in divine timing, the right situation will be made present.

Why don't you give it a try?

Set your intention:

Focus your attention: (<u>steps to take</u>)
- <u>Set a timetable</u> for each step that you want to take.
- <u>Carry out your attention</u> for your intention.
- <u>Believe</u>, <u>envision</u>, and "<u>know</u>" that it's so.

Rest and give no-tension
Rest and continue to believe, listen, and follow your inner voice.

Affirmations are powerful statements that support what you want to manifest or create.
- To formulate an affirmation, you want to declare in a statement what it is that you want.
- Often the sentence will start with "I am …"
- Write the statement in the present tense, as if it is occurring now. Do not use the word "will."
- Do not use "no," "can't," "never," or any negative words like pain, anger, fear, cancer, or alone.
- Incorporate how this creation will serve a greater good—not to benefit the Ego.
- Use words that reflect your passion and are true to you.
- Do not be so specific that you restrict or dictate how it comes about.
- Express gratitude in your affirmations to supercharge them.

Here are a few examples:

- I am grateful for all the new friends who have entered my life and the joy we bring each other.
- I am happy volunteering, and I enjoy spreading joy to others in need.
- I am attending the perfect college to study the ideal curriculum that best supports my gifts, passion, and purpose in life.

One additional aspect that I believe is critical to helping affirmations become reality is that they have to be in agreement with what you believe can occur. If you think one way but your words are in opposition to your thoughts, there will be unrest, because the vibration and energy aren't in harmony with each other. For example, you could say, "I am an astronaut." Although you might love this goal, in your mind the truth is that it's unrealistic because you never finished high school, much less college. Make sure your thoughts agree with what you are sending out into the Universe.

Sometimes you need to write an affirmation to change your thoughts. Here's a great example: "I am confident and strong, and I enjoy stepping up to help others thrive." By working on being confident, strong, and joyful in stepping in to help others, you're building your own confidence and courage so you, too, can use it for your own goals.

"When I was a child my mother said to me,
'If you become a soldier, you'll be a general.
If you become a monk, you'll be the pope.'
Instead I became a painter and wound up as Picasso."
—Pablo Picasso

Now it's your turn.

Take the goals that you wrote above and create an affirmation statement that is in support of your vision.

1.

2.

3.

4.

5.

Super! You've just taken a very powerful step in fulfilling your passion that is rising to the surface, and you're honoring that wisdom and embracing this fabulous journey that's about to unfold.

"Love life and life will love you, love yourself and you shall feel loved."
—**Siân Lavinia Anaïs Valeriana** (The Raveness)

The emotional pain we carry is the cause of the pain we live.

WELLNESS AND HEALTH
Vitality and happiness are waiting for you!

Discover techniques to positively impact your health and well-being.

I strongly believe that wellness incorporates the four pillars of health and wealth that I spoke about earlier: body, mind, emotions, and spirit. Understand and appreciate that everything you do, think, feel, and believe has an impact on your state of wellness and health. When we speak about wellness, we usually think more holistically; when we think of health, we focus our attention primarily on our physicality. I believe most, if not all, of our physical health has a direct relationship to our wellness as a whole. You can't separate one aspect from the other.

Wellness is a positive approach to living—an approach that emphasizes the whole person.

- **The National Wellness Institute** defines wellness as "an active process of becoming aware of and making choices toward a more successful

194

existence." The most important words to focus on are process, aware, choices, and success.

- **The World Health Organization's (WHO)** definition of health is "a state of complete physical, mental, and social well-being, and not merely the absence of disease or infirmity."

- **The Alliance Institute for Integrative Medicine** views wellness as "much more than just a state of physical health. It also encompasses emotional stability, clear thinking, the ability to love, to create, embrace change, exercise intuition, and experience a continuing sense of spirituality."

I particularly love that last definition because it incorporates living aspects in to the formula to produce wellness. It includes the ability to change and love, and even includes intuition and spirituality as part of the spirit pillar.

Throughout this book, you have been asked to explore, examine, and enlighten yourself regarding all these areas, and you've learned the importance of resolution, forgiveness, and positivity. Wellness can never be experienced if you live a life of anger, regret, fear, guilt, blame, and restlessness, continuing to hold on to the emotional pain and mental thoughts that no longer serve you well.

There has never been a greater movement toward improving our quality of life, health, and wellness than what we see today. Wellness research confirms that Americans who manage their lifestyles successfully and reduce their stress are healthier, more productive, and have a reduced need for medical services. *The Journal of the American Medical Association* reported the results of one study in which subjects participated in a year-long self-care education program: there was "a 17 percent decline in total medical visits and a 35 percent decline in medical visits for minor illness."

I have reinforced the importance of taking responsibility and ownership, for your life, happiness, activity, creation—everything that impacts *you*! You are the creator of your wellness. Wellness is closely associated not only with lifestyle choices like nutrition, exercise, self-care, proper weight control, sleep, and eliminating alcohol, smoking and drug usage; it also greatly involves our emotional and spiritual well-being.

The choices we make have a significant, pivotal impact on our wellness and health. Traditional medicine focuses on alleviating, managing, or curing disease, while wellness focuses on a proactive, preventative approach to creating a state of harmony and happiness in all areas of your life. Truth be told, when we are happier and at peace, our lives are abundantly filled.

In this chapter, I want to provide you with multiple resources and techniques that you can use that will impact all areas, using different modalities that can bring about powerful results. It is my hope to help you see even more clearly the connection between the mind-body-emotions-symptoms and what you can do to resolve, release, rehabilitate and restore.

> *"You're only just a thought away from changing your life."*
> —**Dr. Wayne Dyer**

The Power of Visualization

The legendary spiritual teacher Esther Hicks said, "Seventeen seconds of focused, pleasurable visualization is stronger than two thousand hours of working to obtain a goal." Wow, talk about time efficiency and effectiveness! Do you feel Powerful Beyond Measure to realize that you hold this kind of power to create and manifest your simplest thoughts? Throughout this book, I have tried to reinforce this concept, but let's go even a bit deeper.

Do you remember Dr. Bruce Lipton, the scientist who worked with stem cells to show that, by changing the environment, new types of cells could be created? He has spoken about his strong belief that it is our subconscious mind that ultimately influences how much success, abundance, health, happiness, and freedom we experience in our lives.

When we create our goals, it's typically on a conscious level. For example, I want to lose ten pounds over the next three months. Consciously, in this moment, I created this goal that I would like to achieve. Now, many of you may or may not have had a similar goal with varying results. What makes one successful? Allowing our goals to remain at the conscious level actually impedes and impacts our success. When we function primarily from our conscious mind, we are actually using only 1–5 percent of our potential.

It is our subconscious mind that reminds our consciousness of all the reasons our goal is unattainable and unworthy; this places negative energy within that specific goal. With *creative visualization*, which occurs in our subconscious, we can raise the vibration, changing and positively reprogramming the blueprint from our past that says we cannot achieve.

The powerful technique of creative visualization has been around for centuries, but today we have evidence that shows remarkable results. Celebrities, athletes, and leaders share openly how they use creative visualization to produce the vision they want to achieve. For instance, a baseball player stepping up to the plate may point to the outfield, envision hitting a home run, and say in his mind, "Watch where this is going." He planted the seed in his subconscious mind; he could see the ball flying through the air and landing in the bleachers.

One of my sons, Dan, was a competitive diver at a very high level. He represented the United States in international competitions, and he was a participant at the 2008 Olympic trials. While he trained at Auburn University with a multinational championship swim and dive team, creative visualization was a huge part of creating the subconscious belief that you could envision and create the energy that supports the results you want to achieve.

Dan holds many SEC titles in springboard and platform diving, and he missed advancing to the final Olympic selection process by the narrowest margin: .04. That computes to less than .5 points being awarded by just *one* judge over the entire list of dives. As crushed as he was at the moment when he didn't advance, looking back, his career and passion were really in another direction, and he is thriving and pursuing his destiny with great ambition and success. I often counsel people to be careful how we define success because the end result we think we want—the grand prize—may not in fact be the greatest treasure.

As you use creative visualization to intensify and strengthen your goals, remember that the Universe/Creator may have other plans that are for your greater good.

Are you ready to visually create your goals and bring them to life?

Choose one of your goals from the last chapter and sit in reverent silence, visually creating what that goal would look like. See how it would impact your life, your facial expressions and how you would respond to it, the way you and others would view yourself. Visually create even how you see or hear the goal being accomplished. Remember, you are the creator of your dreams.

> *The <u>power</u> of our minds is beyond our imagination.*
> *There is no way we could ever know our capabilities,*
> *because they are limitless.*

Energy and Healing

Let's shift and move on to our next modalities that have an energetic connection and influence.

There are many different names for energy, including Ch'i (from China), Prana (from India), astral light (from the Jewish faith), and the energetic pathways called meridians.

You've seen me write of the mind–body connection. As disease and imbalances occur within our biology and energy, they may show up as a result of *unresolved emotional issues*. Our bodies have many energetic pathways that exist between the cells, organs, and tissues. Our emotions can impact our energies and symptomatically appear in one or more body parts. I have found that the longer our emotional pain exists, the more impaired our energy can become, which can increase the intensity of our symptoms or conditions. Until we address the root causes, the symptoms may increase, wax and wane, or become a more serious illness.

The various techniques that I describe below are **not intended to replace traditional medical treatment**; they may be used as an adjunct, complementary form of intervention. If you notice that your symptoms are improving, consult with your medical professionals and allow them to make the necessary adjustments in your treatment protocol.

Where your symptom is located can help you determine
what and/or who may be the root cause or underlying problem.

For example, if you are experiencing a symptom in the upper half of your body on the right and the lower half of your body on the left, this usually represents a male figure (past or present) or a dominant persona (which could be female). If your symptom is in the upper half of your body on the left or the bottom half of your body on the right, it is likely referencing a woman (past or present) or a feminine/passive/nurturing persona (which could be male). The area in the pelvis where the energies cross may be either male or female, depending on the case. The best advice is to trust your intuition.

Physical, Mental, and Emotional Pain

I've created two charts for you below. The first one describes areas of the body and what symptoms in those areas tend to represent. Use it to help identify possible connections between different parts of your body and what they could mean, energetically and emotionally, to you. This chart is **not to be used as a diagnostic tool**, but one that may give you greater insight into your truth. For personal guidance, exploration and intervention, you can contact me through my website at www.PowerfulBeyondMeasureBook.com/contact or email me at info@CynthiaMazzaferro.com.

Location of Symptom	Possible Root Causes
Head	Difficult, traumatic birth; too much confusion; fear; stubborn; not seeing or trusting your feelings
Neck	Fear of flexibility or expressing your side; stubborn; unwilling to turn and look the other way
Ear	Turning a deaf ear; not wanting to hear; unable to listen to the truths or untruths; not being able to hear a higher source

Eyes	Turning a blind eye; not wanting to see (too painful)
Mouth	Sexual shame; unsupported; not valued
Throat	Not speaking up or telling the truth; devaluing yourself, your voice, and your emotions
Jawline	Anger/pride; clenched teeth; repressed frustration; unresolved stress
Shoulder	Carry the world on your shoulders; fear of giving up or holding on to responsibilities; everything is viewed as a burden and your responsibility; unable to lighten your load; may consider yourself not valued
Arm	Need to be loved/hugged/supported. Left arm: receiving support is needed; right arm: our offering to the world.
Elbows	Fear of changing directions or new opportunities; can represent carrying a great weight; not feeling safe
Wrists	Fear of dexterity (e.g., moving and changing with ease); a difficult, trapped, situation; sexual shame; unable to grasp what you needed as a child
Thumb	Stress; worry; tension; needing support
Index finger	Pointing blame and criticism at self and others; fear; frustration
Middle finger	Anger; indecision; lack of caring (e.g., "F*** you"; irritability; fatigue
Fourth finger	Relationships; grief; sadness; rejection; negativity
Pinkie finger	Trying very hard; unhappy; feeling unseen, small
Palm	Not able to hold on; feeling unloved; lacking nourishment
Spine	Represents the support and structure of your life

Neck	Inability to see the total view; left can be about the past, right can be about the future
Upper spine	Fear of being unloved; lacking emotional support; unable to let go; feeling stabbed in the back, betrayed
Middle spine	Fear of guilt; unable to get others off your back; taking on ownership of others' problems; the need to protect self; not feeling safe with your power
Lower spine	Fear of money problems; financial security; feeling unsupported; abandonment by parent or loved one; worry and fear
Chest	Too much pressure; heavy weight or burden; parents or family could have struggled
Lungs	Feeling like you can't catch your breath; the life is getting sucked out of you; ability to breathe (freedom) and sustain life; feeling trapped; bullied or ridiculed by others or life.
Heart	Not listening to your heart/emotions; too painful to feel; pressure in life; rejection; timing in life is amuck
Solar plexus	Loss of power; unsafe; afraid to have power; feeling disempowered or overpowered by others
Buttocks	Lack of humility; birth trauma; sexual hurts; bullying; falling on your butt (embarrassment)
Hips	Anger; fear of moving forward with major decision or having no goals or passions to pursue; sexual trauma; stubbornness; birth trauma
Knees	Fear of giving in, having to bend; defending Ego; afraid to go forward with relationships/projects/career; stagnation; life isn't safe or just

Calves	Loss of bounce in your step; lack of enthusiasm and zest for life and moving forward
Ankles	Fear of flexibility and forgiveness; restricted ability to receive pleasure and love; disconnected; feeling misunderstood; relationships with children; abortion
Spleen	Vulnerability; rupture in life; separation
Rectum	Holding on to fear; trauma; sexual shame
Sinuses	Anger; frustration; grief; expression; powerless
Kidney	Difficulty with filtering, remaining balanced, and in the flow
Bladder	Unsupported; out of control; a form of crying; letting go

Next, let's examine some specific common symptoms and their potential causes. If you're experiencing symptoms, consider whether the related topics resonate with you on a personal level. If they do, I recommend trying some of the alternative healing techniques in the remainder of the chapter to see if you're able to affect your symptoms.

Symptom/Illness	Possible Connections
Arthritis	Meeting against resistance/blocked; butting heads; feeling unloved, unappreciated; criticized/judged/cannot do it right; anger
Loss of Balance, vertigo	Feeling scattered, mentally or physically; disorganized; lack of feeling centered and in balance
Joint pains	Represents changes in life and the degree to which you handle them
Back pain	Feeling unsupported; ready to crumble; financial difficulties; unable to handle events/life

Stiffness:	Being rigid in thoughts and behaviors; unable to bend or work with others effectively
Bursitis	Inflammation of a situation; carrying repressed anger
Bunions	Fear of experiencing joy; feeling unworthy
Weakness and fatigue	Need to rest, mentally and physically
Inflammation	Fear based; scared; thoughts are rampant; very negative; sees no solution; hot-headed
Sprains	Anger and resistance; avoiding certain actions
Fibromyalgia	Pins and needles; agitation; unrest; past traumas; trapped; unresolved emotional stress
Digestion issues	Unloving towards self; anger; resentment
Cancer	Unresolved anger; poisonous emotions; thoughts about individuals/events; avoidance of transparency
Heart issues	Unresolved emotional pain; takes on everyone's emotional pain and may see self as a victim
Sexual or reproductive issues	Sexuality issues; belonging; broken or difficult family ties; afraid of the future; afraid of birth and new life; sexual trauma; incest; rape; religious oppression
Migraines	Sexual frustrations; suppressed feelings
Eczema	Embarrassment; doesn't want to be seen; decreased self-esteem and self-worth

Alternative Forms of Healing

There are many other alternative forms of treatment available to us to relieve and address our symptoms. Homeopathic physicians take a holistic view, including aspects like diet and environment. Acupuncture works with meridians and energy flow as well.

Donna Eden, author of *Energy* Medicine, is one of the pioneers working with energy. Much of her work is focused on meridians, chakras, radiant circuits, and how to improve the flow of energy within the body and your aura, the energetic field that surrounds you. The author of eight books, Donna teaches, trains, and speaks all over the world. I've had the privilege to attend and learn from her, and I was in awe when I first saw what she accomplished on stage. The results were simply amazing: in many cases, the symptoms that audience members presented were gone in just minutes. I have incorporated many of her techniques in my classes and with my clients.

Now let's take a look at some other alternative therapies that you may find incredibly helpful on your journey toward becoming Powerful Beyond Measure.

Jin Shin Jyutsu

Jin Shin Jyutsu is a simple touch therapy that anyone can do to themselves or others to boost your energy and balance your emotions and energy through stimulating the meridians in your hand. With this therapeutic art form of energetic intervention (which is consistently used at the University of Kentucky's Markley Cancer Center, with astounding results), tension is released by simply holding on to the finger(s) for three to five minutes to relieve the various symptoms in the body and the emotional energetic component.

When a baby cries and is fretful or worrying, the most natural thing he or she does is to suck on their thumb. Instinctively, the baby knows exactly how to reduce the tensions and improve their energy flow. Some infants may even choose to suck on their index or middle finger to release their frustration or anger.

If you're an adult and worrying about an upcoming exam, procedure, or presentation, holding each of your thumbs for three to five minutes may reduce or minimize your worry. To summarize: the thumb represents stress, worry, tension, stomach, and spleen; the index finger represents fear, self-criticism, kidney, bladder, digestion, and back; the middle finger is associated with anger, frustration, indecision, fatigue, liver, eyes, and gallbladder; the ring finger represents sadness, grief, relationship, rejection, negativity, lungs, skin conditions, tinnitus, and large intestines; the pinkie deals with low self-esteem, trying too hard, nervousness, heart, throat, and small intestines; and the palm nourishes everything.

Reiki

Reiki, a balancing, Universal form of energy healing that has been around for hundreds of years, helps to address emotional, mental, spiritual, and physical symptoms. It was introduced to the Western world by a Japanese Reiki Master, Hawayo Takata, when she brought this beautiful, powerful healing art form to Hawaii.

Reiki is a relaxing, natural healing treatment during which vibrations are transmitted through the hands of a Reiki practitioner, who acts as a conduit for transmitting energy to the body of the recipient. Almost all cancer and military hospitals offer Reiki to their patients in addition to their other treatment protocols. The benefits of Reiki include stress and pain reduction, increased relaxation and energy flow within the body, removal of blocks (emotional or others), and accelerated natural healing.

The harmonizing, peaceful, balancing energy has an intelligence that knows where to flow and what to address. Reiki can be delivered in person, or it can also be administered over distance and time. Reiki can address issues that occurred many years ago and even during past lives. Time is not a deterrent or a limitation with Reiki.

I have achieved Master level status in the practice of Reiki, and I appreciate the lineage of this beautiful and powerful healing system. I trained with Reiki Master Lourdes Gray, whose husband, John Gray, was one of the four original masters trained and certified by Takata. As a Reiki Master, I have the privilege of working with hundreds of individuals, with amazing results.

One of my clients who will remain in my heart forever is a woman (let's call her M.S.) who had suffered with fibromyalgia for more than forty years. Her pain level was significant (eight to ten on the ten-point scale) throughout her entire day. Over the years, M.S. had been to the best hospitals and seen medical experts, but she had never been able to discover the cause of her fibromyalgia or find any form of pain relief. The pain was debilitating and limited her in every aspect of her life. I first met M.S. when she was attending my ten-week class and making some progress with healing past emotional wounds that stemmed around fear, sexual abuse, and the feeling of being unloved.

I invited M.S. for a complimentary Reiki treatment, and after just one session, her fibromyalgia pain completely disappeared. She still had other pain in her neck and lower back, but the pins-and-needles, achy, throbbing pain throughout her extremities was completely gone. When she got off the table, she said that the whole room looked bright, sparkly, filled with an energy of light and love. Something special had definitely occurred. Ironically, she had a regularly scheduled doctor appointment the following week, and she couldn't wait to tell him the good news. Her doctor was amazed and thrilled about her pain relief and encouraged her to continue with Reiki and the personal work she was doing.

If you would like to explore and learn more about Reiki, visit www.cynthiamazzaferro.com/energy-healing/reiki-master; to schedule a session with Cindy, please visit www.cynthiamazzaferro.com/store and pick the best package for you. Reiki can be delivered remotely all over the world; time and distance are no obstacles.

Tapping

Tapping is one of the simplest techniques you can use for self-healing. Give it a try—it's super easy, and you can even do it on a daily basis.

Before you try some tapping to improve your energy flow, pay close attention to how you're feeling. Identify your symptom and location, and assign a number to indicate your level of discomfort. Write that down as your base line.

Tap on the various locations listed below and see which one improves your symptoms. Keep a record to help you identify which one is best for you to continue with. Wait a few minutes in between each location and tapping cycle to get a clear understanding of your results.

Below are just a few points that you can tap on that affect your meridians and improve your energy flow.

- Use both hands if there is a right and left location; use one hand if it's a central location
- Tap five to ten times (approximately five to fifteen seconds, or as long as you feel is necessary) at each of these locations:
  a. Top of your Head—Crown Meridian/Bladder Meridian
  b. At your temples—Triple Warmer and Gallbladder Meridian
  c. Under your eyes—Stomach Meridian
  d. Above your lip—Governing Meridian
  e. Below your lip—Central Meridian
  f. One to two inches below your collar bones (each side of where a necklace would typically fall)—Kidney Meridian, point #27
  g. Mid-sternum (between your breasts)—you're tapping on the Thymus Gland
  h. Start at the side of your body, under your lowest (floating) ribs, and move to your midline. This is part of your spleen meridian. As you tap from the side of your body moving to the center of your body, if you come upon a tender spot, tap a bit longer until the blockage is released and discomfort improves—Spleen Meridian
  i. Lateral side of your hand (between pinkie and wrist)—often called the Karate point; affects the Heart and Small Intestine Meridian

Many people think they should only tap on a meridian if they have a diagnosis for a specific organ, but that is *not* necessarily the case. When you are trained and work with a practitioner, they can assess and be more specific about which meridian needs work. Because we grew out of two simple cells (the sperm and the egg), there are many connections within those energy pathways.

Emotional Freedom Technique (EFT)

Nick Ortner, author of the #1 *New York Times* bestseller *The Tapping Solution*, is known for creating a wonderful tapping routine that helps to release emotional stress, energy, and pain. Using many of the points I included above, his technique has you go through them in a specific order and make a statement of how you're feeling. In the initial round, you identify the main situation you want resolution about and identify it at the karate point. Then, as you progress through the other points, you state how you feel. All the negative feelings, anger, hurt, sadness, loss, frustration—you just put it out there. Acknowledging what and how you are feeling is so very important. This fits in perfectly with all the work you've been doing: learning to be open, share, and take ownership of how you're feeling, stopping the old patterns of suppression and avoidance of what you're feeling.

With each tapping round, your statements start to change. In the second or third round, you offer some understanding and rationale for why you are feeling this way. The next round may be more about letting go of feeling that way (and why you need to); the next cycle, you can choose to look and feel differently, and so on. You can tap as many cycles as you need to and state whatever feels right to you. There are no magic words you must repeat. Being honest with your emotions and how you're feeling is the basis of the healing. Tapping on the various points is stimulating and improves the energy flow in those meridians.

Tap into the powerful subconscious mind

Tapping is a gateway to overcoming challenges, including, but not limited to: emotional blocks, anxiety, fear, anger, traumas (past or present), phobias, physical pain, weight management, financial limitations, relationships, trust, and intimacy, just to name a few.

Fabulous results are often achieved in a very short amount of time. If you want to try this technique, you can find plenty of YouTube videos that use tapping to address many topics including health, finances, guilt, pain, forgiveness, freedom, peace, career, love, relationships, abundance—just about anything you can think of.

Sedating the Triple Warmer

The science of impacting our energy is so vast, and I've offered you only a glimpse of the many various methodologies available to you. I would like to demonstrate one very specific technique that you can use if you suffer from a post-traumatic experience, have severe anxiety or panic, feel overwhelmed, or have fibromyalgia or arthritis—these are just a few conditions that can benefit from it. This technique involves sedating your Triple Warmer (Fight-or-Flight Response) Meridian. When we experience a threat or something quite painful or dangerous, our Fight-or-Flight Response is triggered and can remain in overdrive. By quieting this meridian, you allow it to return to normal, and the symptoms that you have been experiencing may reduce or completely disappear.

To sedate the Triple Warmer Meridian (TW), you are going to trace the (TW) meridian flow line backwards to quiet the energy. You begin by taking one hand and placing it on the opposite temple. Move your hand up and backwards behind that ear, come down the side of your neck along the top of your shoulder, down the lateral aspect of your arm and forearm, and out past your fourth (ring) finger. *Don't stop* at the tip of your ring finger—allow your hand to extend past the ring finger, as if you're throwing that excess energy out of your body through your fourth finger. That's it. It's very simple, and only takes seconds to do. Do you remember M.S., the woman with fibromyalgia that I talked about earlier in this chapter? She used this technique to continue to work on releasing all her past emotional trauma and panic.

As your symptoms abate (disappear) in times you will not want to sedate the triple warmer any longer because the energy flow will have returned to normal. Working with an energy practitioner is very helpful to make adjustments and continue to access your energy flow.

It is important to note **that if you have an autoimmune condition or you're pregnant, it is always best to seek someone trained in working with energy before participating in this work on your own.**

Forgiveness and Prayer

Another wonderful form of healing that occurs on a very deep spiritual and emotional level is one used by John Newton. John is able to bridge the gap between thoughts at will for extended periods of time, which enables the clearing of unresolved negative imprints from our current life and ancestral lineage. With this process, he is able to help establish new patterns and the elimination of emotional, mental, and physical wounds.

When you use his technique through forgiveness, prayer, and gratitude, there is a profound shift that ends up impacting all areas of your life. After attending John's certification program and using it with many of my clients, I have found his process to be an extremely beneficial, transformative, and therapeutic approach that allows the emotional release and subsequent healing that truly brings about huge shifts. We are, in fact, addressing the root cause.

Healing can occur on so many levels and in so many ways. Just being by the ocean or getting a massage can be just as relaxing as a sedative, and you don't have to introduce any chemicals into your body. A glorious revolution is brewing that uses the arts to promote healing. There are numerous coloring books, art classes, music therapy, and many more activities that can support and promote our wellness. Once you accept that your emotions, feelings, and thoughts are impacting your internal health and happiness, you can embark on a new path that will affect you and your life in wonderful ways.

There are many alternative resources available to you, and I hope you'll explore your options for congruent, wellness intervention. The *most important thing to remember* is that your thoughts and emotions are the biggest contributors to your health and wellness. Do your part and work on resolving your emotional pains and those self-limiting thoughts!

When you address the (root) cause, you *affect* the *effect*!

Envision the success
YOU DESERVE

Discover the infinite possibilities as you become
Powerful Beyond Measure

Which one are you: Optimist/Pessimist or Skeptic/Visionary?

What determines if someone lives in fear or if they live to succeed? I think the way we live is determined in large part by whether we view life as a pessimist or an optimist. A **pessimist** sees life from the viewpoint of expected failure. Often this viewpoint stems from an ancestral line of failure, difficulties in life, or even feeling like a plague or bad karma looms over your entire family, leaving no escape. You expect and believe, even before you start, that less than desirable results will occur, and usually it ends badly. Getting started can be very difficult because you think, "Why bother? I already know the outcome."

An **optimist** is someone filled with hope, excitement, and anticipation of good things to come. They look at life with enthusiasm, but that doesn't mean they don't still have the doubts and self-limiting thoughts that arise to hold us back and cause us to question our passions and goals. In some ways, if you're an optimist, there is an even greater internal struggle: you're excited and ready to go, but your mind often derails you, leaving you frustrated, disappointed, and unfulfilled.

While pessimists and optimists both have their own unique problems, let's throw two more categories into the mix: the skeptic and the visionary. A **skeptic** sees only the obstacles, the problems, and the impossibilities, and questions everything. This creates the negative vibrational resonance of anguish, unrest, and disillusionment with their reality. You would typically hear a skeptic say things like "What if this," "What if that," and "How can we trust this?" There's a lot of fear expressed, and they want desperately to try and maintain control because they know that is safer than the unknown.

The **visionary** is someone who looks to the future, sees possibilities, embraces the unknown, and routinely doesn't let fear stand in their way. Doubts can still be present, but they are always searching, striving, creating, and envisioning. They are often looking for something better or ways to make a contribution to society or the world. A visionary is more often an optimist, striving for success, expecting to reach a specific endpoint or realize a particular accomplishment. Visionaries and optimists tend to be more positive and can hold that vibration in their work and personal lives.

No matter which role you've taken on in the past, you don't have to continue to play that part. Are you ready to be empowered to create the conscious reality that your desire? You have the innate Power Within that allows you to be **Powerful Beyond Measure**. When you harness the passions, desires, and purpose that call to you, miracles become even more abundant to support you on that path.

Are you ready to create a miraculous life, the one you were meant to live? It all starts from within. Your heart and Soul have *seeds of desire* that were planted long ago—maybe even before your physical birth—and they need to be nourished to thrive and be present in your life.

"Plant your own garden and decorate your own Soul,
instead of waiting for someone to bring you flowers."
—**Veronica A. Shoffstall**

Your ***perception*** of all your dreams—the seedlings of your desire—either allows fertilization or decay to occur. If you doubt them or think they're impossible, than you'll create that reality! You're an expert now, and you understand that your *perception* becomes the *reality* you *choose* to live.

A good friend of mine, Joel Roberts, was a famous, respected radio announcer for many years with WABC in Los Angeles, CA. One of his ears was severely damaged at work, and he was unable to continue broadcasting. He recalls his devastation, anger, and pain as the work he loved dearly was stripped so suddenly from his life. He was forced to change his career, and now Joel empowers thousands of people around the world by teaching them about the *impact of language*. He may have a profound hearing loss, but in a way, his hearing is even more acute now because he listens to the words that resonate from his students' Souls. Joel has worked with heads of state, the pope, Fortune 500 companies, students, and authors, and if you've ever had the privilege of seeing Joel's language-impact magic, you know exactly what I mean. When he is able to get an individual to speak from the Soul, the language that is revealed and later tweaked by Joel's genius is pure music to the Soul's ear.

Joel's story illustrates a message that I feel is extremely important: if you want any positive change to ever occur in your life, you must have the desire and the will to make that change. Joel had been horribly wounded, both physically and emotionally, but he was open and willing to change. If he hadn't considered a shift in his *perception*, he would have most likely continued on, to live a life filled with resentment, grief, and anger. No one can find the peace and joy they want in their life if they aren't willing to receive it.

Your potential and possibilities are infinite. The only limits are the ones you *choose* to place upon yourself. The energy you hold within becomes the fuel for your vision and goals. Throughout this book, you have been reprogramming your subconscious mind and using various tools to remove the emotional pains and blocks and take steps to remove your negative thoughts. It takes practice, and I know you can already see a shift in how you're feeling about yourself, others, and life in general.

Think for a minute about what your daily thoughts consist of. How much of your day is filled with questioning, trying to understand, frustration, anger, comparison, stress, unrest, and dissatisfaction? How could your life ever change with that type of influence? Who wants to live that life? The good news is that you no longer need to. You have everything you've ever needed, and as you learn to unleash your inner *power*, your strength, confidence, and wisdom increases, resulting in success and happiness.

> *"Life is 10 percent what happens to me*
> *and 90 percent how I react to it."*
> **—Charles Swindoll**

Fear vs Success: Who Will Be the Victor in Your Life?

We can be plagued by so many questions, doubts, fears, struggles, pains, guilt, and feelings of being inadequate, insignificant, and incompetent. When we don't have the answers, we create our own self-doubt through our negative feelings and beliefs. This then creates our own fears, which always seem to end in failure, or at least that's the way it looks through the lens of our perception.

The Formula for Failure

The greater our negative feelings are, the greater our fears become and, subsequently, the greater our failures will be. I refer to this *Formula for Failure* as the **"Triple-F"**:

<u>F</u>eelings + <u>F</u>ears = <u>F</u>ailure

How many times have your own *negative feelings* been expressed (internally or by others) that only add to your own insecurities? From these, we create *fears* and justifications that support our inability to proceed; this ultimately affects the outcome, which will never be enough and therefore is considered a failure.

Positive feelings and fear cannot coexist.

The Law of Attraction simply states that like vibrations are attracted to each other. Therefore, the feelings that accompany fear must be negative and self-limiting. If fear is present, then failure will be the end product. You can't escape what *fear* creates!

Some of you might be saying, "But it's scary to dream, to put yourself out there." You're absolutely right—it is, but are you more scared of *trying* or more worried about the *results* and whether you will or won't succeed? As soon as you make a choice not to try, you've already failed yourself!

Where, in any part of this formula, is the belief in self-love or the knowledge, passion, purpose, and ability to succeed? Nowhere. When fear and negative feeling combine, there is only one possible outcome: *failure*. You may actually try to convince yourself that you had a positive result and were successful on some level, but the true realization of the outcome is still filled with the underlying belief that you're still not enough, that you were in some way incompetent, undervalued, and inept. The underlying negative energy still exists within you and continues to fuel this repeating formula for failure.

The Formula for Success

If there's a Formula for Failure, surely there's a **Formula for Success**, right? You bet there is! I call it the "**Triple-S Success System**":

Self + *Sustenance* = *Success*

The first integral variable that promotes success is *Self*. This includes every aspect of what makes you *you*—your beliefs, emotions, knowledge, understanding, and purpose all rolled up into one beautiful package. This is *you*, and only *you* can create and be *you*. Throughout this book, you've been examining, digging deep, and learning to see your brilliance and be empowered by your greatness. That greatness has always existed, but, like most of us, you may have lost your way somewhere along your path. The fact that you're reading this book tells me that you're ready to reclaim it, here and now.

Remember that anything the mind tells you is most likely a distortion of the truth. As you know, your energetic, Soulful being is actually separate from your physical body. Your body is only a vessel that holds your spirit during this physical life incarnation. In many ways, we have created an image of understanding that is dependent on our senses. This limited understanding only leads us to judge and criticize. What if we could tune into our Self and sense who we are through those senses that are fueled by our intuition of truth?

Self and Success

If you were unable to see and could only experience life through your other senses, would your perception of **Self** be any different? Your eyes measure, judge, and place value on everything, which ultimately means you often end up feeling that you're "not enough."

I love this quote by Helen Keller: "Death is no more than passing from one room into another. But there's a difference for me, you know. Because in that other room I shall be able to see." I often think that, although she couldn't see with her eyes, her vision was much clearer than people with perfect sight. How often do we turn our imperfections into our nemeses when in fact they can become the gateway to our truest wisdom? After reading much on Helen Keller's life, I think she would concur with a quote I created in her honor: "I may not have traditional vision, but my sight is so much more truthful."

Right now, after all your personal exploration, healing, and growth, take a few moments and try to be open to seeing who you really are without any visual sensory limitations on Self. If a quality comes to mind that requires vision, don't include it. If you said you are beautiful, how would you know? If you said you are 6'4", how would you know? How about caring? Does vision play a role in being a caring person? I think not. What about being unhappy, cold, old, or young?

Being quiet and present in the moment, experiencing your oneness, is the first place you need to start. Here is a fabulous exercise to help you do just this.

Take ten to fifteen minutes and quiet your mind. Open your heart, listen closely to your inner voice, and express the many characteristics that are reflected by your inner expression of Self and Soul.

Self-Reflection Exercise

Without using your five physical senses, list your Soulful feelings of Self here with love and appreciation :

_____

_____

_____

_____

Now look back through your list. Draw a line through any feelings that required your physical senses to observe and identify. These may be ones that you've come to believe but know in your heart are not really you. Don't let what others have told you, become you.

It's not about how many items (feelings) you can write down here; it's about sensing and owning your unique, divine self. Judgment is not allowed in this exercise. Some of you may only have one word listed, and that's perfectly okay. It may in fact be your greatest gift to yourself.

You've already accomplished so much personal exploration and growth regarding ways to see and love your true, authentic Self. You're the only one who can affect how you feel about yourself and your life. Someone can throw you a life preserver, but you have to be willing to reach out and grab on to it. I can't encourage you enough to enthusiastically take on the responsibility of finding your beautiful internal self. No one can make you be someone you don't want to be! Ultimately, you decide how you let anything and everything affect you—in the past, present, and even the future, which of course is your present, only a moment away.

Congratulations! I hope you're feeling really awesome about your work here, because you're halfway to creating the success that you desire by just sensing, feeling, and accepting your divine essence, which is part of the Power Within that is beyond our comprehension. This power emanates from God/the One/ Infinite Source/Universe and is an extension into you.

Sustenance and Success

Sustenance, the second ingredient needed for success, is the nourishment that you choose to fuel your ambitions, desires, and passions. When you embrace, empower, and embody what you desire, success has already been achieved.

You can provide sustenance for yourself in many ways. Here are just a few:

- Allow yourself to express your inspiration and creativity
- Provide support, encouragement, and love to yourself
- Receive support, encouragement, and love from others
- Obtain resources that sustain and offer growth and advancement
- Nourish the mind, body, spirit, perception, and emotions
- Implement actionable steps that move you forward toward your goals and dreams

It's important to reinforce here that your own internal support is far more important than any external support if you're going to achieve success. Having people and situations that foster you is awesome and extremely valuable, but if your internal personal work is still coming from a place of lacking, then the external influences will have little impact.

We must take care of our inner house if we're ever expected to take care of our outer world. One cannot occur without the other. The same is true with success!

What are some of the things you feel that you need to provide the *sustenance* to achieve your passions and goals and reach success? Try and incorporate your Soul Lessons (aspects that you need to grow and learn) into the sustenance that you're providing yourself (e.g., compassion, empathy, strength, cheering, support, belief, persistence, commitment, etc.).

Let's look at a simple example. Say you want to bake a cake from scratch. First, you need the desire (**intention**) to bake the cake. Next, you need the necessary ingredients: some are external (eggs, flower, and water) and some are internal (talent, persistence, and interest). Then you follow the directions with actionable steps, giving it **attention**. As the cake is baking, you wait while there is **no-tension** (no action is taken), allow the creation to be realized (manifested), and you are filled with anticipation and excitement. Sounds like a simple recipe to achieve success!

"But what if ...?"

Oh yeah, here's where our thoughts get us into trouble: what if the cake falls, or it doesn't come out tasty, or people don't like it—and dang, I want a piece, but all those calories! *Why* do we do this to ourselves, removing all the pleasures we just experienced?

We can self-defeat everything we do, no matter how small,
but we must realize that we are doing it to ourselves.

As the aroma fills the air, your stomach starts to gurgle, your salivary ducts kick in to prepare for digestion, and your mind creates a fabulous picture of your guests as they rave about the final delicious outcome.

What if we could look at all of our goals with this same approach to success and enjoyment? How wonderful, delightful, and engaging would the pursuit of our dreams be? We could remove the stress, worry, and fears and bask in the joy of our creations.

Deciding—and here's the catch—how *you* define success for each goal will in fact be the deciding factor in whether or not you're successful. I used to create tons of goals for myself. I was great at creating and executing projects, but my sustenance started to fall apart when it came to my expectations. My mind told me that *success* was determined by how others felt about my outcome and had nothing to do with what value *I* placed on the project.

How ridiculous was that? I just took all the work I did and said, "Now *you* decide what my worth and value is." I had totally disempowered myself. I know now where those thoughts originated from: my need to be confirmed because of my fatherless childhood. My personal insecurities and need for external reinforcement could, and *did*, influence every part of my life until I finally said, "Enough!"

Success is <u>always</u> attainable!

Success is attainable because, when you match the positive energetic vibration of Self with Sustenance, success is the only possible result. Success isn't a one-size-fits-all concept; there is no single mold for what we all aspire to attain. Success means something different to each of us, and it doesn't apply only to major goals. It can mean accomplishing little things, like exercising three times a week for three months; remaining sober for one hour, one day, one year; and sharing your truth with your partner. Success starts with just believing and trying to fulfill a desire that stirs from your heart, Soul, and spirit.

Your inner knowing, passion, and destiny wait patiently for you to respond. That fire that resides within you wants to come to life, but as long as you ignore it and refuse to give it life, your Soul most likely will continue to feel unfulfilled.

Your life is important. You have a purpose and
the strength to fulfill your heartfelt dreams!

Sometimes the Little Steps Can Be the *Biggest* Steps!

Let's get you started right now. What goals would you like to work towards? Before you even start, I suggest closing your eyes and connecting to your heart and your inner intuitive voice. Listen to hear what's central and important for you right here and now.

Don't list the goals that you thought about a week or a month ago; start fresh with a new vision that stirs from within. It's often best to start with goals that can be obtained in a short time frame when you try out the **Triple-S Success System**. You can always come back, revisit, and create new short- and long-term goals.

Try to be very clear about what you desire and want to accomplish. In this process, you're not necessarily stating what success would mean. Remember that it's your inspiration and creativity that stirs and allows your passion or goals to take form. Then you'll be able to look at how you can provide yourself with the sustenance necessary to accomplish your desires. The magic is that you're already 99 percent there, and success is just waiting for you to revel in the experience. Ask yourself the powerful question that Marcia Wieder, CEO and Founder of Dream University, suggests in her revolutionary DreamSteps Methodology: "How do I want my life to be, and what am I willing to do about it?"

Passion, Purpose, and Prosperity Exercise:

Success is only a few steps away. Answer these questions to provide a jumpstart to help determine what you need from *Self* and *Sustenance* to yield *Success*. For a printed copy, go to www.PowerfulBeyondMeasureBook.com/forms.

1. *Self*: what do I desire from my heart and Soul?

2. *Self*: how can I best support my inner needs and use my *inner sight* to know that I can achieve and believe in this goal, desire, or purpose?

3. *Sustenance*: what do I require from my *Self* that supports this goal?

4. *Sustenance*: who and what can the external world provide in support of this goal? How and where can and will it be provided?

5. *Success* would look like_____?

6. I am passionate about this goal, and I want to succeed in order to benefit myself and others in what ways?
   a. Benefit me:
   b. Benefit others:

Congratulations! You're *stepping up*, showing that you're *willing* and *ready* to do everything in *your power* to allow the Universe/God and others to help support you in your ambitions. I'm so excited for you! Remember: no goal, dream, or passion is too small or too big.

Affirmation to Support your Vision

Create an affirmation statement in support of the goal you wrote above. Please go back to Part III, Chapter 2 ("Own and Create Your Happiness") to refresh your memory on how to write an affirmation statement correctly.

Write your affirmation statement for your stated goal above:

_____

_____

Here is an Affirmation example

"I am successfully completing my online educational course with enthusiasm, consistency, and personal satisfaction that open doors to employment that brings financial abundance into my family's life."

How does that affirmation really sound? Let's examine it in detail.

1. Breakdown of personal goal
   a. I feel good about furthering my education and skill set.
2. *Self* aspect
   a. I participate with confidence and consistency, and I complete my work.
3. *Success* aspect
   a. I secure a job that I know I can do and enjoy, and that brings the financial security that my family and I deserve and need.

Notice how the affirmation statement is positive, supportive, and benefits you and others. The positive energy and vibration offers hope, belief, benefits, abundance, and the potential for your individual growth. Remember that the affirmation must be written in the present tense and cannot use "will" or any negative words.

Each step you take is a step forward, and with that, success has already been achieved.

When you live, dream, and believe in the flow that allows personal growth that is aligned with your heart, passion, and purpose, the Universe (God) offers abundant opportunities to support your successes. Remember to believe that what is happening around you has been created for your success. Janet Bray Attwood, a friend and author I mentioned earlier in the second chapter of Part III, puts it this way: "Everything is a Gift in service of me." I encourage you to ponder these powerful words if and when you're feeling like a victim, unhappy, and discontent; maybe, just maybe, what is happening in your life is a gift that is in service of you.

"Your vision will only become clear
when you can look into your own heart.
Who looks outside, dreams; who looks inside awakens."
—Carl Jung

"There is a candle in your heart, ready to be kindled.
There is a void in your soul, ready to be filled.
You feel it, don't you?"
—Rumi

REJOICE—YOU ARE POWERFUL BEYOND MEASURE!
Awaken the Divine Intelligence Within

Voids are spaces that must be filled.

Our physical bodies become our house of existence during this physical life. In our vessel, there is a space that allows Spirit to exist. Without this space we wouldn't be present. Where ever there is space, a void, there is a natural order to try and fill it. The question is, "What are we filling this space with?"

So often we fill our void, our emptiness, with thoughts, emotions, and items that don't serve us and in many cases, actually becomes toxic to our true existence. In that process to fill in, or fill up, we can actual feel irrelevant, not important, and experience a loss of self.

Throughout this book, you've done much reflection, which took you through self-discovery, healing, and revealing your passions and purpose; all those efforts have brought you closer to enlightenment which is acceptance of your infinite power and knowing the connection to Oneness with the Universe and/or the God of your understanding.

Your Soul is a force unto itself—an entity that exists in space and time with a presence, power, and purpose. It needs to come to life, breathe, and claim its energetic birthright. When we disengage from the Source, ignore our divine spirit and greatness, and snuff out our Soul's light and power, our lives can feel completely empty and hopeless.

You may be asking yourself, "How do I maintain space where my Soul has the capacity to thrive and fulfill its passion and destiny?" This inner power, or presence, is an extension of God (or the word you use for your understanding of the Divine), which means that each and every one of us is an integral part of that power. It is always *with* us and *within* us, without limitation. Its Source is so much greater than anything we can imagine—infinite, forgiving, loving, and supremely intelligent. Since we are One with this Greater Source of Pure Love and Light, we are brilliant manifestations of its magnificent, radiant purity.

Be Patient with Yourself

"There's a momentary silence in the space between your thoughts that you can become aware of with practice. In this silent space, you'll find the peace that you crave in your daily life."
—**Wayne Dyer**

It's only natural that you might be feeling a bit unsteady and unsure of yourself right now. You're just like a newborn baby, figuring out ways to live and be true to your Self in that big old world out there. You've done a lot of painful searching, asked yourself a lot of very difficult questions, and explored the darkest, scariest places in your mind, heart, and Soul. Don't beat yourself up when you feel those negative emotions or hear those untruths whispered in your ear. You're a

Soul warrior now, armed with the tools you need to recognize and fight those powerless foes. *They can never, ever hurt you again.*

Give your <u>Soul</u> the power it deserves and needs to simply <u>be</u>.

It's my sincere hope that you feel like you've moved mountains of emotional residue that held you back and prevented you from achieving everything that you desire. Reading and participating in this book was an action step that *you* took into uncertainty, where *you* acknowledged your inner desire for healing, peace, and direction.

You're not the same person you were when you first started this book. Something magical, powerful, and transformative has occurred. I suspect that you have acknowledged this shift in some form or another. You've learned to heal your past through forgiveness, acceptance, and ownership of the perceptions and beliefs that shaped who you became and the life you're living. You were able to connect the dots and identify those repetitious patterns that continued to negatively impact you.

You've taken control and empowered yourself in the present by seeing the beautiful, Divine Soul that you know to be true, stopping the destructive *Dis-Cycle of Self* that had become your nemesis and limited you in so many ways. You've removed the protective walls that prevented you from learning, growing, and engaging with people, opportunities, and life. Understanding the impact of your emotional pain from the past and present is an integral component of your continued emotional and physical health, and you can now embrace your fears and limitations as you travel along the road of freedom and infinite possibilities.

You've learned how to envision and face your future with excitement as you began to trust your intuition and open up to your inner communication with Self and the greater Universe or God of your understanding. Your inner calling—that ravenous hunger, that unquenchable thirst—comes from the Power Within you that wants to take form and be expressed. When you're aligned with your Soul's truth, your life is abundantly supported in the pursuit of your greatest desires and passions. Igniting and awakening your desires, passions, gifts, and purpose allowed you to create and take action steps towards achieving success, living in the miracle zone, and following your spiritual path and destiny.

You may be feeling happier, more hopeful, open, authentic, compassionate, and loving. You may even feel unsure in this unfamiliar new state of being. That's okay—your Soul is quite possibly more alive now than ever before, and guess what? There's even more greatness to claim and be! Your journey is never-ending. Your personal and spiritual growth is continuous, limitless, and meant to be desired and enjoyed.

Throughout our time together, you've done a great deal of reflection which took you through self-discovery, healing, and revealing your passions and purpose; all those efforts have brought you closer to enlightenment, which is the acceptance of your infinite power. In your search for truth, understanding, and direction, you've discovered your own light that shines from within. Your Soul desperately wants to share its presence and be a blessing to the world.

***Do you acknowledge and connect with this wisdom,
the voice from <u>within</u> and <u>beyond</u>?***

When you sense and embrace your inner power, you'll find yourself in a state of completeness and peace. You'll be able to turn toward your inner "intelligence" because your power will become the source of all your creations, your guide along the path that you're meant to follow. You'll walk side by side and hand in hand with the great invisible power of divine greatness.

To be **Powerful Beyond Measure** is to engage your inner calling, ignite your inner light and fulfill the destiny you were born to live. There is no greater place to be than in complete wholeness, no longer lacking and able to live in a place of unconditional love, acceptance, forgiveness, and trust.

Now comes the time to activate, supercharge, and rekindle your inner fire—the **Power Within** that allows you to be **Powerful Beyond Measure**.

Your Journey Forward

It is so very important that you don't judge, criticize, or ask yourself, "Did I get enough from this book with all that I put into in this healing process?" As soon as you do that, you're looking at the experience again from a place of *lacking* instead of a place of gratitude and appreciation. I have faith that you have noticed a profound shift, both personally and in what's occurring in your life. Trust me; the words, lessons, healing, and inspiration you've taken in will continue to work within you, often in ways you may not even notice or be aware of.

I invite you to return and read this powerful book again and again. Each time you do, you'll be starting from a new place of exploration with greater opportunity for healing and growth. You most likely will return to the chapters that spoke to you most profoundly and use those tools that you found helpful on a regular basis. Repeat the exercises and meditations until you *know* how special you are. Make a loving, heartfelt promise to your beautiful Self to take the time you *deserve* and honor your path, your calling, your passions, and your unique, amazing Spirit. Write, draw, sing, laugh, hug, and inhabit your joy like it's the only place you could ever truly call home. Growth never stops. Be open to visions of things that can't be seen, healing words that can't be heard, and sweetness that can't be tasted. Feel with all *six* of your senses, allowing your heart to be the window into your Soul.

<u>The Heart's Home of Healing</u>

Whenever you're feeling those ugly remnants of fear, doubt, anger, unworthiness, and mistrust (and you will), I urge you to repeat the Heart's Home of Healing meditation in Part I, Chapter 2, or listen to the recording at <u>www. PowerfulBeyondMeasureBook.com/HeartHomeOfHealingMeditation</u>. During this meditation, which can be used on a regular basis, your heart is *filled in* with unconditional love, forgiveness, freedom, light, and presence of being, filling in the void that was created when all those negative foes were removed. As we come to a close in this book, I would love for you to participate in this meditation one more time to release any residual emotions, fears, and limitations that may have a shadowed presence within you. You may be surprised at what you find or do not find. Take the time to once again do this powerful Heart Healing meditation.

Meditation Reveal:

What were the four items that you found in each chamber of your heart during the meditation? Write them here, and name their existence:

_____,_____,_____,_____

Were you able to let them go and clean your heart's chambers of that debris? Go back and see if the four items you identified here and now are the same ones you acknowledged when you first participated in the Heart's Home of Healing meditation in Part I, Chapter 2. If they were the same, that only reinforces that these areas are continuing to try and limit you in some way. Knowledge is Power, and having identified your nemesis allows you to ensure that you do not "feed that wolf" and give it power in your life. *You* are the master of your existence, and *you* get to *choose* what you experience.

If your four items were different from the previous time, this is reasonable and should be expected. These new aspects of awareness are another layer in the healing and growth process. No judgement, positive or negative, is required (or allowed). Simply be open to accepting your feelings and ask yourself if they offer you expansion and growth or contraction and continued self-perceived limitation.

The more often you are able to disengage from your insecurities, doubts, and fears, the more your life will be filled with freedom, joy, and abundance.

The Power Within Me

Whether or not you participated again in the Heart's Home of Healing Meditation, please take a few minutes to answer these following questions that support your expansive future.

1. Although I am at peace, I know I lack knowledge in this area:

2. In my peaceful state of uncertainty and unknowing, I need direction and guidance to:

3. My old habits of Dis-Cycle of Self no longer exist, and I place my focus on these areas:

4. I am Powerful Beyond Measure and await the Divine wisdom. I'm open and receptive to:

Now that you've cleared out any old emotional residue in your heart center, it's time to **Awaken your Divine Intelligence**. This is a *twofold process* that includes a powerful guided meditation and subsequent communication with your Divine Intelligence. Let me share with you each component prior to actually listening to the meditation.

Awaken Your Divine Intelligence

Awaken Your Divine Intelligence meditation integrates your energies with Mother Earth and Father Space in a spiral of connection of infinite energy that brings harmony, balance, and peace. It stirs and rekindles your Soul's fire of creation which is supported and fueled with the masculine and feminine energies from the Universe and Mother Earth respectively. When you complete this meditation, clarity, vision, and guidance is revealed and you're able to move forward with your passions, desires, and goals with confidence, courage, and success. You're empowered with inner strength, inner wisdom, and inner peace, knowing that your path is Divinely created and aligned with your greater good, spiritual gifts, and purpose work. You may choose to listen to this meditation often in your life to reconnect and find the answers that you seek.

I've found that when you listen to the audio of *Awaken the Divine Intelligence Meditation,* the results are even more powerful, so I've provided the link to access the Awaken the Divine Intelligence Meditation here: www. PowerfulBeyondMeasureBook.com/AwakenDivineIntelligenceMeditation.

At this time, go to the site, locate the meditation, but please do not begin yet.

The second component, Divine Intelligence Soul Writing, will follow immediately after the meditation. I need you to locate multiple pieces of paper and a pencil or pen—you'll need them immediately following the conclusion of the meditation.

After completing this powerful guided meditation, you'll be directed to return to your paper and pen and write for approximately five minutes without censoring yourself. I've termed this portion of the process ***Divine Intelligence Soul Writing***, *which allows your soul to have voice.*

During Divine Intelligence Soul Writing, there is no conscious thought given to determine what you should or want to write. The sentence structure is often not correct, and the words may not even make sense at the time, but you allow your inner wisdom, the voice of your Soul, and the connection to the Divine Intelligence to be expressed in written form. As you write undisturbed, if and when you sense a pause in your flow of understanding, ask your Self, "What more do I need to know?" or ask a specific question you're seeking an answer to.

Now that you know the process, at this time, I invite you to take a few minutes to quiet yourself, silence your conscious mind, and open up your heart to connect inward to Self and Source.

Be very still. Hear and sense the vibration *outside of yourself.* Next, turn *inward and experience your physical body.* Finally, be present and *allow your voice from within to have presence.*

After you've taken the time for this contemplation, take note of any impressions and understandings that may arise. They may be positive, supportive, and with direction, or they may be negative energies that are brought to your awareness. Allow them to be present and take note *without judgement.* Ignoring them will not make them go away.

Let's Begin:

- *Press play* and enjoy the powerful audio of **Awaken the Divine Intelligence Meditation.**
- Return to your paper and pen and begin Divine Intelligence Soul Writing for between five to ten minutes or until you feel that your Soul's voice has been revealed to you.

- If there is a pause in your flow of words, ask yourself: "What more do I need to know?" or ask a specific question you need an answer to.

Wonderful! What did you think about that guided meditation and the words you wrote?

- I encourage you now to return to your paper and reread your words of insight, focus, and direction. Underline or highlight the words and phrases that really resonate for you at this moment.
- **If you had to summarize your Divine Intelligence that was revealed in two words, what would they be?**
  _____and _____.

Acknowledge what you're *feeling* with each message that you received, without judgement.

- If it's forgiveness, let it be so.
- If it's moving forward, trust that all is as it should be.
- If it's to set boundaries and stay out of other peoples' business, then allow it to happen.
- If it's trust, then believe and welcome it.
- If it's _____,
  know it to be so.

Save your paper and consider your combined voices of Self and Source over the days that follow. Some people look at their notes as their **Soul's Power Map to Oneness and Happiness**.

Divine intelligence is always available, encouraging, supporting, and opening pathways towards your calling and greater good.

Final Thoughts

Throughout this book, there has been one main integral theme that's been consistently expressed in all the work that you've accomplished: *loving and embracing your authentic truth.*

You're truly a beautiful, loving Soul, full of grace, compassion, and strength that is just waiting to be revealed to the world. It has been my honor to travel with you on your powerful, transformative journey towards discovery, healing, acceptance, engagement, and activation towards fulfillment of your desires and passions. When you allow your light to shine, we all are touched by your beauty and graced by your presence.

> *"People are like stained-glass windows. They sparkle and shine when the sun is out, but when the darkness sets in, their true beauty is revealed only if there is light from within."*
> **—Elisabeth Kübler-Ross**

Powerful Beyond Measure is an *active miracle* that's been unfolding as you've read these pages and explored your Power Within. Your personal experience has allowed healing and forgiveness to occur, facilitated growth and expansion, and awakened your desire and purpose. *You* are **Powerful Beyond Measure,** and the world eagerly awaits your gifts and the love you have for yourself and others. Please, never forget that your life matters and that you're a very special part in the master plan of Creation.

My wish for you is simple: love yourself and others, fill your heart and actions each and every moment with happiness and joy, and fulfill your dreams, passions, and destiny.

**Powerful Beyond Measure is my gift to you,
with the hope that you found much peace,
healing, love, hope, direction, inspiration, and wisdom
for the path you're meant to follow.**

If you would like to contact Cynthia Mazzaferro for transformational life coaching and healing, speaking engagements, or to share your thoughts or testimonies about Powerful Beyond Measure, **please email me at info@CynthiaMazzaferro.com**

Our Deepest Fear

Our deepest fear is not that we are inadequate.
Our deepest fear is that we are powerful beyond measure.
It is our light, not our darkness that most frightens us.
We ask ourselves, "Who am I to be brilliant,
gorgeous, talented, and fabulous?"
Actually, who are you *not* to be? You are a child of God.
Your playing small does not serve the world.
There is nothing enlightened about shrinking
so that other people won't feel insecure around you.
We are all meant to shine, as children do.
We were born to make manifest the glory of God that is within us.
It's not just in some of us; it's in everyone.
And as we let our own light shine,
we unconsciously give other people permission to do the same.
As we are liberated from our own fear,
our presence automatically liberates others.
—Marianne Williamson, *A Return to Love: Reflections*

ABOUT CYNTHIA MAZZAFERRO

Cynthia Mazzaferro is a best-selling author and highly sought-after transformational speaker in the field of self-development and personal responsibility. She is also a renowned vibrational, intuitive energy practitioner, and Reiki Master, and coaches hundreds of high-profile clients. As a retired physical therapist, ergonomist, and founder of Industrial Ergonomics and Educational Services, Cindy spent twenty-five years teaching, evaluating, and playing an integral role in rehabilitation and redesign to reduce stress and debilitating symptoms.

Cynthia is a featured columnist in the e-magazine *Wellness Woman 40 and Beyond*, founded and produced by Lynnis Woods-Mullins. Cindy's column, Powerful Beyond Measure: Intuitive and Emotional Fitness Expert, allows readers to leave stories or ask for advice and receive intuitive and plausible connections between their physical symptoms and their emotions, behaviors, and difficulties. Mazzaferro is a contributing author in the best-selling book *Shine Your Light: Powerful Practices for an Extraordinary Life*, along with *New York Times* #1 best-selling authors Marci Shimoff, Janet Bray Attwood, Chris Attwood and Best-selling Author Geoff Affleck.

Cindy holds numerous workshops, trainings, and summits featuring the Power Within, Intuition, Energy Healing, and Powerful Beyond Measure programs. Empowering people is one of Cindy's greatest joys, and she uses her expertise to inspire, transform, and facilitate creating change and success. Cindy loves to work with people individually, in group settings, or in the corporate arena. If you are interested in speaking with Cindy regarding coaching, a healing session, or a speaking engagement, please send your request to info@CynthiaMazzaferro.com.

Cindy has a wonderful, loving husband, Thomas Mazzaferro; two fabulous sons, Thomas and Daniel; and a delightful daughter-in-law, Nicole. Cindy is blessed to have her mother, Janet Moore, in her life, along with sisters and many wonderful friends. When Cindy is not working on Powerful Beyond Measure opportunities, you may find her playing tennis or cards, painting fine art, enjoying the family's lake house, and traveling.

She lives in Cheshire, CT.

Website: www.CynthiaMazzaferro.com
Website: www.PowerfulBeyondMeasureBook.com
Fine Art Website: www.StreitGallery.com
FB page at www.facebook.com/ThePowerWithinCynthiaMazzaferro/

Enjoy becoming *Powerful Beyond Measure*
when you embrace your Power Within!
Claim your FREE
Powerful Beyond Measure Additional Gifts for you at
www.PowerfulBeyondMeasureBook.com/bookgifts

Congratulations! Whether you are just beginning to scan the pages or have concluded this life-changing book, your spiritual journey of transformation is an ongoing and life-fulfilling experience. Growth never ceases, and we are continually provided with opportunities and places to find the power we all hold within and transform it into the gifts we can nourish and present to the world. You are part of the Creator's Master Plan, and we each need to do our part in fulfilling our destiny. To help you continue on your beautiful Soulful path, I've created the following free gifts for you:

FREE *Powerful Beyond Measure* Workbook

The *Powerful Beyond Measure Workbook* includes all the various forms used in the book, *Powerful Beyond Measure*, along with the Emotional Fitness Program and special bonus material.

FREE *Powerful Beyond Measure* e-P-O-W-E-R-zine

Every few months, I will send you new fun and inspiring exercises, tools, and the latest breakthrough information that may assist you in your personal growth, goals, and success. This e-P-O-W-E-R-zine is a way to keep you informed about what's going on and how to increase your health, happiness, and harmony.

FREE *Powerful Beyond Measure* Intuitive Weekly Reading

Every week, a new pictorial collage is created with beautiful, inspiring Soul Messages located behind each image. Your intuition assists you in the image selection, and the *Powerful Beyond Measure* Soul message lies waiting for you to reveal. This empowering Intuitive reading is an additional way for you to connect to your inner wisdom and focus your attention on the insight that is revealed each week. People are always amazed at the relevance of the message, and it is often just what they needed to hear.

www.CynthiaMazzaferro.com/cardreading

For these and other gifts, visit: www.PowerfulBeyondMeasureBook.com
To access free gifts, users must provide their first name and e-mail address.
Offer subject to availability

Powerful Beyond Measure

offers many programs and services to embrace your Power Within, heal your broken heart, self-limiting doubts, and past falsehoods, and facilitate success with any goals, passion, and purpose that you envision.

Check out other powerful programs or services that might be right for you or your business.

Powerful Beyond Measure **webinar**
www.PowerfulBeyondMeasurePrograms.com/webinar

- An online, interactive book-study webinar that walks alongside you as you read *Powerful Beyond Measure* and rediscover self, resolve any emotional or energetic influences, and create goals to accomplish your greatest desires.

Powerful Beyond Measure workshop
http://www.PowerfulBeyondMeasurePrograms.com/workshop

- An off-site, multi-day workshop to be arranged to meet your specific individual or group needs, bring focus to specific areas, and build results on your objectives. This program can be used for individuals, couples, and small or corporate groups.

Powerful Beyond Measure Coaching Programs
www.PowerfulBeyondMeasurePrograms.com/life-coaching
http://www.CynthiaMazzaferro.com/life-coaching

- *Personal Coaching Program*—geared toward facilitating personal changes in any areas you want to address. Throughout this powerful, integrated coaching program, profound healing, awakening, forgiveness, and emergence of Self are accomplished—transforming your life in positive ways that are beyond what you may have ever dreamed of.
- *Professional Coaching Program*—helps business executives raise their game by becoming stronger within, which translates across all areas of their lives. Build confidence, courage, and management skills through self-discovery, empowerment, and resolution. When you affect who you are personally, you affect the professional that you are as well! Success, happiness, and the bottom line are all positively impacted beyond even what you may imagine. Creating balance creates harmony, building *self* builds inner strength, and manifesting your desires manifests results and success. Personal, group, and corporate rates are available.

Intuition Mastery Summit
www.IntuitionMasterySummit.com/bundle

- Intuition Mastery Summit Bundle—where twenty-eight transformative and intuitive experts share their beliefs and tools to develop and strengthen your intuition. Your intuition is the voice from within and beyond that holds all your answers. An Intuitive Treasure Chest filled with thousands of dollars' worth of free gifts is waiting for you.

A free eBook edition is available with the purchase of this book.

To claim your free eBook edition:

1. Download the Shelfie app.
2. Write your name in upper case in the box.
3. Use the Shelfie app to submit a photo.
4. Download your eBook to any device.

Shelfie

A *free* eBook edition is available
with the purchase of this print book.

CLEARLY PRINT YOUR NAME ABOVE IN UPPER CASE

Instructions to claim your free eBook edition:
1. Download the Shelfie app for Android or iOS
2. Write your name in **UPPER CASE** above
3. Use the Shelfie app to submit a photo
4. Download your eBook to any device

Print & Digital Together Forever.

Snap a photo

Free eBook

Read anywhere

CPSIA information can be obtained
at www.ICGtesting.com
Printed in the USA
BVOW08s1232281016
466036BV00002B/5/P